Rooted on Blue Stone Hill

Rooted on Blue Stone Hill

A HISTORY OF
JAMES MADISON UNIVERSITY

BY NANCY BONDURANT JONES

with Forewords by Linwood H. Rose and Ronald E. Carrier

CENTER FOR AMERICAN PLACES
SANTA FE, NEW MEXICO,
AND STAUNTON, VIRGINIA

in association with
The Community Foundation of Harrisonburg and Rockingham County

Dedication:
For "Schoolma'ams" of every generation,
past and present and future—
and to those men brave enough to follow their paths.

Publisher's Notes:

Rooted on Blue Stone Hill: A History of James Madison University is published in an edition of 4,000 hardcover copies in association with The Community Foundation of Harrisonburg and Rockingham County, a nonprofit organization established for the purpose of developing endowed funds for the community's benefit. For more information about the Foundation, see www.the-community-foundation.org. For more information about the Center for American Places and the publication of this book, see page 288.

© 2004 The Community Foundation of Harrisonburg and Rockingham County and the Center for American Places.
Photographs © James Madison University, unless otherwise indicated.
All rights reserved. Published 2004. First edition.

Printed in Korea on acid-free paper.

Center for American Places, Inc.
P.O. Box 23225
Santa Fe, New Mexico 87502, U.S.A.
www.americanplaces.org

Distributed by the University of Virginia Press
www.upress@virginia.edu
9 8 7 6 5 4 3 2 1

Library of Congress Cataloging-in-Publication Data is available from the publisher upon request.

ISBN: 1-930066-17-1

Contents

Contents

(continued)

THE DAZZLING LIST of present-day achievements that have secured James Madison University's pre-eminent position in higher education across the Commonwealth of Virginia might lead us to lose sight of the rich traditions that have influenced that progress.

But now comes Nancy Bondurant Jones, popular writer and historian, to remind us of this remarkable institution's deep roots and how they have extended shoots up through the soil of ninety-plus years of history to create the region's most vital center of higher learning. She details the tenure of the first four presidents—Burruss, Duke, Miller, and Carrier—and opens into the future with my inauguration.

Through the last decade, Jones has unearthed a treasure trove of resources, some familiar, some never before examined and shared. Like me, you will be amazed and delighted by the scope of these materials—including rare photographs that depict with disarming directness the richness of campus life as it evolved over the span of decades. One moves forward through the book well able to discern the links that bind together different eras, the elements that have made up who we are.

Much has been written about our university, but now—under one cover—we have what may be confidently described as a highly readable history of JMU. Every alumnus, every student's family, every friend of JMU will want to add *Rooted on Blue Stone Hill* to his or her library for hours of enjoyment.

LINWOOD H. ROSE, *President, James Madison University*

Foreword

WHEN I FIRST VISITED MADISON COLLEGE IN 1971, I found a small-town school that was primarily a teachers college for women with around 4,000 students. At the time I was vice-president at Memphis State University, a campus with 18,000 to 20,000 students in the midst of an urban area with all the excitement of a sprawling urban institution—its athletic programs, cultural events, and academic challenges. And my wife Edith and I were part of the very satisfying social life of Memphis. Why would I trade the job at Memphis State for a presidency at Madison College?

Because I also saw an institution with a potential that mattered more than the reality. It stood on so solid a foundation that it could carry unlimited change into the future. I realized this was a place where I could have an impact. Things I had already done at Ole Miss and at Memphis State, and my knowledge from coursework at East Tennessee State and the University of Illinois, were just so natural for this institution to implement. And so I began twenty-nine years as president—a great journey, a wonderful challenge, and a broad band of opportunities.

Also, as the growth and change continued into my latter years as president, I understood more fully how the story of James Madison University's evolution from a small-town normal school for women to a nationally recognized coed university mirrors the story of higher education across the United States. When the Normal and Industrial School for Women at Harrisonburg was built in 1908, compulsory education for the nation's children was not yet a reality. One- and two-room schools dotted the landscape under teachers who often had no special training. And few students ever completed the eleven grades needed for a high-school diploma. Nine decades later, in our public schools today, the majority not only finish twelve years, but a greater number also enters college than at any time or *in any country* in history.

I felt this remarkable change was worth recording. So I commissioned Nancy Bondurant Jones to write a popular account of JMU's first ninety years. She has fleshed out life on the campus under the administrations of the first four presidents. *Rooted on Blue Stone Hill* captures the history and sets the stage for the next decades of excitement and transformation throughout the twenty-first century.

RONALD E. CARRIER *President Emeritus, James Madison University*

Part One

Burruss:
The Founding Years,
1908–1919

I N SMALL TOWNS ACROSS THE NATION, civic actions taken during the first decade of the new twentieth century set unimaginable patterns for the end of the 1900s. Suburbs, interstate highways, mass media, universal education, antibiotics, world wars, and genetic engineering loomed unseen ahead. The United States was an agricultural land wrestling with the change to an industrial economy. Few citizens could envision the impact of discoveries around the corner, the somersault lifestyle where the family farm and rural town became exceptions rather than the rule. Just as waterways and railroads

patterned population growth in the 1800s, so highways would in the next century. And every town eagerly sought growth and something to wrap that growth around.

Thus, in rural Rockingham County, the county seat of Harrisonburg offered land along its Main Street at the south edge of town to win the new college being established by the General Assembly. Other towns across the Commonwealth vied for the same, provoking a fierce legislative contest that ended at quarter past ten o'clock Tuesday night, March 10, 1908. By ten-thirty the excitement in Richmond had pulsed beyond the Blue Ridge. Small-town Harrisonburg in western Virginia's central Shenandoah Valley had won the new state normal school.

The 1905 Firemen's Parade drew citizens to Court Square and porches along Main Street to honor Hose Company No. 4. The men had won the state competition in Richmond for their crew's fastest response time after a pre-arranged alarm, a deciding factor in Harrisonburg's selection as the site for the Normal School. (Photo: Courtesy Nancy Garber)

Through the early evening hours in the town itself, the newspaper offices had taken on the air of an election night. Citizens thronged the papers' rooms, eagerly waiting for word from the capital city. As the hours passed without tidings, the crowd waned, but hopes did not. Then came the results of the final roll call. The next edition of the Harrisonburg *Daily News* summarized the legislative details plus the instant local response:

The entire [*Daily News*] building was then illuminated for the first time. . . . To those citizens who had retired to dream rather than hear of normal schools, a prolonged blast of the fire whistle announced the result. This . . . made trouble for the central telephone office, where dozens of inquiries were turned in as to the cause of the alarm. The announcement that it was merely a normal school salute served to appease anxiety and . . . no doubt furnished the basis of still sweeter slumber.

The rival *Daily Times* bannered headlines equally jubilant the next day. Its March 12th edition announced "KEEZELL AND GOOD/Monster Ovation to Be Tendered Rockingham's Representatives/ THEY WON THE NORMAL" and urged citizens of the town and county to join in welcoming the train bringing the senator and the delegate home from the General Assembly in Richmond. The welcome drew an estimated 2,500 of Harrisonburg's population nearing 4,500. The *Daily Times* reported:

> When the train pulled in there were fully five hundred people on the platforms or immediately around the station. While every factory whistle in town was blowing, the band played 'Dixie' and hundreds cheering, Messers Keezel [*sic*] and Good were escorted to a large automobile and the march to the court was begun. West Market Street was lined from the station to the Square, and many were in the court yard.

Mayor O. B. Roller called it the "proudest moment in the history of Harrisonburg." Shrill whistles pierced the air and church bells pealed in answer. Families streamed out of doors to cheer their representatives and congratulate one another amid laughter and shouts of, "It's come, it's really come!" Confused toddlers must surely have wondered if Santa Claus had arrived in the midst of spring.

Indeed, a gift had been given, with Senator George B. Keezell as the jolly old elf who managed to achieve the miracle climaxing four years of legislative battle. He and Delegate P. B. F. Good had directed the fight in their respective chambers, but others had marshaled support as well. Citizen groups had campaigned vigorously to convince visiting legislators on the selection committee that Harrisonburg was the ideal site for the school.

On March 13, 1908, Editor Adolph Snyder's *Daily News* carried the following poem on the back page, a gleeful stab at the towns which competed and lost:

THE NORMAL'S COME AT LAST

The Normal's come to Harrisonburg,
 And Oh! my lawsy daisy—
All the folks around this town
 Are just a-running crazy.

Snatched it 'way from Fredericksburg,
 Knocked Manassas silly'
Good and Keezell are the men—
 They got it willy-nilly.

Now they're looking for a site;
 I wonder if they'll find it.
Somethin'll happen, sure as fate
 Unless they stand behind it.

The Normal's come to Harrisonburg,
 And how our heads are swelling!
Keep your mouth shut, Staunton dear,
 We know it without telling.

Nothin' more to talk about
 Since this thing has ended;
Papers now will quit the biz,
 Unless they are befriended.

Raymond Dingledine, Jr.'s history of the school published in 1959 describes the earlier campaign. After the visiting legislators had been ceremoniously escorted to the Clarendon Hotel from the train station, "[they] were treated to an exhibition by the Harrisonburg fire department to demonstrate the efficiency of the fire alarm system and the excellent water pressure. Responding quickly to a prearranged alarm, the volunteer firemen impressed a large crowd by the speed with which they got three streams of water playing on the courthouse."

At 6' 7", Sen. George B. Keezell stood out in any crowd. Here he confers with President Burruss at a reception where faculty and students enjoy a rare opportunity to leave the boardwalks and stroll on the grass. In the background is Jackson Hall, circa 1909. (Photo: JMU Special Collections)

Safety worries allayed, the visitors feasted. Dingledine records, "The meal began with caviar, included fish, roast beef, fried chicken and spring lamb, and ended with ice cream, fruit and cheese."

Legislators recognized the urgency for decision, the pressing need for construction. Ninety percent of white teachers in the state were women, yet only one state-supported school for the training of women existed in 1908, that one at Farmville. Both the Rockingham County Board of Supervisors and the town council of Harrisonburg acted on acute awareness of local need. They offered dollars as well as land. The county would put up $10,000; the city, $5,000. Rockingham County had a larger enrollment of white pupils and employed more white teachers than any other county or city in the state. Each governing board recognized that compulsory education loomed in the immediate future, increasing the demand for qualified teachers.

Local newspapers carried the fight forward. Aware of prevailing ideas that varied climates and health conditions made it dangerous for people in one part of the state to attend school in a different climate and at a different altitude, Adolph Snyder, editor of the *Daily News*, strenuously touted Harrisonburg's advantages. He wrote of the town's "healthy and pleasant location at 2,000 feet above sea level" (embellishing the actual 1,300 feet) and the resulting cool breezes and protection from extreme winter weather. He also noted the "ideal purity" of a water supply sufficient to serve 12,000—well above the current population. In addition, a school at the center of such a rich agricultural area was assured of quantities of nourishing food at low cost. Easy access by railroad weighed as a further advantage.

Despite the widespread campaign to win selection, not everyone realized the magnitude of the prize for which a dozen towns had been contending. But

Left: President Julian Burruss in 1908 at the start of his illustrious career, beginning in Harrisonburg and ending in Blacksburg as president of Virginia Polytechnic Institute. (Photo: JMU Special Collections)

Right: Newlywed Rachel Burruss, the Normal's *first* first lady, took in stride inconveniences such as living in the dorm and constant scrutiny from students and townspeople. She chaperoned outings, held supper parties at Massanetta Springs (before "Hillcrest" was built), and enlisted her mother to help make identifying bows in blue and gold for girls to wear whenever traveling. (Photo: JMU Special Collections)

the senator and the editor fully grasped the educational, social, and commercial ramifications—and realized that Harrisonburg would never be the same.

The town would never be as small or as unknown again. During the school's first years, Harrisonburg's very provincial character personalized the connection between school and town until both seemed almost one. In the beginning, the townspeople felt such ownership that they assumed their voice should carry weight in all aspects of executing the legislative mandate. Choosing a site came first, so residents hotly argued location. But the board of trustees, newly appointed by Governor Swanson, would render that decision.

Dr. Dingledine's history describes the board members' initial inspection: "Riding in a yellow surrey with a fringe around the top . . . They hoped to find an area larger than the thirty-acre minimum required by the legislature. They visited the Newman farm on South Main Street, a group of tracts on South Mason Street, the Rosenberger-Houck property along the top of the hill on the south side of East Market Street and the Waterman site at the northwestern edge of town."

Fields and farms ringed Harrisonburg. The Waterman site, for instance, offered "fifty acres at a very reasonable price." The forty-two-acre Newman farm fronted on Main Street at the opposite southern edge of town and gradually rose to the crest of a hill. As the *Daily News* pointed out, a school built there would be in full view of the Valley Turnpike (U.S. Route 11) and the Baltimore & Ohio and Chesapeake & Western railroads. So the committee selected the smaller, more expensive Newman site and immediately moved to the next step, the search for the man to seize the dream and lay the foundation.

FIRE-FIGHTING POWER WON THE DAY

Perhaps surprisingly to modern readers, the efficiency of the local fire department was a major deciding factor in 1904 for state legislators traveling from town to town to select the site of the new normal school. Fear of fire threaded the daily lives of every family and business of the time. Few places had central heating. Most homes used fireplaces or, like offices, stores, and one-room schools, depended on the potbellied stove. The thought of housing dozens of young ladies without proper defense against fire aroused deep concern.

Details of a past tragic fire in Lowell, Massachusetts, on January 10, 1860, haunted the present. There, young female textile workers were housed in a five-story brick building. Of the ninety who died, fourteen were unidentifiable. The numbers of workers hospitalized and crippled staggered the imagination. (A few years later the nation would witness another deadly fire in 1911, at the Triangle Shirtwaist Company in New York City, which killed more than 150 women working there.)

But one didn't have to travel that far to cite disaster. Within the memory of most adults, awesome burnings had consumed homes and whole sections of nearby towns and cities. On December 24, 1870, the largest fire in the history of Harrisonburg had destroyed almost the entire block south of Court Square, spreading down Main to Water Street and down Water almost to Blacks Run. Ten houses burned out, the fire presenting such a solid front it was impossible to get to the center. Fire fighters pressed bystanders into their lines, passing buckets filled with water from hand to hand, while another line returned the buckets to the spring at the corner.

Hose Company No. 4

Named as Harrisonburg fire chief after that historic fire, John R. Saum worked to assure the school selection committee that the current fire companies had the finest men and equipment in the state. They had won yearly statewide competitions and held a world record of twenty-eight seconds to get couplings broken and nozzles attached to hydrants.

The town had purchased two fire engines shortly after Saum's tenure began, and the new engines successfully hosed down adjacent buildings to retard the spread of flames more than once. In 1902, J. C. Staples's large livery and feed stables had burned and endangered Harrisonburg's business district. The firemen had contained it. And when Dayton's largest fire occurred on March 3, 1903, Saum's team had saved much of the triangular block comprising the business district, though the Waverly Hotel and three residences had been gutted and destroyed.

In addition to adding fire engines, Harrisonburg had also dug an artesian well on North Main for an increased water supply. Eager to demonstrate to legislators the power of their fire-fighting efficiency, they conducted the visitors to the Clarendon Hotel on the south side of Court Square and swung into action. At the sound of an alarm, the volunteer firemen impressed a large crowd by the speed with which they spewed three streams of water on the courthouse. The show played well to allay fears and helped make Harrisonburg the choice site for the State Normal and Industrial School for Women.

Board interviews of candidates quickly narrowed. One finalist was Julian A. Burruss of Richmond. Although a youthful thirty-three years old, he had impressed those watching with his implementation of a manual training program for the Richmond schools. Only three years after his graduation in 1898 from Virginia Polytechnic Institute in Blacksburg, he had been appointed principal of Leigh High in his native city. From that position, he moved to director of manual arts in the public schools where he introduced and supervised Richmond's first vocational education system. Furthermore, he had pursued advanced studies at Columbia University in New York City during the summer months. In addition to educational zeal and youth and energy, he offered the rare combination of vision and pragmatism needed to build a school.

The board tendered a contract and Burruss signed. For a salary of $2,500 yearly, plus school-related travel expenses and a house when available, he began his duties as president of the State Normal and Industrial School at Harrisonburg, Virginia, on July 1, 1908.

Any doubts about the selection of one so young for a position of major responsibility were dispelled by Burruss's immediate action. And two of the characteristics that had led to his selection became strikingly clear—his vision and practicality. He immediately withdrew from Columbia, postponing the doctorate almost at hand, and crisscrossed several states to take counsel with the heads of other institutions. Observant as ever, the new president probed for details, studied campus layouts, questioned equipment choices, and weighed faculty concerns. He sought what to avoid as well as what to do, increasingly aware of the uniqueness of his situation, of the gift of time to plan ahead. Too many colleges seemed to have grown like Topsy, with no larger agenda behind the addition of classes and buildings.

Throughout the summer of 1908, he urged:

> The greatest possible foresight should be exercised, and the school should be planned for the future as well as for the present . . . a large school, capable of ultimately accommodating at least a thousand students, with boarding space for about three-fourths of that number. The complete scheme should be projected now, and every building erected as a permanent part of the original plan . . . buildings substantial and modern in all respects, but simple and appropriate in design, and distinctive in type . . . and the same type of architecture must in all events be maintained throughout the group.

Richmond architect Charles M. Robinson drafted the far-sweeping vision onto paper. Robinson's bird's-eye view established forty buildings around an open green to accommodate an evolving school. His detailed plan for a future complex of distinctive blue limestone walls and red, Spanish-tiled roofs impelled belief in that future—and offered a design for gradual growth. Not since Mr. Jefferson's dream of a state university had a public school in Virginia been given such careful forethought. In mid-September the trustees approved the blueprint for an institution emerging at once and stretching into the future. "The next twenty-five years" became a keynote phrase for the first year.

Top: Richmond architect Charles M. Robinson's grand vision for the school.

Bottom: The Normal's first halls—(pictured left to right) Science (Maury), Dormitory No. 1 (Jackson), and Dormitory No. 2 (Ashby)—adhered to the architect's plan. During the next twenty-five years, red-tiled roofs and bluestone walls, from stone quarried locally, instantly became campus identifiers and gave rise to the name Blue Stone Hill, two words in the beginning and one, *Bluestone*, for the yearbook starting in 1962. (Photo: JMU Special Collections)

Burruss, however, never mistook piles of stone and mortar for the real goal of molding young women into useful adults. The dreamer and pragmatist wrote, "The development of a strong, noble, womanly character is of first importance. . . . We believe that thought which does not function in action is largely wasted, that it is the duty of the school to teach its students to do as well as to think."

"Competent teachers" and "competent home-makers" became pet phrases of his. He wanted to send young women out whose husbands might safely trust them to manage their households with skill and economy—"no clerk should be tempted to dishonesty" because of a graduate's lack of knowledge. And he voiced hope that "in the not very distant future it will be impossible for anyone to teach in the public schools without adequate specific preparation." Then would come "better salaries and a better recognition of the teacher's work in many ways." His ideal school had to "meet conditions, anticipate needs, encourage everything that makes for progress."

He also asserted, "Any Normal School worthy of the name can make a good teacher better and can frequently make a success out of one who would otherwise prove a failure." He emphasized not only academic background, but also methods and principles of teaching as the cornerstones of the Normal curriculum.

He needed, though, to draw those potential teachers to the fledgling school. From his office in the *Daily News/Rockingham Register* building, or at his desk in the rented rooms he and his bride took in a house on Main Street in sight of the new campus, he wrote the first "Prospectus." In it he painstakingly drafted ideals as well as requirements. Underscoring all was his belief that the opportunity for schooling should be within reach of any who wanted to learn. He resolved that dormitories should be the best available, yet available at cost—with almost everything except clothing and books for only $14 a month. He vowed, "It will be the aim of the management to be able to say, 'No worthy student has ever been compelled to leave the school on account of the lack of financial means to continue.'"

By February 1909, Burruss and his secretary Evelyn Liggett had completed the 112-page *Normal Bulletin* detailing information about the school. Ninety classes in a dozen departments would begin the next fall. Ground-breaking the prior November 25 had set Harrisonburg contractors W. M. Bucher and Son (forerunners of Nielsen Builders, Inc.) at work on the first academic building and first dormitory to be ready by September.

Through the spring rains and into the summer heat, Burruss kept a discerning eye on the construction, often making a round of inspection in evenings after the workmen had gone. His manual arts background rendered him sensible of details and he liked what he saw. But as absorbed as he was in building and promotion, he knew not to isolate himself—and thus his school—from the community. He embraced every offer to speak in public, explaining the school and emphasizing the importance of teacher training plus the uniqueness of manual arts education.

This school, he proclaimed, would break new ground. It was the first Virginia institution to be set up on a four-quarter system and also the first to give complete courses in industrial education. Burruss insisted, "Education must be brought close to the lives of the people . . . must result in industry and thrift; it must pave the way to productive work with skilled hands. . . ."

The sixty-seven students at the Normal School who expected to graduate in 1914 and who planned to enter the teaching profession came from more than sixty counties and every geographical section of Virginia. Although room and board had been raised from $42 to $45 a quarter, or $126 for the three-quarter year, enrollments continued to rise. (Photo: *Schools of Rockingham County*)

Burruss understood that Virginia was an agricultural state, so he demanded that the school prepare teachers to serve that aspect of their children's lives. Rural arts was to be as valuable a department of the new school as English language and literature. In addition, there were departments of education, foreign languages, geography, history and social sciences, household arts, manual arts, mathematics, music, natural science, and physical education.

State Superintendent Eggleston praised the ideals as those of "a really great school—one worthy of the Valley of Virginia. When completed . . . beyond comparison the most beautiful, the most comprehensive school of its kind in the South—indeed will have few equals anywhere."

Throughout the spring, Burruss interviewed applicants to find a faculty to match the curriculum. In May, he produced a briefer *Bulletin* announcing the "Kindergarten Course" and arrangements for the creation of a training school, to replicate the actual conditions of a public school. Such a model would better prepare student-teachers. He instituted a cooperative system with Harrisonburg to utilize Main Street School for training, then added nearby rural schools in Rockingham County. The *Bulletin* set forth the rationale: "the value of . . . facilities for observations and practice teaching under real public school conditions cannot be overestimated. There are no specially selected classes of pupils and no artificial environment of any sort. The teacher-train[ee] meets the same conditions that she will face when she takes up her work after graduation."

Beyond his attention to the logistical details of establishing curriculum and selecting staff, he personally read each application for admission and then

Faculty not only greeted students in September, but also saw them off in June, and made certain that individual bows (shown in the hand of the woman left of center) tagging the women as Normal School students were prominently pinned in place. Any respectable young woman of the day appeared in public carefully chaperoned. (Photo: Dingledine's *History of Madison College*)

answered each prospective student. The first letter of acceptance went to Eleanor Beatrice Marable of Prince George County.

By the last week of September 1909, though construction debris still littered the campus—and its president carried his broken wrist in a sling from having tripped on the rough boardwalk entrance to Science Hall—the school was ready for the incoming students. Both faculty and townspeople proudly awaited the first arrivals to the Normal and Industrial School for Women at Harrisonburg.

And those first arrivals, excited and anxious in equal parts, came by train from across the state, arriving by Chesapeake & Western, Baltimore & Ohio, or Southern rail lines. Each girl found a faculty member waiting to greet her at one or the other of Harrisonburg's two passenger stations, located on West Market Street, opposite Wetsel Seed stores, and at the corner of Bruce Street and Chesapeake Avenue. President and Mrs. Burruss had met each incoming faculty member. Observing propriety, no Normal school female would ever move through town sans chaperon.

One of those first arrivals was M'Ledge Moffett, later dean of women at Radford College. She recalled her early days in an article published twenty-four years later in the May 1933 *Virginia Teacher*.

RULES FOR TEACHERS—1915

Teaching can be demanding in any age, but looking over these rules published by the "Buckeye Farm News" in 1915 makes one question why any young girl would choose such a strait-laced profession. And Virginia was probably no different in its demands than Ohio.

"You will not marry during the term of your contract."

"You are not to keep company with men."

"You must be home between the hours of 8 P.M. and 6 A.M. unless attending school functions."

"You may not loiter downtown in any of the ice cream stores."

"You may not travel beyond the city limits unless you have the permission of the chairman of the board."

"You may not ride in a carriage or automobile with any man unless he is your father or brother."

"You may not smoke cigarettes."

"You may not dress in bright colors."

"You must wear at least two petticoats."

"Your dresses must not be any shorter than two inches above the ankle."

"To keep the school neat and clean, you must: sweep the floor at least once daily; scrub the floor at least once a week with hot, soapy water; clean the blackboards at least once a day; and start the fire at 7 A.M. so the room will be warm by 8 A.M."

I was one of the first students to arrive. Miss King met us at the station. There were surries galore and in the midst a four-seated carry-all. I chose this and there, perched high amid telescope suitcases, bandboxes and umbrella, I with about thirty other girls formed the first parade of Normal girls the public square of Harrisonburg ever saw, and they saw us.

The first dining hall was housed in the basement of Dormitory No. 1, Jackson Hall. The first meal included baked apples from the former farm orchard that became a part of the campus. Girls had to bring their own napkins, but in Duke's day napkins were furnished and the dining hall moved to the newly constructed Harrison Hall. (Photo: *History of Madison College*)

Everyone in Harrisonburg knew the Normal was opening. Triumphantly we rode up South Main Street, around to the corner of the dormitory (Jackson Hall). Marshalled about by zealous faculty committees, I finally landed bag and baggage in Room 21, my home for the next two years. That night we ate the first meal ever served in this college (the dining room was in the basement). We had baked apples ('shriveled witches'). We continued to have baked apples until we had depleted the [campus'] apple orchard, drunk the cider, and eaten the last 'gnarl' from the Science Hall basement.

The next day (September 28, 1909) we registered. The preliminary organization of the faculty functioned. Each one at his station served us with a card. I can still see those cards, large ones, small ones, white ones, pink ones, blue ones—they had a card for everything. Having divested myself of fourteen dollars, the charges for one month's board, I shuffled my pack of cards and chose the color which stood for Household Arts. I little realized that in that choice I was making history. The five of us who chose household arts as a major that day were the first Virginia women ever to start training in a Virginia institution for that greatest of women's callings, home making education. (Three of us are still 'old maids'.)

Thus our college life started. Every one had an equal start; there were no old girls to steer us about; there were no organizations to flaunt their virtues in our face, only girls who had the faith to try a new school.

Faith proved essential to carry Miss Moffett through the initial, universal homesickness. Her letters home distill the flavor of those early innocent times:

Students returning after Christmas break in 1911, their skirts clearly the prescribed inches from the boardwalk. (Photo: Dingledine's *History of Madison College*)

Friday night there was a called meeting to form two literary societies. . . . After the meeting we played folk games and danced. Saturday I went to Manual Arts. . . . I hemmed napkins until dinner and cheered up homesick girls. After dinner I went down town again to get another clothes bag—I can't go down town again for two weeks—well. Saturday night the Bible class of our church gave a reception to Presbyterian girls—I wore my white dress. It was a swell affair. Perfectly beautiful dresses. The hostess wore a garnet dress trimmed in rich garnet velvet and gold braid. One of her daughters wore pink silk, the other green. The dresses of all the town people were fine.

I had seven girls helping me dress. Really our room is full all the time. Virginia (my roommate) has the reputation of being the prettiest girl in school. . . .

I think every young man in Harrisonburg has been out here this P.M. They act like they had never seen a girl. . . .

We had cooked-to-death chicken today, and O dear, we have had chipped beef three times this week, twice in one day. We have burnt rice, potatoes and tomatoes or corn, and tough beef every day. . . . I get up at six o'clock. Books cost like forty here. I paid $1.40 for one book and thirty-five cents for notebooks . . . the girls are after me to wear a rat (hairpad), but I flatly refused and I solemnly mean to stick to it.

Of course, not every girl had been lucky enough to be housed in the dorm or renovated Newman farmhouse (later known as Cleveland Cottage). The berths on campus for seventy-five proved fewer than the number needed for the 128 students from around the state. Some students roomed in town and

Members of the Lanier Literary Society pose costumed for a patriotic performance, circa 1910. Such participation groomed future teachers for days ahead when they would organize school events—write, direct, and costume pupils of their own. Note the forty-six-star flag. (Photo: JMU Special Collections)

took meals in Jackson, others found both room and board in nearby homes. But, on campus or off, all bonded in one grand sisterhood of being "Normal girls."

The faculty nurtured that bond in every possible way. If classes separated girls according to major interests, daily assemblies in Science [Maury] Hall brought them all together. The faculty also encouraged formation of an all-school YWCA to be the guiding organization on campus under Miss Natalie Lancaster.

Other faculty members sponsored smaller groups. Professor John Wayland mentored the Lee Literary Society, and Miss Elizabeth Cleveland the Lanier Literary Society. Those two groups soon became the most prestigious on campus. In fact, society colors gave rise to the school colors: purple derived from the violet and white of Lanier, gold from the gray and gold of Lee. In addition, clubs emerged around subject fields such as art, home economics, and foreign language, as well as springing from geographic locales, as in the Tidewater or Harrisonburg clubs. In a few years, the Mary Club—for girls named Mary—became one of the largest on campus, excluding the two grand literary societies.

The 1913 *Schoolma'am*, dedicated to Elizabeth "Lida" Cleveland who had given the yearbook its name, lists sixteen different organizations to enrich the social life of students. The *Normal Bulletin* that year touted the social opportunities present:

The people of Harrison-burg socially are cordial and hospitable. Many cultured homes are open to the young ladies of the school. The churches . . . offer opportunities for social intercourse. [Each girl was expected to attend the local church corresponding to her home denomination.] Wholesome development of the social side of student life is necessary and valuable, and organizations for promoting the social welfare of the students are encouraged, receptions and social evenings are held, and entertainments, public lectures, and musicals are given from time to time.

The *Bulletin* also reassured parents that "Care is taken that all social affairs be kept within the bounds of propriety for young ladies, suitable chaperonage being provided at all times; and they are not allowed to interfere with the progress of the student's work in the school."

The school view of "propriety" and "suitable chaperonage" was strict and unyielding. The administration clearly understood its charge to be *in loco parentis,* and it established rigid rules with harsh consequences for breaking them. Eight decades later, a member of that first class shook her head and smiled in disbelief recalling one incident. Alumna of 1912 Ruth Conn said, "Two girls walked out on the [C&W] railroad tracks [edging the school] to meet two boys one Sunday afternoon. They were seen and the faculty immediately convened in a long meeting that lasted all evening trying to decide what to do with the girls. Since it was so close to graduation, they were confined to campus for the remainder of the year instead of being sent home. All they did was walk and talk, but it was a terrible offense."

Conn also remembered cleanliness as a greater problem for her than strictness. "The campus was so muddy, we couldn't keep our dresses clean. We had to walk on boardwalks everywhere—new grass was planted but we were not

MARGARET CAMPBELL KINNEAR
HOUSEHOLD ARTS
"Blest with each talent and each art to please,
And born to write, converse, and live at ease."

Y. W. C. A.; Home Economics Club; President Lanier Literary Society; Cherokee Hockey Team; Editor-in-Chief SCHOOLMA'AM, '15; Rockbridge Club.
DESTINY: Around Margaret's head we can almost see the twining laurel wreath of America's most famous novelist.

CORINNE SNOWDEN JONES
KINDERGARTEN
"It's the songs ye sing, an' the smiles ye wear
That's a-making the sun shine everywhere."

Y. W. C. A.; Secretary Senior Class; Kindergarten Club; Pinquet Tennis Club.
DESTINY: Mistress of a farm, and that right soon.

LAURA LEE JONES
REGULAR NORMAL
"Known by few, but prized as far as known."

Treasurer of Lee Literary Society; Pinquet Tennis Club; Hockey Team; Glee Club; Vice-President Class of 1913.
DESTINY: Professor of History in Columbia University.

A sample page from the 1915 *Schoolma'am* reveals a diversity of desired destinies. The annual's name derives from the purpose of the school to produce "schoolma'ams," as teachers called themselves. (Photos: 1915 *Schoolma'am,* Carrier Library)

allowed to sit or walk on the new growth."

The only saving grace for the girls' complaints was that President and Mrs. Burruss suffered the same problems they did. The couple lived in two rooms at the southwest end of the second floor of the dormitory (now Jackson Hall) and ate in the dining room. Students occupied the rest of that floor, the first floor, and the Newman farmhouse. Conveniently, the dining room and kitchen were in the basement but the majority of classes were in Science Hall.

Although Mrs. Burruss assumed no formal responsibility for the girls, they "coveted her attention and counsel," according to M'Ledge Moffett. One incident shows why she was so loved. Although the girls were forbidden to sleep outside their rooms, even the most law-abiding felt the event of Halley's Comet in 1910 could negate ordinary rules. Moffett gives the details: "After several fruitless efforts to see it from the porch rooms, we moved ourselves

Top: This informal "Hiking Crowd" led by President and Mrs. Burruss, circa 1910, had hiked roughly nine miles to the John S. McLead's farm in Bridgewater, demonstrating the new interest in feminine fitness. Later years would see the formation of a Hiking Club and annual treks to the top of Massanutten Peak. (Photo: JMU Special Collections)

Bottom: Offering a rare early view of the back campus, this photo shows members of the Class of 1910 proudly aligning themselves along the grounds now overlooking Bridgeforth Stadium, thus making them perhaps the first "Hillside Gang." (Photo: JMU Special Collections)

upstairs and doubled up. At 2:00 A.M., we aroused the dormitory to see this glory of the heavens. Mrs. Brooke was horrified, but we scored when she discovered Mrs. Burruss in our midst."

What the president said is not recorded, but certainly dorm living must not have been his favorite style. And in the broader picture, he knew that limited space meant limited success. A new dormitory was the immediate need. Enrollment for the winter quarter in 1909 was 209, the next year 249. He knew the spiral would continue upward. He had, however, underestimated the appeal of summer school. The very first summer brought 207 students—men as well as women; enrollment during the second summer (1911–12) enrollment was 360. Housing in a single dorm and the Newman farmhouse obviously fell far short of needs.

The cornerstone was laid in October 1910 for a second dorm (Ashby) to house 109 students and one chaperon in thirty-eight rooms. Pride flows with each line in Burruss's 1913 prospectus to describe the campus and assure parents about the safe, modern facilities. In an era when most farm families had neither electricity, central heating, nor inside plumbing, he could write:

> The dormitories are built of stone, with red tile roof . . . are heated by the automatic vacuum steam system, lighted by a large number of windows and by numerous electric lights. The stairways are entirely fireproof . . . and extinguishers placed in easy reach on every floor, with sufficient water supply and pressure to cover every part of the building, which are only two stories in height. All electric wiring is run in conduits in the safest and most approved modern manner. . . .
>
> The shower and needle baths are equipped with white marble walls and nickel and brass fittings. The lavatories are of white porcelain enamel with mirrors above the basins. The floors of the halls and rooms are of hard wood. The halls are wide and well lighted, and a wide portico runs the full length of the front of the buildings. Besides the bedrooms for students, the dormitories contain parlors and rooms for the Matron and several teachers. Dormitory No. 1 contains a dining-hall, kitchen, and pantry; Dormitory No. 2, the gymnasium, with baths, lockers, and bowling alley. Single iron beds are used in all the rooms.

In addition to the true gymnasium located in the basement of Dormitory No. 2 (Ashby) was another large fireproof room equipped for student use in ironing the long, cotton dresses that took an allotted time from each

This view toward Main Street, across the future quad, shows the "Normal Line" marching in 1912 along the boardwalk to a baccalaureate service at a church in downtown Harrisonburg. Churches rotated holding the service, and if too small for the anticipated crowd, as the Episcopal Church was, the event was held in the Virginia Theatre or the Assembly Hall in the Courthouse. (Photo: Dingledine's *History of Madison College*)

girl's day. Personal appearance was a high priority. On any occasion the "Normal girls" descended on the town en masse, the line made an impressive statement of proper decorum. Hatted and often gloved, the students marched two-by-two—sedate "young ladies" clothed in the simplest fashion of the day, white dresses hemmed exactly six measured inches from the ground, regardless of the wearer's height. Chaperons often checked each hemline with a ruler before the procession embarked.

Townspeople were not the only ones impressed by the marching line of girls and the rising bluestone buildings. As the *Normal Bulletin* circulated statewide each year, readers sensed that something special was occurring beyond the Blue Ridge. In 1908, the total enrollment had been 209 from forty-seven counties. By 1914, summer school alone listed 642 students from eighty-three counties. And graduates taught in classrooms across the Commonwealth.

Early commencement exercises could not be held in a state-supported school today due to the clearly religious overtones indicated in this program. (Photo: JMU Special Collections)

Commencement Exercises

of the

State Normal School

Harrisonburg, Virginia

June 11, 1912, 8:30 p. m.

Hymn—Love Divine . . . . *Wesley*

Invocation . . . . Rev. H. H. Sherman

The Glee Club—Last Night . . . . *Kjerulf*

Address . . . . . . Hon. Henry D. Flood, Member of Congress

The Glee Club—Ye Happy Birds . . . . *Warner*

Delivery of Diplomas

Benediction . . . . Rev. G. C. Minor

(The audience is requested to stand during the singing of the Hymn and to remain standing until the conclusion of the Invocation.)

Chapter Three

"The great adventure
of getting the
school going"
(1914–1917)

THROUGH THE FIRST DECADE OF GROWTH, faculty and students shared a unique bond as they strove together to create the new school "bound by no traditions . . . unbiased by questions of the past. . . made to fit our own time," as Dr. Burruss summarized in 1916. And the faculty consciously concerned itself with almost every aspect of student life.

In frequent meetings lasting two to four hours or more, the entire staff labored over details from general policy to daily life. Burruss repeatedly countered complaints about the length of meetings with, "We must bear in mind we are here to serve the State in any way we can." Topics ranged from the momentous to the trivial, justified if they bore any tie to the school.

Random examples from faculty meeting minutes reveal "problems" such as students' careless handwriting, the propriety of girls wearing male costumes in a student production of "Mrs. Wiggs of the Cabbage Patch," and the wisdom of allowing students to attend a football game in Charlottesville.

In 1917, the faculty worried enough about student health to mandate forty-five minutes of outdoor exercise each day. Then they

The students pictured here with "Indian clubs" are in the original "gymnasium-assembly room" in Science (Maury) Hall. But by 1914 the expanded school gym in Ashby offered Indian clubs, ladders, a jumping board, and other equipment heralding a fresh approach to feminine fitness. Even the up-scale new Lord & Taylor in New York City had set aside a dining area, roof promenade, and exercise room with Indian clubs for employees. (Photo: Dingledine's *History of Madison College*)

debated whether to close the library early in order to force students outside. Also, from 1916 on they granted Senior Privileges each year, extending the curfew to 10:00 P.M., rather than 9:30, for seniors to return from downtown.

Firmly believing the old adage about safety in numbers, the faculty decreed that groups of three seniors might leave campus without chaperons not only for church, social affairs, and movies, but also for calling, shopping, walking, driving, and dining out in private homes. The girls had to sign out, of course, by name and destination, but the freedom to go driving with a gentleman, even limited to daylight, was a coveted concession. And walking or driving, a favorite student destination was Fletcher's Drug Store for a "Kum Back Puff"—a

Middy blouses and canvas shoes allow free movement for participants in the first tennis tournament on Saturday, November 12, 1910. Frances Mackey, Eva Massey, Willye White, and Amelia Brooke find their enthusiasm paralleled in a popular postcard—the girl in a middy carries a racquet and flag emblazoned HNS, for Harrisonburg Normal School. (Photo: JMU Special Collections. Postcard: Courtesy Nancy Garber)

delectable concoction of ice cream, chocolate sauce, and trimmings for a mere ten cents—"a trifling sum for such a delicacy," insisted one young lady.

Few girls questioned the strict regulations. Years later an alumna recalled that once, when skirts cleared the floor by a few inches, one freshman was restricted to campus for too short a skirt—though the length had been acceptable at her high school. At the conclusion of a lengthy rebuke, the student left the matron's presence with a courteous, instinctive "Thank you," spoken without a trace of resentment in her attitude.

The same alumna reported in 1917, "One girl, and only one, in the student body had bobbed hair. The comment was made by a fellow student, 'No school board will employ her unless she lets her hair grow.'"

Spotswood Hall in 1917 followed the same architectural plan that guided construction of prior dorms Jackson and Ashby. Sunshade umbrellas were *de rigueur* to protect porcelain-pale complexions still in vogue. (Photo: JMU Special Collections)

COPY OF A HANDWRITTEN LETTER

Sunday Morning
Jan. 16, 1916

Dearest Papa,

I received your postal last night . . . that was welcomed. I also received my coat which you sent. I certainly was glad to get it. I had been wearing that old blue coat which I have had for at least five years, but is still a good coat, wonder if you could sell it. I use to cover up with at night now, it has been freezing up here. Rachel and myself have been sleeping together, even our ink which was on the table froze, my bath robe is the comfort of my life.

I certainly am sorry that Mamma is sick, I missed her usual letter. I hope she is much better by now. The Infirmary is full of sick girls and there are several sick ones in the dormitories. They all have the La grippe and sore throat, it is always the case after the holidays.

I was elected Monitor last week. I have to keep order on my end of the hall at night, it is no easy job, but a person who shirks responsibility does not amount to much in this world. The Stratfords (this is the society I belong to and also the best in school) is going to give a Shakespearian pageant next Saturday night. I am going to be Shylock in the play. I hope it will be a great success. At the Faculty Meeting the other night they decided to lighten the work of the students, they think we ought to get out of classes earlier in the afternoon and take more exercise and get more fresh air. I do not think that our work this year will be shortened any but the work next year will be lighter. If Katherine comes to school up here year after next this ought to interest her. . . .

I wish you would please send me some writing paper, stick a five-cent paper of pins in too if you can. I have been thinking about applying for some schools, but Mr. Smithey told us not to worry about getting a school because he could get some good positions for us. One of the girls up here from Waverly, Virginia told me she thought there would be a vacancy in the fifth and sixth grades next year and thought I could certainly get the position if I applied. There are eleven teachers in this school, and the grammar grade teacher gets from $60 to $65 per month. I think I can get this amount. If I can get $60 per month in Virginia, I do not care to go to West Virginia, it is so far from home, and the people of West Virginia are not always so desirable, and the climate no doubt is different, don't you think it better to teach in Virginia if I can get a desirable position?

I am just living now for graduation day and to be obtaining a position. I would not take anything for my Normal Training. Papa, I will have to have some visiting cards, can't you get them cheaper than I can, fifty will be enough, of course the Old English print is prettier I think but the other prints are real pretty too. I wish if you could get them you would do so as soon as you can. I might need them very soon, we never know.

A great Evangelist is going to preach at the Virginia Theatre this afternoon on "A Woman's Worth," a crowd of Normal girls are going, I am going also. I have seen several of my pupils since I have been back and they seemed delighted to see me. . . . Papa, please also send me three pairs of black stockings, two pairs of fifteen cents ones will be all right, and one pair of twenty-five cent ones. I guess you will not want me to write to you anymore as I have asked for several things. . . .

I will close as it is time for Church. Give my love to Mamma and hoping she will soon be all right. Kiss the children and save much for your own dear self and write sometimes too.

Your loving daughter,
Mary Coles
[With twenty-nine girls called Mary on campus, most went by double names as did Mary Coles Hankins of Halifax County.]

The cloistered atmosphere, in which decorous young women moved at that time and which they accepted as normal, saw few serious breeches of school regulations. But when graver breaches of discipline occurred, they were considered by the faculty at large. Raymond Dingledine's history relates several examples:

> A student was placed on a quarter's probation for attending a
> dance downtown without permission, knowing that she could not

get such permission. Another student was suspended for rudeness to a teacher. . . . A girl guilty of repeated thefts was expelled. Two students who went riding with young men one October without permission were campused, one for the rest of the quarter, the other for the rest of the session. This latter young woman was allowed to remain in school only because five girls agreed to help her keep the rules and regulations. The attempt to 'save' this student failed, however, and, on the advice of the faculty, her guardian withdrew her from School.

President Burruss and his faculty could keep a tight rein on campus, but they could not hold Mother Nature in check. In 1913, unbridled hormones defeated the campus mores in a dramatic incident that brought unsought publicity to the school.

Banner headlines in the Harrisonburg paper for February 15, 1913, reported "PRETTY SCHOOL GIRL ELOPES FROM NORMAL." Immediately below in small caps ran, "MISS LILLIAN CAMPBELL, LEAVING DORMITORY BY MEANS OF IMPROVISED ROPE, JOINS LOVER AND HASTENS TO BE MARRIED—STUDENT BODY SHOCKED."

The faculty was more shocked. It quickly convened, and less quickly concluded. The dilemma was that no specific school rule banned elopement. After deliberating from four-thirty in the afternoon to after midnight, according to Dingledine, "The faculty, however, rose nobly to the occasion. The romantic young lady was expelled for leaving school without permission. . . . The sister of the fiancé was asked to withdraw from School. The other roommate was suspended for a year."

The story had made the *Washington Post* as well as other newspapers around the state, which named the two lovers from prominent Bedford families. The marriage announcement was conspicuously absent, however, from the annual list of weddings in 1913's *Schoolma'am.*

The unexpected also brought unwanted excitement in the fall of 1913. One October morning while classes were in session, the laundry shack caught fire. Students and teachers rallied to save the clothes and ironing boards; the local fire company saved the building. Harrisonburg proudly boasted a "motabile" fire truck that quickly responded to the alarm. Soon the students' initial panic was replaced by delight at the scores of young men on campus. As one young lady was quoted in the Harrisonburg *Daily News-Record*, "Sure enough, there they were—scores of men, real men, tearing across the campus. They came from every direction—men running, men on horseback, men in buggies, men in automobiles. Nothing short of a fire could explain that phenomenon."

The next disruption due to natural events came one evening in February 1914. The dam on the Shenandoah River broke and waters flooded the electric power plant to deprive Harrisonburg of electricity. Senior Mary Wallace Buck (later Rowe) recalls the night in a 1957 letter to Dr. Dingledine:

> The power went off one Sunday night, of all times, and arrangements had to be made to open the stores and get lamps for all those dormitory rooms, and in a hurry. At first, while we were waiting for the lamps, it was something of a lark. All the girls gathered in the living room of the dorm, that monstrosity of leather upholstered Mission furniture, and sat around on the floor, by the light of a few candles. Someone thought it would be a good idea to tell ghost stories in such an eerie setting, but apparently nobody knew any to tell!

For a month all evening activities were lit by lamplight—about 200 oil lamps enabled studies and recreation to continue. Each night brought a holiday air to the campus with lanterns placed at intervals along the walks like festive luminaries to penetrate the bleak February darkness. One night the "Normal line" carried lanterns as the girls walked to town to attend a comic opera.

Candlelight also cast a soft, reassuring glow through the windows of the newly erected "Hillcrest" as Dr. and Mrs. Burruss completed their evening routine. The president and his wife had moved from the dorm to "Hillcrest" in 1914, and the whole campus took pride in the new quarters. Prior to the

Built at a cost of $14,800 in 1914, "Hill Crest" (original spelling) housed in succession presidents Burruss, Duke, Miller, and Carrier, until 1986 when the latter left campus for "Oakview" at 916 Oak Hill Drive, across I-81. (Photo: 1920 *Schoolma'am*)

change, excited home economics majors were allowed to help Miss S. Frances Sale, the department head, estimate the yardage for all the matching drapes, cushion covers, and slipcovers, among other items, to adorn the presidential living room. Margaret Kinnear Patton ('15) had been one of those home economics majors, and years later she recalled that, at a tea the Burrusses held for the students afterward, "Miss Sale proudly reversed one cushion to show that the [total] yardage had come within 18 inches of being exactly right. That one cushion had been pieced on the back."

Patton's same memoir depicts the awe with which students regarded Miss Sale:

> My class must have been one of the first to have a group of Home Ec majors. There were twelve of us. . . . in the class following, there were 48. . . .We cooked in one room, with long counters divided into desks with deep drawers, where we each kept our allotment of spoons, measuring cups, and such, but we had a small room that could pinch hit for a dining room.
>
> Miss Sale had us prepare and serve to ourselves a formal dinner. Well, I remember how the twelve of us sat around the table, gazing with fixed smiles at Miss Sale, who sat at the head of the table, making what was supposed to be light social conversation. Every time she lifted her soup spoon to her lips, twelve spoons rose and lowered in time with hers. I don't recall how we ate the turkey, but I suspect we chewed that in unison, too, and the light conversation rather petered out. I doubt the present day Home Ec majors are *born* as bashful as we were then!

The "home ec" cottage was on the south campus, the president's house to the east. From his vantage on the hillside President Burruss could watch the campus expanding. True to the architect's initial concept, the new buildings extended bluestone walls and red-tiled roofs around the greensward. Spotswood Hall completed the basic building plan. In only eight years, the beginning school of two buildings and a farmhouse had grown to six limestone buildings, a president's home, an expanded farmhouse, two barns, and a laundry shack. At the graduation ceremony in 1917, Burruss announced new names for each of the main structures.

Dormitory No. 1 had been affectionately christened Burruss Hall by the 1913 graduates, but had to be renamed after the president and board agreed that no living person should be commemorated. A permanent name was to be delayed until the fifth reunion of the Class of 1913. (They would decide on Jackson Hall for General "Stonewall" Jackson.) Dormitory No. 2 was christened Ashby Hall after Confederate General Turner Ashby, a local resident who had been killed nearby in an 1862 engagement. Dormitory No. 3 honored Gov. Alexander Spotswood, leader of the first English expedition into the Shenandoah Valley. The Science Building became Maury Hall, aptly named for the distinguished Virginia scientist and oceanographer Matthew Fontaine Maury. The Students' Building, as Harrison Hall, recognized Gessner Harrison, a notable educator born in Harrisonburg in 1807 and a member of the founding faculty at the University of Virginia. The home ec cottage emerged as Cleveland Cottage, after the Normal's own beloved Miss Annie Cleveland, who had died the past December.

Seniors march for the last time to take their seats on wooden benches behind the Science Building, now Maury Hall, during a 1914 commencement. (Photo: JMU Special Collections)

Girls from Richmond and the Tidewater region were still entranced with the view westward from the upper windows of Maury. Their native flat landscapes had sent them off unprepared for the breathtaking seasonal shifts in color along the Allegheny ranges marking the skyline for miles. Autumn's vivid golds, reds, and bronzes and spring's distant dogwood and nearer apple blossoms delighted everyone. The two apple orchards adjacent to the campus on the east and south invited picnics and outdoor performances.

Girls from Tidewater Club (circa 1917) loosely encompassed students from Norfolk, Newport News, Portsmouth, and small towns along the Northern Neck—and filled several passenger cars on trains to Harrisonburg one day each September. They made up a quarter of the student body. (Photo: JMU Special Collections)

An unknown motoring copilot parked on Main Street sits in a sidecar (before the campus's future quad) in a widely admired machine in 1915. Harley-Davidson was five years younger than the school. Both company and school would celebrate centennials in the next century. (Photo: JMU Special Collections)

Toward the close of the first decade, the school grounds appeared more like an established campus than the isolated buildings that rose initially on a muddy field. Trees, shrubs, and flowers had been planted with careful fore-thought, with clubs and classes contributing. Arbor Day established a cere-mony each spring to add a formal touch of beauty to the landscape. In 1911, the first senior class planted a maple tree. Dressed in white, all twenty mem-bers of the class marched around the tree, singing "Here We Go Round the Maple Tree," and then each one dropped into the hole some memento of her course at the Normal and removed a blank diploma.

On Arbor Day in 1913, fifty seniors planted a sprig of ivy from Warwick Castle in England at Maury Hall and tenderly created a miniature English flowerbed with seeds of sweet peas, larkspur, forget-me-nots, and daisies from the same place. Then, with great formality, they passed their spade to Miss Keezell, junior class president, so that next year's class might continue the proud tradition.

Such traditions held on through the 1914 name change when the State Nor-mal and Industrial School for Women at Harrisonburg became the State Nor-mal School for Women at Harrisonburg. As external improvements continued, cement walks began to supplant the old boardwalks. A concrete porch con-nected the three buildings on the south side, and the Class of 1918 gave lamps for the entrance to Harrison Hall. Blue Stone Hill was still on the outskirts of Harrisonburg but had established a look of permanence and a style of its own.

The girls, too, were developing permanent ties to the school and forming lifelong friendships. Year after year, alumnae returned to visit with former classmates, pay respects to former mentors, and marvel over changes taking place. For example, 1916 brought major academic shifts to Harrisonburg. The General Assembly authorized the school to offer a four-year course leading to a Bachelor of Science degree in education. In addition, entrance requirements were gradually tightened until by 1918 completion of three years of high school was mandatory for admission. The previous minimum requirements had stipulated that the entering student be at least fifteen years of age, have completed seventh grade, and be of good moral character.

And there were changes to report off campus. As graduates filled teaching positions around the state, their proficiency burnished the Normal's reputation. A compulsory education bill failed to pass the state legislature in 1916, so schooling remained a local option, but many districts had eight-month school years and the demand for trained teachers grew. In Rockingham County, for example, each of five district school boards offered an impressive $40 a month for teachers with a professional certificate and set the goal of at least one grade school per district.

Practice-teaching lessons under Miss Rachael Gregg's strict supervision might evoke for the women sleepless nights preparing lesson plans and nervous moments in the classroom, but they were a necessary baptism by fire for earning professional status. More than one complainant "tired to a peanut" or "worn down to a nub" managed to keep going, sneaking into the bathroom to work after lights out. Care packages from home with fudge and cookies refueled fading energies.

Afterward, no first-year teacher who had undergone the rigorous demand ever complained it hadn't been worthwhile. The growing roster of alumnae at the end of each *Schoolma'am* gave an indication of how widely the Normal's influence spread.

Naturally, moments of frivolity broke the nights of study. After any snowfall, sledding down the hill in back of "Hillcrest" set girls cavorting boisterously. Winter or summer, any evening before study hours found hopeful dancers gathered in the gym, where practice made perfect prior to the formal dances given during the year—with and without men.

Birthdays brought additional excuses for parties, all faculty sanc-

Just as it does today, any snowfall lured students outside. These girls welcomed a chance to abandon boardwalk rules and staid behavior. The yearbook described the scene as a "mer de glace"—sea of ice—behind Jackson Hall. The house in the background is Cleveland Cottage, the original Newman farmhouse. (Photo: *Images of James Madison University*)

The populations of "town and gown" were energized to present together the Shakespeare Pageant of 1916. Top left: actors are shown here leaving campus; top right: parading around Court Square; and bottom left: performing in the amphitheater (next to today's Joshua Wilton House). Bottom right: the supporting audience may hint at the popularity that would seventy years later greet Professor Ralph Cohen's Shenandoah Shakespeare Express, which was first based in Harrisonburg, before relocating to historic downtown Staunton in the late 1990s. (Photos: JMU Special Collections)

tioned. Miss Lida Cleveland, Mrs. R. B. Brooke, and Miss Frances Mackey attended the one on January 30, 1915, but escaped an outbreak of mumps after the evening's fun. According to one of the girls, "One of the twins was taking mumps at this party. Nine of us had mumps afterward and were in the infirmary at the same time."

There were class parties, YWCA functions, literary society socials, basketball games, and tennis and hockey matches—all designed to let off steam. One unique annual tradition was the May Breakfast, served out-of-doors under the apple blossoms, featuring the first strawberries. Mary Buck Rowe ('14) recalled, "The girls blossomed out too, with their bright new spring dresses, and it was a lovely and colorful affair. There were attractive posters advertising it, and dainty place cards."

A sensitive faculty tried to balance students' academic pursuits with wholesome outings for R&R. For example, Laura Lee Jones Mohler's ('15) diary for 1914–15 includes the entry, "Miss Spillman, our critic teacher, and her 7th grade took the three of us who were teaching in that grade to Raleigh [Rawley] Springs [eleven miles west of Harrisonburg] on Saturday. Went in a big five seated tally-ho and drove four horses."

Off-campus outings were encouraged. In November 1914, Mr. Harry Byrd, president of Valley Turnpike (U.S. Route 11), gave free passes through the toll-gates for an excursion by automobile for fifty ladies and gentlemen to inspect the underground palaces of Weyers Cave at Grottos. In an area "replete with historical interests and natural curiosities," according to the *Normal Bulletin*, the school frequently scheduled excursions in winter, weekly during the summer terms. An annual favorite was the hike to the top of Massanutten Peak (now a resort) with President Burruss or Professor Wayland. On April 4, 1915, the Harrisonburg newspaper reported on one of the trips to Weyers Cave:

> This wonder of nature is visited every year by a number of our students and teachers—especially by those who are not to the mountains born. Even those who are natives of the Valley never tire of seeing such natural wonders as Weyers Cave, Luray Cave, Massanutten Cave, the Natural Chimneys, the Natural Bridge, Peaked Mountain, Brock's Gap, Mole Hill, the Giant's Grave, and Lovers' Leap [in Rawley Springs]."

That same issue of the paper reported:

> Easter came on the wings of the storm and departed on a wave of sunshine, leaving all sorts of memories for the girls who spent the time at Blue-Stone Hill. . . . Among the many boxes and packages that filled the incoming mailbags, those marked 'Perishable—Rush' seemed to predominate. Inside were found violets, carnations, sweet peas, daffodils, and roses, and all the fair hues of flowers seemed reflected in the blushes and smiles of those who had the privilege of opening the packages.

No doubt the opening of packages was accompanied by soprano trills of "Don't you just *love* it?" or "Oh, it's the *essence* of bug juice," popular expressions of delight. Those Easter corsages remained visual reminders of popularity, laid out to keep fresh on the windowsills, in lieu of other refrigeration, before being pressed between the leaves of the heaviest textbook for preservation. Drying laundry in the windows was banned, but flowers were fine.

A fine school, a fine faculty, and fine young ladies received public recognition when state senator John R. Saunders of Middlesex addressed the graduates in 1917. The faculty, resplendent in academic robes (worn for the first time the year before at the groundbreaking for Spotswood Hall), felt no small pride as each girl received her diploma. For the second year, commencement took place on campus in Harrison Hall. Seniors graced the stage in white dresses, sitting stiffly erect, correctly solemn, and justly proud.

Three decades later Lida Cleveland wrote, "I have great pride to have been a part of those first inspiring years and to remember the unselfish spirit, the loyalties, and efforts of each one and the complete cooperation in the great adventure of getting the school going. We knew then—and we were right— this was going to be a great school."

State Normal and Industrial School
HARRISONBURG, VIRGINIA

Report of Miss _Susie Maloy_

For the Quarter ending _March 19, 1915_

CLASS	GRADE	REMARKS
Education 62	A	
Education 68	Passed	
English 61	B	
English 64	B	
History 61	A	
Manual Arts 64	A	
Mathematics 35	B	
Physical Education 61	A	
English 2 (Special)	B	
		Very good

In students' reports A is considered *very good*; B is considered *good*; C is considered *passable*; all being above 75%, which is the *standard pass mark*. A student receiving D on any study is *conditioned* in that study and is allowed to take another examination. E signifies *failure*, and the entire work of the quarter in this study must be repeated if credit is desired.
Residence at the school during *any three* quarters is counted as one year.

19-11-1-'12—5,000

Source: JMU Special Collections

FOR ANYONE WORRIED about complacency from success of the established routine, the war years soon altered the Normal pattern. In April 1917, President Woodrow Wilson dispatched General "Blackjack" Pershing to Paris to head the American Expeditionary Force. Suddenly, distant events unified a nation that had been divided over entering the war. The nation was *at* war. The YWCA held a special vesper service on campus.

Faculty and students shifted focus and realigned priorities to join the war effort. Girls mobilized by compressing study hours to free up time to produce surgical dressings for the Red Cross. Music teacher Elizabeth Harris chaired a Red Cross Auxiliary that met each Saturday morning to roll bandages and knit sweaters—sweaters that proved an awesome undertaking for many just grasping how to knit and purl. More than one recipient in the trenches must have marveled at the model of deformity for which his woolen covering had been designed, with too-long sleeves of different lengths and uneven stitches throughout.

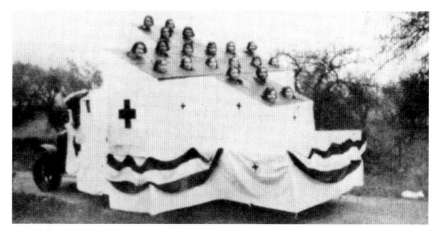

Student patriotism rode high on motorized floats, a coveted addition to the Red Cross parade in 1914, with World War I a distant rumble in Europe. (Photo: *Images of Madison*)

First aid classes, taught by the superintendent of nurses at adjacent Rockingham Memorial Hospital, filled up with patriotic ladies from the county, town, and school, all determined to be ready for any emergency. Academic offerings added special classes in food conservation and Red Cross dietetics. Culinary classes learned how to make "war bread" and "potato biscuits" and attempted to render meals palatable without using precious flour, sugar, or butter. As their patriotic duty, the girls swallowed fish and meat substitutes without complaint.

To waste anything, food especially, was unpatriotic. According to Dingledine's history, "On one occasion, students in Institutional Management made a study of the amount of food left on plates after each meal and reported to

First aid classes sponsored by the Red Cross during World War I actually provided sound preparation for future teachers who would have to deal with children's minor scrapes or more serious playground accidents. (Photo: JMU Special Collections)

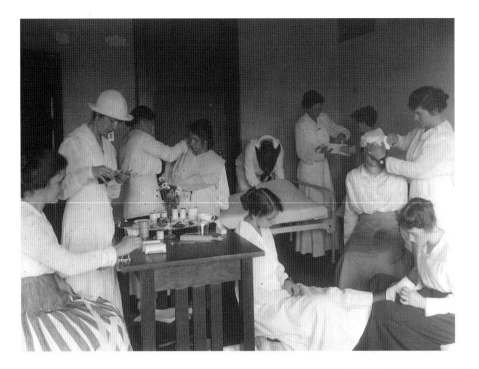

The Practise [*sic*] House, adjacent to the campus, housed household arts seniors in groups of six for a quarter at a time "to practise what they teach." During their six weeks, students spent one week in each household position, beginning as second maid, then first maid, dishwasher, assistant cook, head cook, and lastly housekeeper. The tight budget allotted ten cents per person for each meal even after wartime had necessitated another increase in room and board, to $180 a year. (Photo: 1918 *Schoolma'am*)

the student body." The execution of that study boggles the imagination. Whether the report influenced behavior is not given.

H. Mae Hoover ('18) of Roanoke recalled:

When war came to the nation, colleges were not untouched. It was felt in the mail which brought tidings of loved ones going to camp or "Over There," in the songs we sang—"Keep the Home Fires Burning," and in the substitutes for flour used in the kitchen. Potato bread was really quite good. Muffins of oatmeal were somewhat gooey. With deep concern we watched and waited while a very bright and stable girl decided whether to marry or not to marry before her lover went over seas. A married person probably could not have remained in school. [She did not marry.]

In our patriotic fervor we marched in a parade in the interest of the sale of War Bonds. Headdresses of red, white, and blue produced a moving American flag. Viewed from an upper window, the display was probably effective. Uniformed boys from A.M.A. [Augusta Military Academy] added to the color and interest of the occasion for the girls.

Immediately following that Liberty Loan parade in April 1918, the girls delighted in the incursion of men on campus. Three hundred A.M.A. cadets took dinner in the dining hall that evening. And the Normal girls' formation of that moving American flag drew such accolades that the next month sent their marching platoon in red and white hats to form a moving Red Cross in the Red Cross parade.

The Red Cross parade, however, proved the last march until war's end on November 11, 1918. From the opening of school on September 25 to the first week of November, an epidemic of influenza gripped the campus and brought activity to a standstill. Statewide, college presidents, including Burruss, met to determine how to head off the impending disaster. There seemed no barrier to the scourge sweeping the nation.

Dingledine's history records conditions by the end of the second week of school:

War couldn't totally dampen enthusiasm for extracurricular activities. Girls named Mary formed a club of their own—as did those named Virginia and Helen/Ellen, though the latter were shorter lived. (Photo: 1918 *Schoolma'am*)

So many girls were sick that Jackson Hall was, bit by bit, turned into an infirmary—half of the first floor at first, then all of that floor, and then the whole building. . . . [The regular infirmary in Cleveland Cottage was already filled.] President Burruss, himself, came down with the flu on Tuesday, October 1, and was confined to his room for three weeks. . . . Appeals to the State Health Commission for nurses were virtually fruitless. Serving meals to the sick, which by this time numbered sixty or more, was a heavy burden. Miss Lancaster became ill and other faculty and Post-Graduate student assistants had to carry on.

By Sunday, October 6, the shortage of help was so desperate that Dr. Wilson . . . appealed for volunteers at his Sunday night service at the Presbyterian Church. . . . The next day classes were suspended for two weeks. [Plus churches and many stores were closed.] All well students, except student assistants and Post-Graduates who stayed behind to help, were sent home. Without the burden of constant new cases, conditions at the School rapidly improved. The suspension of classes was extended for two more weeks to allow time for full recovery and to allow students to help at home if needed. . . . On Wednesday, November 6th, the Normal reopened with virtually all the students present.

Amazingly, not a single life had been lost on campus. State- and nation-wide, the tale had a more tragic ending. In the last week of October, while a total of 2,700 American soldiers died in battle "over there," 21,000 civilians died of flu on the home front. Before the epidemic ran its course, more than 500,000 Americans and twenty million people worldwide had perished. Furthermore, forty-five percent of the deaths occurred in the fifteen-to-thirty-five age group. One doctor commented, "The disease simply had its way. It came like a thief in the night and stole our treasure."

When the Normal held Thanksgiving services in 1918, the prayers of thanks were for the end of "the War to End All Wars" and the banishment of "Spanish flu." Classes were held that day to make up for time missed, but the YWCA conducted a special assembly in the afternoon, and the dining room staff served a traditional holiday dinner that evening.

Their world at peace again, the campus returned to normal, and students moved to a familiar pace—except during drills. President Burruss had seldom expressed disappointment in his girls, but he had been less than satisfied with their lack of precision in marching. As an ex-cadet officer at Virginia Polytechnic Institute, he knew how to turn lackluster marchers into precision troops. In January 1919, he instituted a course in military drill and organized a battalion of four companies. The grand finale was a competitive exhibition before local military men to judge the best company as color bearers for graduation.

Dressed in white middy blouses with black skirts and ties, white shoes and white hats, Company B under Virginia Zirkle of Harrisonburg won the competition. At the commencement in June, a battalion parade became the feature presentation of the field day program. The military touch added panache to Burruss's last official ceremony as president of the Normal School. He had

accepted a new challenge, to begin that summer: the presidency of his alma mater in Blacksburg.

From the first 209 girls willing to risk enrolling at an untried school of two buildings and a farmhouse bordering a little known town, Burruss had nurtured "his" school to an institution respected statewide. The number of buildings had grown from two to six, and the initial faculty from fifteen to twenty-six, presenting an equally broader curriculum.

A freshman entering at the end of the first decade found herself on a forty-nine-acre campus (slightly enlarged from the original forty-two) with three dormitories, Cleveland Cottage to house the infirmary, and Maury Hall, the location of the home economics department, laboratories, and classrooms. Harrison Hall held the dining room, auditorium, library, and mail boxes—a daily scene of great expectations. The gymnasium occupied Ashby's basement. Spotswood stood slightly apart from the other buildings, but not as aloof as the president's house.

From his hillside vantage that final June, Burruss certainly must have faced ambivalent feelings as he heard the girlish voices rise from dorm to dorm, carried on the soft evening air through the open windows at "Hillcrest." Hoover's description captures the nostalgia:

President Burruss's final event before departure to VPI was the 1919 Field Day. Firmly a proponent of military-style drills to teach both self-confidence and self-discipline, he unfurled his newly formed battalions holding high the now forty-eight-star American flag. Rockingham Memorial Hospital is pictured in the background. (Photo: 1919 *Schoolma'am*)

A rare closeup (below) of Cleveland Cottage (the old Newman farmhouse), between Maury and Jackson halls. The longer shot (above) demonstrates President Burruss's love of trees. He prevented the clearing out of as many trees as possible, including a variety of fruit trees nearly concealing the cottage. (Photo: *The Virginia Teacher*, May 1920)

On an evening during the final days of the session, girls gathered on the steps of their dormitories to sing. Voices floated across the campus from Spotswood, the strumming of ukuleles and "Sleep Kentucky Babe" answered from Jackson, and a refrain followed from Ashby. There was an undercurrent of sadness in the notes, which heralded the breaking of ties. We were leaving the sheltering walls where we had gained ideals which we should transmit to the rising generation.

But with the nostalgia, Burruss must have also found a heightened satisfaction for the job he had done.

Part Two

Duke:
The Building Years,
1919–1949

Samuel P. Duke and his family at "Hill-crest." His wife Lucille, a teacher when they met in graduate school at the University of Chicago, was educated and civic minded. In her new Harrisonburg community, she taught Sunday school, headed a garden club, helped organize the city nursing service, and entertained the usual bevy of visitors from on campus and beyond from 1919 to 1949. After her husband suffered a stroke in 1948, she cared for him until his death in 1954. She then remained in Harrisonburg until her passing in 1980 at age ninety-two. (Photo: *Images of James Madison University*)

THE APPOINTMENT OF SAMUEL P. DUKE to succeed Julian Burruss as president created a volley of criticism. Duke assumed the position in 1919. Private papers fail to reveal how the Normal's new head felt about the very public support his rival, William Sanger, had received. Nevertheless, Samuel P. Duke was aware that he was not a unanimous choice to follow in Burruss's footsteps—supported neither on campus nor around town, where opinion carried no power, nor universally on the Virginia Normal School Board, where votes counted. As the Harrisonburg *Daily News-Record* clearly reported on July 23, 1919, the vote was "7 to 4 in favor of Prof. Duke"—the paper not even according him the title of state supervisor, a position he had served for high schools throughout the Commonwealth, nor listing his many achievements.

The story went on to emphasize the local favorite who lost:

> Dr. Sanger was solidly supported alike by the educators and political leaders of the Shenandoah Valley, and was not opposed by any local political party or faction. He had the endorsement of Prof. Burruss, of every county school superintendent in the Valley, of the superintendent of Schools of Harrisonburg and the Harrisonburg School Board, in addition to the Merchants Credit Association and political leaders, including Senator Conrad and Delegate Rolston, Democrats [*sic*], and Prof. Wright, the Republican delegate. He also was endorsed by the Harrisonburg Chamber of Commerce, the faculty and the alumni of the Normal School.
>
> During the morning, telegrams were received asking if Prof. Heatwole would be acceptable locally in the event Dr. Sanger could not be elected. So far as known, the replies made were that the Valley had but one choice—Dr. Sanger—and desired to see him elected.

Public sentiment did not prevail. Neither Cornelius J. Heatwole, one of the original faculty who had moved to the University of Georgia, nor William T. Sanger, the Normal School's registrar, director of summer sessions, and first dean, won the coveted appointment. Instead, Duke assumed the presidency on August 26, just nine days before his thirty-fourth birthday.

WILLIAM SANGER

Dr. Sanger, Professor of Psychology and Education, in 1918. (Photo: 1918 *Schoolma'am*)

When the Board of Visitors named Samuel Page Duke as president of the State Normal School for Women at Harrisonburg, the local outcry was loud and disapproving. William Thomas Sanger, the popular choice who lost, must have been deeply disappointed. Born in Bridgewater in 1885 to Brethren minister Samuel F. Sanger and his wife Susan, he lived there until the family moved to Indiana during his teens, and returned to attend Bridgewater College.

An outstanding student, Sanger was offered a position there on graduation in 1909. He taught history and philosophy, then took a year to earn his master's degree at Indiana University.

Returning to the Harrisonburg area, he soon moved to the Normal School as its first dean. In addition, he headed the school's department of education and directed summer sessions. By 1919, he'd also garnered the first of several doctoral degrees.

Hometown sentiment favored Sanger over the locally unknown Duke. Consequently, after failing to obtain the Normal school presidency, Sanger taught briefly again at Bridgewater, then at the universities of Utah and Virginia. But his reputation today derives from his presidency of the Medical College of Virginia (1925–56 in Richmond.

As MCV graduate Dr. Jean Wine of Harrisonburg said, "Sanger was the greatest thing that ever happened to MCV. He took a mediocre school and raised the standard to make it one of the class-A medical schools in the nation." Fellow alumnus Dr. George Nipe agreed: "He was the man for what they needed. Most faculty prior to his time were private practitioners who taught when they could. He attracted great leaders."

As MCV's first full-time president, Sanger drew notable national figures. To head surgery he brought in Isaac "Ike" Bigger, who would pioneer heart surgery. Sanger also hired William Branch Porter to head medicine; Lee E. Sutton to be dean and pediatrics chair; and Porter P. Vinson, who was one of the only men in the country doing endoscopic work at the time.

Sanger also pioneered the concept of regional professional education by arranging with West Virginia University for its students to attend MCV in their final two years of medical school.

He was further skilled at winning funds from the legislature, funding to underwrite a five-story hospital, a library, clinic facilities, dorms, and renovation of the original Egyptian building. By the end of his tenure, the value of MCV's plant had risen from around $1 million to more than $24 million. Enrollment had doubled and the number of hospital beds increased from 400 to 1,000. At his death in April 1975, one editor applied Sir Christopher Wren's inscription from St. Paul's Cathedral to Sanger: "If you would see his monument, look around you."

Never physically imposing, bald and seriously myopic, he had to hold a paper almost to his eyes to see through his thick lenses. Dr. Robert Bondurant (the author's uncle) of Roanoke recalled, "He had to get right in my face to talk, leaning forward about six inches from my nose." Yet he read and wrote with an amazing memory for facts and people.

Had Sanger won the Normal presidency, no doubt he would have served the school well; that initial defeat, however, propelled the right man to the right school at just the right time—the Normal's "loser" proved MCV's exceptional gain.

His youthful enthusiasm would be a major asset. He inherited the Normal's unexpected financial distress. September's first monetary statement revealed a balance of only $324.34 in the school account. Yet enrollment for the first quarter had reached the highest in the institution's history. So Duke, like his predecessor, knew that continued growth depended on adequate facilities for housing and teaching students.

Surveying the campus that first autumn, he realized that he lacked facilities for desired growth, yet he concealed his dismay. A positive attitude became his trademark. In an opening address evincing confidence and enthusiasm, he outlined his agenda to the faculty, a faculty that by then had unified and tendered its loyal support with a formal statement read aloud and entered in the minutes at their initial meeting. From Duke's immediate agenda, historian Dingledine capsules the budget requests:

"Duke placed first the need for a new dormitory . . . pointed out the capacity . . . with two students to a room, was 190, whereas 252 students were actually housed in them. . . . In addition, thirty students had to be housed . . . off campus, an expensive proposition. Twenty-five prospective students had been turned away because of lack of facilities."

In addition to a new dorm, Duke cited the need for a new heating and laundry plant, for finishing Harrison Hall, and for adequate baking, refrigeration, and kitchen equipment. He proposed building a practice house—as now required under the Smith-Hughes Act of 1917. He sought lab equipment for the home economics, agriculture, chemistry, and physical education departments. He prioritized Maury Hall renovations. And finally he suggested that the rough, "unsightly" grounds of the campus be landscaped into a more suitable appearance for a girls' school.

A typical dormitory room had two electric lights, with cords dangling from outlets in the ceiling. During the first decades, an electric lamp seemed a wonderful innovation to girls from rural areas across the state, with electricity on farms not a reality until the mid- and late 1930s, after the passage of the Rural Electrification Act in 1936 under President Franklin Roosevelt. Parents sometimes needed assurance that harmful electricity did not leak out of the wire when the light was off. (Photo: *History of Madison College*)

Then he turned to less visible but no less urgent needs. In his official "Requests for Support and Capital Outlay" on October 22, 1919, he pressed for more adequate faculty compensation, with "an average salary scale of $2,250 for department heads, $1,600 for instructors and $1,200 for assistant instructors, with $3,300 for the president."

These initial requests, however, held no hint of the creative way Duke would address fundraising over the next thirty years as he earned the nickname "Builder." The public soon recognized that the young president brought special assets to his job. Coupled with energetic ambition was the imagination to fuel his enterprises. That first recognition came at an alumnae luncheon in Richmond on November 26 of his second year when he launched a unique plan to raise money for an Alumnae-Students' Building.

Firing the enthusiasm of 121 gathered alumnae, he set them a challenge: *they* were to sponsor a drive to raise the enormous sum of $50,000. Thrilled at his confidence in their ability, the women fanned out into communities throughout the state to extend his creative approach with imaginative actions of their own. In Norfolk, former Normal students opened the Cinderella Tea Room in which alumnae served as waitresses and profits were turned over to the building fund. Graduates living in Harrisonburg and Staunton presented a minstrel show at the New Virginia Theatre. Statewide, card parties, plays, food sales, ball games, and individual pledges poured in. In addition, the Normal faculty also pledged more than $2,000, and the student body matched the professors' effort.

With more courage than currency, Duke and his stalwart supporters scheduled the cornerstone laying during commencement week in June 1921. Subsequent construction progressed—or was delayed—in direct proportion to income until the new building was ready for the summer session of 1922. While Duke hadn't gotten all the funding he'd asked for from the state board, he had done so from his public call. Public opinion had turned around magnificently, and solidified behind him.

Not that "his girls" were surprised. They had backed Duke from the first. The lanky, handsome young president set hearts to fluttering as he strode across the campus. These were romantic crushes of the most pristine and proper quality, while his wife represented a feminine ideal to which each undergraduate aspired. A college graduate herself, Lucille Campbell had met her future husband while she was teaching at her alma mater in Georgetown, Texas. Then, when she fell in love, she had happily set aside her own career to become the model wife and mother, to devote her life to her children and husband—her success thereafter reflected in his achievements, a customary attitude of the day and one inculcated in Normal women.

As if to underscore the mood on campus, the 1920 *Schoolma'am* was dedicated to Burruss *and* Duke, "With/ All love for the past/ All loyalty to the present/ and/ All faith in the future/ Of Our School." Excited students on the cusp of change heralded their new president with enthusiasm, an excitement that flowed through the roll of 259 names, from Margaret Louise Abbott of Evington, Virginia, to Madge Yeomans of Rayord, North Carolina.

Distribution of *The Schoolma'am* generated high excitement each year. It was printed and picked up from McClure Printers at Staunton in a flatbed truck and never failed to be on time in twenty-two years. (Photo: 1920 *Schoolma'am*)

W HILE THE REST OF THE NATION careened into the "Roaring Twenties," movement on the Normal's campus remained sedate. News headlines screaming of flappers, speakeasies, bathtub gin, and jazz in New York City or Chicago simply solidified moral opposition in small-town America, Harrisonburg included. President Duke and his faculty determined to maintain a safe enclave for young ladies in the midst of moral disintegration elsewhere. With God in His Heaven and Christians in college, all would become right with the world.

"A Word from Mr. Duke," opening the *Handbook*—issued yearly to each girl by the Young Women's Christian Association (YWCA)—affirmed his position: "A state-supported college for teacher-training must be non-denominational, but it cannot be non-religious if it is to send out into our state teachers of high moral and religious character. . . . Here all the students of all religious beliefs can meet on common ground and consider those big problems of one's attitude toward God and his Word."

Chapter Six

"The Roaring Twenties"
(1920–1926)

Main Street (U.S. Route 11) is still unpaved but concrete sidewalks replaced wooden walkways by 1922. The gate accesses the driveway to "Hillcrest" in the distance. (Photo: 1923 *Schoolma'am*)

Friddles Restaurant on Main Street off Court Square continued as a favorite destination through the years. Today, Jess' Lunch occupies the same place and carries on as a favored site for students to chow down. (Photo: Harrisonburg-Rockingham Historical Society)

Sometimes the faculty had a hard time determining details of the right attitude, but on behavior guidelines it generally followed a popular saying of the day: "When in doubt, don't." The "don't" covered a long list. The 1920 annual illustrated a few of those "Forbidden Fruit[s]." Outlawed were lollipops, public dancing, joy riding, cutting campus, electric attachments such as curling irons and hotplates, Friddles Restaurant, and Staunton or Augusta Military Academy cadets.

Coveted senior privileges, formally granted by the faculty each October, waived very few restrictions. On October 6, 1922, the faculty granted that:

• Seniors will be allowed to leave the campus for the purpose of going to church, calling, shopping, attending social functions and entertainments, or dining out in private homes without chaperonage . . . provided school work be completed, they travel in pairs, return by 10 P.M., and register destination with the Social Director [SD].

• Seniors will be permitted to have an engagement with a young gentleman one night a week in addition to Friday and Saturday nights and they will be allowed to attend Church with young gentlemen . . . with the approval of the SD.

• Seniors will have the privilege of missing eight meals each quarter.

• Seniors will not be required to go in line to any school function downtown except the commencement sermon or some other occasion when special condition may require it.

• Seniors will be allowed to practise [sic] basketball or rehearse for entertainments two nights a week, provided one of these nights be Friday or Saturday.

• Gentlemen may accompany seniors from Church, social functions, entertainments and movies, provided they have accompanied them there.

Violations, of course, happened and punishment followed. Each year, reams of the president's correspondence flowed to and from students' parents in consequence of retribution—giving explanations and answering appeals. One example, during the summer session of 1924, captures the times:

My dear————,

I regret very much that M———— has violated one of the very significant regulations of the college, that is, automobile riding with men without permission, and has therefore been recommended to the Administrative Council by the Student Council for suspension. This action was approved by the faculty Administrative Council and will remain in effect for four quarters. M———— not only went riding on Sunday without permission but she went with boys who were on the ineligible list and were not allowed to go with any girls at the college. This act also involved leaving her rooming place on Sunday without permission which is another rule violated and the college did not approve at all of spending a portion of the Sabbath at a swimming pool at one of the summer resorts. I regret very much that this has happened, but I tried in every way possible to impress upon your daughter the necessity of strict observance of the college regulations. I instructed your daughter to go directly home but find that she was still in Harrisonburg a day or so ago.

> With kindest regards, I am
> Very truly yours,
> SPD/R   President

If M———— did not take the rules seriously, other girls did. A delightful remembrance from Delphine Hurst Parsons ('31) of Chitham, Virginia, evokes a freshman's fear of failure. New girls spent "nightly sessions with the handbook for quite a while after arriving, but even then the 'don'ts' were so numerous that we dreaded Monday nights when the student council met. Then, when lights were out, we lay in our beds with doors open and listened for footsteps in the hall, which meant that a council member was coming for somebody. It was with a sigh of relief that one heard the footsteps go by her door—for as hard as one tried to keep all the rules, they were so numerous that one was never sure."

"Boys" offered the greatest temptations, on or off campus. One girl remarked that so many of the town boys were blacklisted that she was never certain if it was safe even to smile. "Safe"—a term never defined—boys were on an eligible list. Additional names of any out-of-town boys permitted to call had been submitted by each girl's parents with the name cards filed in the office of the dean of women. Naturally, when a young man appeared who was not on the list, resourceful girls found instant kinship. Parsons wrote, "Sometimes these boys became 'Cousins,' 'Uncles,' etc., but Mrs. Varner's piercing eyes seemed to look right through the subterfuge."

Auburn-haired, attractive Bernice R. Varner succeeded Natalie Lancaster as dean of women in 1924 and brooked little nonsense. Poised, vivacious, and able, she set an example in good taste with a sensibility for modern life yet wholesome values. Dingledine cites two examples of conduct that endeared her to the student body, if not the school president:

> The administration and faculty were still valiantly trying to hold the line against bobbed hair. While increasing numbers of girls were cutting their hair, student teachers were expected to keep theirs or disguise the shorn locks. . . . Then Mrs. Varner went to a meeting in Atlantic City and . . . treated herself to the new style. Upon her return to campus, President Duke gave up the fight—the girls of H.T.C. [Harrisonburg Teacher's College, the new name given to the Normal School in 1924], even student teachers, could follow the example of their dean of women. . . .

The girls of H.T.C. did. Shorn locks pervade the senior portraits in the 1926 *Schoolma'am*. Later Dr. Henry Converse confessed, "When Elizabeth Rolston (president of the Student Association, 1924–25) cut hers, I couldn't help but think of 'Trees' and paraphrased it thus: 'Bobbed hair is made by foolish girls in dresses,/But only God can grow long tresses.'"

Left: Dean Bernice Varner shows the latest styles with bobbed hair, a head wrap popularized by the Rudolph Valentino film *The Shiek*, and a mouton jacket. (Photo: 1929 *Schoolma'am*)

Right: SGA President Elizabeth Rolston's bobbed locks moved Dr. Henry Converse to poetic despair and proved "nice" girls could cut their hair. (Photo: 1925 *Schoolma'am*)

A second Varner escapade did not sweep the campus. It began when she adamantly refused to give a young man permission to take a student for an airplane ride. To ease the aviator's disappointment, however, Varner said *she* would go up. Up they went, and over the campus the plane swept low to buzz those below just as Duke was playing the golf course. "The indignant president was ready to 'have the fool arrested' when he found that his dean of women had been in the plane," writes Dingledine.

The golf course, with three holes on the south front and six on the back campus, was one recent addition. Another was an outdoor swimming pool, in which the president had taken the first plunge. Four new buildings had gone up, and sidewalks had been laid. Erection of Reed Hall (now Keezell Hall) allowed installation of a tearoom in the basement of Harrison,

Left: A limited nine-hole golf course added recreational pizazz, kept President Duke happy, and attracted players from on and off campus. But with maintenance a problem, when Senior Hall was built in 1935 and eliminated one hole, it was doomed. By the end of the 1930s, golf offered only practice rounds on the back campus. (Photo: 1931 *Schoolma'am*)

Below: The rural landscape viewed from the outdoor pool set in a depression southeast of Cleveland Cottage, now the site of Varner House, reminded many students of their own farm roots. The pool was funded by Summer School fees in 1924. (Photo: 1925 *Schoolma'am*)

with kitchen and service space in former classrooms. Operated by the local alumnae association, profits supported selected college activities.

"College" was the correct term now. For three years, Duke had led the voices advocating that the four state normal schools be upgraded to teachers colleges. His persistence paid off. In 1924 the Normal School Board in Harrisonburg recommended the proposal to the General Assembly. The bill, drafted by ex-Senator George N. Conrad of Harrisonburg, was signed into law on February 13, 1924, and the Normal School for Women at Harrisonburg became the State Teachers College at Harrisonburg, familiarly called Harrisonburg Teachers College.

H.T.C. girls met their dates in the reception room at Alumnae Hall, and said goodbye there as well. The couples strolled to town even when a car sat outside in pouring rain.

The lone campus policeman, Walter H. Early, kept a watchful eye on parked cars. He also watched "the Rock" outside Alumnae Hall to make sure "sitters" stayed upright in its folds, since streetlights didn't illuminate the campus. Many wanted to remove the Rock and suggested as much to George Warren Chappelear, head of the biology department as well as building and grounds. His daughter Nancy Chappelear Baird ('39) recalls when he was overseeing landscaping for the campus and decided to take out the Rock:

Once Alumnae Hall was finished in 1922, the Rock outside (far left in the photo) was lit by a new streetlight that reduced lone campus policeman Walter H. Early's patrol duties after dark. (Photo: *Images of James Madison University 1908–1983*)

"In the process of using a tall spud to probe in connection with putting in the dynamite, the spud slipped out of the workmen's hands and vanished into what they feared might be a cavern, so that stopped the project."

Like the Rock in front of Alumnae Hall, rules served a purpose; no one knew just what dark voids loomed beyond their bounds, what would happen if they were removed. When families entrusted their sixteen- and seventeen-year-old daughters, and many were sixteen, to this home away from home, they expected the most vigilant and watchful protection and guidance. While the restrictions seem ludicrous to modern minds, they often only extended the ordinary rules enforced at home. Consequently, most students really didn't mind them.

Mary Louise "Sally" Kent Oslin ('29) expressed her loyal gratitude sixty-four years later:

> Dear Harrisonburg State Teachers College! What a joy to be a student there in the 1920's. Just girls! In spite of the rigid discipline and rules, what a freedom we had to explore our capacity for leadership and independent growth that is always hampered by male competition. . . .

After formation of clubs with geographic bounds such as Rockbridge, Roanoke, and Tidewater, girls from different states formed the Ramblers Club. This 1922 group proudly marked their luggage with their state initials. Higher hemlines and changing styles of hats mark the start of the Jazz Age. (Photo: 1922 *Schoolma'am*)

BUILDINGS FROM 1909–1929

1909—Maury Hall. Honors Matthew Fontaine Maury, scientist and oceanographer. Housed the first gymnasium, library, and president's office.

1909—Jackson Hall. Honors Confederate General Stonewall Jackson; the school's first dormitory.

1911—Ashby Hall. Honors Confederate General Turner Ashby, who was killed near the campus in 1862; the school's second dormitory.

1914—"Hillcrest." President's home until 1986.

1915—Harrison Hall. Honors Gessner Harrison, distinguished educator, born in Harrisonburg in 1807, who later held administrative offices at the school; housed the school's first dining room.

1917—Spotswood Hall. Honors Alexander Spotswood, Colonial governor, who led the first English expedition into the Shenandoah Valley, crossing the Blue Ridge near present-day Elkton; housed the school's third dormitory.

1921—Harrison Hall Annex

1922—Alumnae Hall. Honors the alumnae who supported with financial contributions.

1923—Sheldon Hall. Honors Edward A. Sheldon, leader in the nineteenth-century movement for creating normal schools.

1926—Reed Hall. Honors Walter Reed, noted Virginia scientist, who discovered the source of yellow fever, and whose father had a seasonal residence in Harrisonburg.

1927—Keezell Hall (formally Reed Hall). Honors State Senator George B. Keezell, a leader in establishing the school in Harrisonburg.

1929—Varner House. Honors Bernice R. Varner, a popular dean of women.

1929—Johnston Hall. Honors two early faculty members: James C. Johnston, a chemistry and physics professor, and Althea Johnston, who was head of the physical education department. This hall was touted as the school's first completely "fireproof" building.

I know James Madison University has grown to take a prominent place among the Eastern universities but I also know that, as in all growth, a sacrifice has been made in spirit and inspiration that grew in that small college of young women, flowering in a secure environment and personally cared about as a unique person by a dedicated faculty who really cared about one's moral well being as well as academic achievement.

From the pinnacle of 88 years, one thinks that bigger is not always better. But my good wishes go with her as she grows.

Chapter Seven

"No tragedy of recent
years has touched the heart
of the city as this one"
(1927–1928)

IN THE LATE 1920S, girls from Tidewater were first to board the railway "special" bound for Harrisonburg Teachers College. Through Richmond, Charlottesville, and Staunton, the train rumbled west, its scattering of empty seats disappearing under a cacophony of shrill greetings at each stop along the way.

"It was truly an all day trip, and by the time of arrival everybody was soot-smeared and bedraggled," described Delphine Hurst Parsons ('31), adding that the absolute *"must* for everybody who made the trip was the stopping for some of Gordonsville's wonderful and different fried chicken."

From student rituals on the journey to faculty ones on campus, a comfortable camaraderie marked the annual return to school. The "old" girls explained to novices that long gowns should be worn for the freshman reception at "Hillcrest," that chapel was mandatory three times a week, that Dr. Wayland might begin class with a song, that Sunday breakfast brought bananas and Sunday night meant brown-bag suppers, usually bread, cheese, fruit, candies, and often a hard-boiled egg.

Soon most of the girls had formed informal "supper" clubs to supplement their Spartan Sunday night brown bags, sharing food bought in town or saved from "care" packages sent from home. Into the semester, friendships formed more often than feuds as roommates swapped clothes back and forth, sustained one another through projects and papers, and whispered dreams far into the night after lights out at 10:30—or gathered for clandestine study in the bathroom.

Day students, of course, missed the special bond forged by dorm living but formed their own coterie in the Day Students' room at the basement of Harrison Hall. A large room filled with Mission-style furniture, it was near the tearoom and central to the other buildings. Virginia Wilson Miller ('31) wrote, "About ten of us girls from the 1927 graduating class of Harrisonburg High enrolled in the fall of 1927. It was almost a continuation of high school. Most of us spent a lot of free time in the Day Students' Room. We played auction bridge and once in a while we would get ambitious and give the place a good cleaning!" Their brown-bag lunches fueled a continuing daily battle with ants.

The popularity of regional clubs soon gave rise to Day Students Club with the motto "Grasp the Opportunity." Dr. Duke had a room added in the basement of Harrison for day students to study or rest between classes. Many of the surnames remain familiar in the area today. FIRST ROW: (left to right) Lola Davis, Priscilla Harmon, Ethel Argenbright, Virginia Holsinger, Virginia Earman, Kathryn Shenk; SECOND: Josephine Sullivan, Lera Bowman, Vada Steele, Vesta Landes, Janie Shaver; THIRD: Ethel Hollar, Ruth Western, Mary Spitzer, Mary Shaver; FOURTH: Virginia Sanger, Catherine Wampler, Dortha Cline; FIFTH: Alice Bolton, Camilla Dovel. (Photo: 1931 *Schoolma'am*)

Miller recalled the "very good workout" from walking a mile to school, then playing hockey in first-period gym class. She also said, "May Day was quite an event. The whole countryside would come to see the May Pole wound and lovely dances round it."

Faculty minutes for the years 1927–29 seem routinely mundane, month by month. At those gatherings in Harrison Hall, President Duke presided over a faculty in concert with his own views and goals, the overriding goal formally stated on March 12, 1928: "The function of this college is the preparation of teachers. We have some general culture courses, but the fundamental aim of the institution is to prepare young women to teach. The term 'preparation' is used advisably, as of broader scope than the term 'training'."

Of course, no faculty concurs totally. That statement evoked the question from Dr. Henry Converse of whether "it's of value for a student to study a subject that she'll never have to teach." From the list of participants in the ensuing discussion—recorded without their comments—it must have been a lively evening. The college had been admitted to membership in the Association of Colleges and Secondary Schools of the Southern States in December 1927, and the weight of that honor was taken seriously in establishing standards for classrooms.

The standards had always been high. As Dr. Wayland writes, ". . . we took ourselves seriously. This was true of all—from the president and teachers down to the youngest student. And we worked hard." The hard work paid off. The school was commended by the ACSS for its students' advances in other

Above: The Training School, built in 1908, stood in front of the Main Street School to house high school students and teachers. The structure now serves as Harrisonburg's Municipal Building. High school football games were played on the grassy lawn in the back across from the current *Daily News-Record* building. (Photo: *The Virginia Teacher*, May 1920)

Left: The original part of Harrisonburg High School on South High Street is pictured after completion in 1928 at the edge of town on the old fairgrounds. Some parents complained that the isolated site forced students to walk too far. The C & W Railway crosses Grace Street, where three Normal girls lost their lives in a tragic collision with a train. (Photo: Courtesy Jim Suter)

colleges and universities: they passed 624 courses out of 628 taken. Such accolades were memorable.

But the 1927–28 year became even more memorable for its worst moment. On May 29, two weeks before the scheduled graduation, a school car carrying four student-teachers back to campus was hit by a train at the railroad crossing on Grace Street. The tracks ran parallel only blocks from the college.

The train slammed into the school's new four-door Chevrolet, shearing its top and wheels off and throwing the twisted frame fifty feet across a wire fence. Witnesses saw the girls hurtle through the air. Margaret Knott of Portsmouth and Pauline Vaden of Sutherlin died on impact; Florine Sedwick of Shenandoah died later at the hospital. Lorraine Gentis and Thomas Armentrout, the school driver, were seriously injured.

President Duke called an immediate faculty meeting. He quickly assigned specific roles—Miss Waples, Miss Wilson, and Dr. Weems to visit the hospital "to extend any courtesies possible to relatives"; Mrs. Milnes, Mrs. Moody, and Miss Hudson to render the same at the undertakers; Mr. Chappelear, Miss

TRAGEDY ON THE TRACKS

Seventy years ago, front-page stories of automobile or train tragedies occurred almost daily. But the story that swept Harrisonburg's entire community into mass mourning involved both. On May 29, 1928, a school car transporting four student-teachers from Pleasant Hill School back to the college was hit by a train at the railroad crossing on Grace Street. Three of the girls were killed and the other passenger and driver seriously injured.

Then as now, trains crossing city streets were commonplace and engineers expected to be given the right-of-way. The coroner's report stated, "I hereby find that the said [girls] came to their death . . . the result of being struck by the Baltimore and Ohio Electric Motor Bus train coming north into the city at a rate of speed in excess of that prescribed by the city ordinance."

The ordinance prescribed 15 mph within city limits. The train was doing 25 or 30 mph, according to eyewitness accounts. (By comparison, the speed limit for cars on campus today is 25 mph.) Engineer T.A. Riley admitted to 25 mph but not to any blame for the tragedy.

"As I approached this side of the crossing, I blew for the street crossing as usual. After I did that, I saw those autos coming and I blew my whistle continuously. I was under the impression that the car was going to stop. It was not running fast, and I was under the impression when he came over the Chesapeake-Western track he was going to stop. . . . The whistle sounded continuously until I struck him."

"How fast were you going?"

"I guess 20 to 25 miles an hour."

"What effort, if any, did you make to stop?"

"I did not make any effort when I first saw. He was down fifty feet below this crossing and another car behind him. . . . He kept on coming. I thought he was going to pull over the crossing and stop but he just kept on coming. . . ."

Witnesses afterward agreed that a Chesapeake & Western freight going the other way might have obstructed the driver's view of the second train on the parallel track. The Chesapeake & Western as well as the B & O ran tracks across Grace Street between Main Street and the Dayton Pike (High Street). The location had special importance to the community, for at the end of the block, a new high school (still a part of Harrisonburg High School) was being erected on the old fairgrounds at the edge of town. The school was scheduled to open in September.

The accident galvanized the Parent-Teacher Association into demanding safeguards. Chesapeake & Western immediately ordered its trains to "come to a full stop before proceeding over this crossing," and promised that, if that weren't sufficient, it would "assign a crossing watchman during weekdays to protect the public and children."

Local organizations joined the cry for action. The Kiwanis Club called for a culvert or bridge, not only at Grace Street, but for protection at other crossings as well. Church groups echoed the plea. For the immediate future, watchmen were assigned to city railway crossings, and engineers heeded city speed limits more closely. Eventually trains would travel less frequently across the city's byways, although they would still rate the right-of-way. Even today, traffic halts on Grace and other downtown streets, as well as on the JMU campus itself, as the massive freight cars lumber backward or surge forward across the roadway.

It wasn't until 1970 that Cantrell Avenue was extended via a bridge that links Main and High streets with an unobstructed span over the railroad tracks near the high school.

Turner, and Miss Wittlinger to assist the Armentrout family. Others volunteered to drive to Staunton for the arrival of the night train from Norfolk and offered their homes for housing. The college focused on its grief.

The three caskets lay in state in Alumnae Hall from Tuesday night into the next day. At the memorial service on Wednesday in front of the hall, speakers included presidents of the student body, the senior class (Knott's and Vaden's classmates), the sophomore class (Sedwick's), and the YWCA as well as President Duke and Dr. Wayland.

At 3:00 P.M., a hearse left for Charlottesville with the body of Pauline Vaden, and another started to Shenandoah with Florine Sedwick. Shortly after 8:00 P.M., undertaker K. M. Higgs returned from Page County to set out again,

MARGARET SAWYER KNOTT
Senior

PAULINE FRANCIS VADEN
Senior

FLORINE ODELL SEDWICK
Sophomore

The students who were killed in the accident on May 29, 1928, while returning to campus from student teaching. (Photos: 1928 *Schoolma'am*)

this time for the C. & O. station in Staunton with the body of Margaret Knott. All day and into the soft May twilight, staff and students "walked around, talking in whispers as though death had entered their own homes," wrote the Harrisonburg *Daily News-Record*. With fewer than a thousand students, the campus reacted as a family.

Graduation was rescheduled two days earlier, made possible by cancellation of all traditional activities. The senior play, class day exercises, class and faculty receptions, the senior-sophomore dance, and the field day programs all were canceled. And even along the streets of Harrisonburg, activity seemed subdued. "No tragedy of recent years has touched the heart of the city as this one," the newspaper reported in its continuing coverage.

Summer of 1928 provided the necessary parenthesis of peace and healing. But another tragedy that would mark this generation of Americans loomed ahead unseen. When school reopened after the summer session, all again seemed right with the world. Students excitedly registered for classes, with new arrivals sent across the hall by Registrar Converse to find "the man who looked like Lincoln" (Dr. Wayland). At the first faculty meeting, Duke took advantage of up-to-date technology to distribute *mimeographed* copies of "Suggestions and Directions for the Faculty 1928–29." In reviewing the guidelines, special attention was given to course requirements and "the desirability of stimulating wholesome moral and religious attitudes without bias or offense or sectarian lines." The president emphasized the "obligation" of the staff to attend the regular assemblies each Monday, Wednesday, and Friday.

THE SUMMER OF 1929 drifted hot and humid into a colorful, crisp autumn while life moved at a leisurely pace on campus and along country roads. Bound by gleaned fields, laden apple trees, and soft-shouldered mountain ranges, the Valley pulsed to a slower beat than the rest of the world. For students and faculty wending their way under the shaded portico of Jackson or along sidewalks of the South Lawn, life seemed distant from rumblings on Wall Street or European capitals far removed.

On campus, pre-opening enrollment showed a slight increase, although it was down elsewhere in the state. The drop was attributed to crop damage by late summer storms and subsequent flooding. Fiscally, the previous year had proved so promising that, by September 1929, the school allocated funds to purchase thirty acres of farmland from Grover Hook on the Middle River of the Shenandoah for a college camp. Yet there was an unexpected statistic cited at the faculty meeting in early October: enrollment had fallen by about seventy students. Duke indicated a need for tight economics and energetic recruiting.

On Wall Street, however, after a summer of surging stocks, October 1929 brought a devastating collapse. Sensing danger, leading bankers had frantically pooled millions to prop up the stock market. They failed. On October 29— forever after called "Black Tuesday"—thousands of investors lost all they had plus more. The shock waves rippled nationwide.

The Valley, however, scarcely felt those first waves, at least on the college campus in Harrisonburg. In faculty meetings throughout the year, although President Duke urged professors to conserve electricity, trivial concerns consumed equal time with discussion of economics. Business in the two-hour meeting for March 11, 1930, consisted of announcements that certain students were anxious to work in faculty homes to pay college expenses and that professors must avoid "crushes," and a vote to continue to participate in the Apple Blossom Festival in Winchester. Then followed a promise by Burruss to begin classroom observations; a plan to take "Mr. Switzer's motion pictures of the college activities" to alumnae gatherings to spark recruiting; and a reminder that visitor cards, issued daily, must be secured from Duke's office by faculty wanting to take guests on the college golf course.

Chapter Eight

Into the
Great Depression
(1929–1933)

Above: In the 1930s, a weekend off campus might be a trip to the College Camp, a six-room brick house on thirty-seven acres along the Shenandoah River near Port Republic. There, girls cooked on a wood range, washed at an outside pump, and sang around a campfire "until long after midnight," according to Dingledine's history. The camp also offered hiking, rock climbing, boating on the river, or just lazing around. It was a favorite retreat until World War II restrictions closed it for three years in 1943, gas being unavailable for recreational trips off campus. (Photos: 1934 *Schoolma'am*)

Right: The float of the State Teachers College in Harrisonburg won First Prize at the Apple Blossom Festival in Winchester, VA, during April 27–28, 1927. (Photo: 1927 *Schoolma'am*)

APPLE BLOSSOM FESTIVAL
Winchester, Va.
April 27-28, 1927

FLOAT OF
State Teachers College
Harrisonburg, Va.
Winner of First Prize

With golfer Bobby Jones winning 1930's "Grand Slam" (four world championships), the game's popularity soared. H.T.C. girls learned the game for credit in physical education classes, and townspeople, who always felt a proprietary interest in the school, saw no reason they should be restricted from using the newly completed facility.

Local citizens had always shared with the campus its pride in its growth and renovations, and such feelings were especially apparent in May 1931 at the dedication of the long-awaited main administration building. The structure fulfilled the original plans for the quadrangle, adding an air of completion and permanence. Beyond internal improvements to Reed and Harrison, and erection of the first totally fireproof dorm (Johnston Hall), and a permanent Practice House, driveways had been macadamized and curbings added. With

The laying of Wilson Hall's cornerstone in July 1930 fueled excitement around the campus and in town as well. Built to house administrative offices, classrooms, the post office, supply room, and a grand auditorium, it would be completed in the spring of 1931. The $200,000 price tag boosted the local economy at the start of the Great Depression. (Photo: *Images of Madison College 1908–1983*)

The contractor for Wilson Hall, Nielsen Company, immediately began work on the foundation and established a relationship that continues into the twenty-first century for James Madison University and Nielsen Construction Company (now Nielsen Builders). (Photo: JMU Special Collections)

grading of the quadrangle finally finished, and mature trees and shrubs lining walkways around an expansive green lawn, the college exuded the charm of a long-established institution.

Since its completion in the spring of 1931, the new building to honor Woodrow Wilson, twenty-seventh president of the nation, towered above all others on campus. Reputedly Wilson's hometown of Staunton could be seen on a clear day from the dome, glassed in only on the south side. In September of that prior year, Duke had announced his major goals as: "1. Finishing Wilson Hall; 2. Preparing for the Dedication; and 3. Recruiting new students."

One student complained: "Every time I saw President Duke that year, all he talked about was the coming dedication for Wilson Hall." She had assessed his focus correctly, apparently immune from her fellow students' excitement.

Mary Sutter Etter ('34) remembers that all-important May 15:

> It was a clear, pretty day—warm enough we didn't have to take wraps. Sister and I wore pretty voile dresses we'd bought the summer before. Mother had bought a new dress at Joseph Ney's [the major department store on Court Square, now a modern office building] where we bought everything. It was beautiful—thin voile, light gray with dark blue flowers. I still have it and the silver bag she carried, lined inside with white leather.

Excitement over the appearance of celebrities at the dedication mounted in town and on campus. Luminaries included the late president's widow, Edith Bolling Wilson; Virginia Governor J. G. Pollard; former governors E. Lee Trinkle and Harry F. Byrd; former state senators George Keezell and George Conrad; and then-president of Virginia Tech Julian A. Burruss, the school's first president. Thirty colleges sent representatives, including alumna Dr. M'Ledge Moffett ('11), dean of women at Radford State Teachers College.

A special luncheon for dignitaries in the senior dining hall followed the opening exercises in the auditorium where University of Chicago historian Dr. William E. Dodd gave the main address. Festivities continued throughout the afternoon with the annual May Day exercises held on the back campus and a dinner at night. The culmination of thrills came that evening when nationally renowned violinist Albert Spalding and tenor Richard Crooks presented the first concert in Wilson Hall.

Etter continues, "Mother was especially excited because Richard Crooks was from her home city of Trenton, New Jersey. And I was excited that we had a real auditorium in town. High school plays and musical recitals had been in the Court House. There was no auditorium anywhere. My high school commencement had been in Reed Hall, and we had to set up chairs for all the assemblies there."

Above: Wilson Hall, dedicated on May 15, 1931, completed the quad and was named for the twenty-seventh president of the United States. Wilson's widow was present for the dedication, here in the first row flanked by President Duke, Governor Pollard to the left, Honorable E. Lee Trinkle, Honorable Harry Flood Byrd, former state senators George B. Keezell and N. B. Early, Dr. Julian A. Burruss; and former state senator George N. Conrad, on the right. Other distinguished guests included Dr. M'Ledge Moffett, Class of 1911, dean of women at Radford College. (Photo: JMU Special Collections)

Left: The auditorium in Wilson with seating for 1,400 claimed the finest stage in the state and soon boasted state-of-the-art technology with sound motion-picture equipment. Campus buildings boosted applications and the State Teachers College at Harrisonburg was on its way to becoming the state's largest teachers college. (Photo: JMU Special Collections)

Historian John Wayland called the stage "the finest in the state." Certainly it befit what had become, with the 1930–31 enrollment, the Commonwealth's largest teachers college. And soon after the dedication, the school added the latest sound and projection technology for showing films. Then the classes of '32 and '33 gave portraits of George B. Keezell and Woodrow Wilson to hang on either side of the stage, large oils in good proportion for the two-story, high-ceiling auditorium.

The faculty moved meetings from Harrison Hall to the new structure on June 4th. The grand surroundings, however, did little to offset fears about job security nagging the professors as realities of the Great Depression spread. Duke allayed concerns with an announcement that contracts simply had been delayed in hope of increases, and now the contracts, though not the raises, would be forthcoming. He also reiterated Governor Pollard's recognition of widespread financial distress, and the governor's urging for economy and retrenchment. Duke informed the group that his administration had never had a deficit, but confessed that possibility was close. In June of 1931, he still had the choice of a deficit. Eleven months later, he would not; the state passed an appropriation act mandating a balanced budget effective May 1932.

School divisions statewide curtailed building programs as well as teaching positions. Rockingham County, for example, had been rapidly renovating and expanding its physical capacity under new superintendent John C. Myers. With the exception of 1927, multiple building projects marked the county sys-

LEVELS OF FACULTY TRAINING INCREASED OVER THE YEARS:

Faculty Preparation*	1909	1919	1930
Holders of Doctor's degree	1	3	10
Holders of Master's degree	1	4	27
Holders of Bachelor's degree	5	11	3
Holders of no degree	8	4	0

*Exclusive of the School of Music and Training School

AVERAGE ANNUAL FACULTY SALARIES

Rank	1919–20	1930–31
Professor	$1,848	$3,100
Associate Professor	$1,320	$2,425
Assistant Professor	$1,065	$2,150
Instructor	$825	$2,067

tem every year from 1917 to 1929. For the next three years, however, construction stood still. Meanwhile, across the county as well as across the state, teaching positions vanished. On campus in September 1932, Dr. Gifford announced that only fifty-seven percent of the school's June graduates had obtained appointments for the winter.

Nevertheless, H.T.C. still drew students. Reasonable costs helped. Registration, tuition, and fees ran $75 for the year; room and board, $225. The number of boarding students fell, but enrollment in 1932 matched the prior year. The deepening financial depression, however, had provoked one member of the General Assembly to suggest that one of the state teachers colleges should be abolished. Fortunately, he was a minority of one. But in December, the holiday mood at H.T.C. was dimmed by notice of another ten percent cut in appropriation from the governor.

Undaunted, the faculty maintained plans for a grand Founders' Day program. The 25th Anniversary Celebration would take place March 17–18, 1933, after the close of the winter term. Something in the Valley's isolation and natural beauty seemed to sustain optimism. A prevailing hope threads through student remembrances, such as this from Elizabeth Thomas Payne ('32), who had graduated from Dayton High School in 1928:

The Midwinter Dance in February was held in the new gymnasium in Reed (now Keezell) Hall. Strict rules governed the major social occasion each year, with dancers instructed by Dean Varner to remain "a hymn book's distance apart from their partners." She meant a book held horizontally; the girls took it to mean vertically. The girls also bid farewell to their dates in the gym, waiting until all the boys had left before they departed for the dorms under the vigilant eyes of the night watchman. (Photo: 1931 *Schoolma'am*)

We [her family of seven] rode in our Oakland car—our first closed car—to my high school graduation ceremony. It had rained that afternoon and on our way we saw a lovely rainbow arched over Massanutten Peak. I thought the rainbow meant a special hope and promise for me.

The Dayton Bank had failed, money was scarce, but for years Payne "had admired the bluestone buildings with their red tiled roofs . . . and secretly hoped that some day I could go to school there." With her application received too late for a dining-room scholarship her freshman year, she traveled back and forth from home with her father each day, dependent on his work schedule. She wrote years later:

> I was at school before 7 A.M. and studied in the dismal "Day Students' Room" under Harrison Hall. It was dark and furnished with drab Mission furniture (now collector's items). There was an old phonograph where we played records like "The Charleston" and "Sweethearts on Parade." Tiny red ants ruined my first day's lunch. We learned to set our lunches on a stand over a pan of water.
>
> No social activities for me but I did go to chapel in Reed Hall. Chapel was required and each row of seats had one student to check on absentees and report. I enjoyed it anyway and still love the hymns we sang. Professors took turns leading the chapel program. . . . Dr. John Sawhill usually played opera music on the big phonograph. Many students snickered at the high arias, but I listened and enjoyed some.

The next year Payne won a dining-room scholarship to pay registration, fees, room and board. The "dining-hall girls" called their awards "24-hour scholarships" in contrast to library ones which held students ten hours and then let them go.

"Ours went on until the work was done. We each set three tables, serving a total of 27 students. We worked in pairs, wheeling in trucks of food. . . . On Saturdays we changed tablecloths and napkins, polished silver, washed spots off the floor. On Wednesdays we turned tablecloths over—clean side up! We paid for dishes we broke—10 cents for a butter [pat-sized] chip!"

Dietician Clara Turner ruled with a firm hand. She mandated air nets, clean smocks, polished shoes, straight stocking seams, and a strong work ethic. But her girls took pride in their work, and many former dining-room workers became generous future contributors to alumnae and college funds in appreciation for the boost that they'd been given during critical times.

Aerial views of the campus in 1934
by the Curtiss-Wright Flying Service
leaves no doubt to the rural character of the landscape and that the
campus still anchors the southern limits of Harrisonburg. Top: The view
north toward downtown Harrisonburg with nearly the entire town
encompassed in the frame of the
photo. Bottom: The view to the
southeast and today's I-81 corridor.
(Photo: JMU Special Collections)

Certainly some of those former students took part in the Alumnae Banquet
on Saturday, March 18, 1933. Assembled to reminisce and praise the school's
first quarter of a century, they alternately laughed, grew misty-eyed, and
roundly applauded the speeches that transported them back through the years.

Dr. Henry Converse, both professor and registrar, revived memories to evoke smiles and pride:

> We had a regular menagerie around here. At one time we had a Lion, a Wolfe, two Bears, a Parrot, a Hare, two Sparrows and a Wren, all at the same time. Since we have had two Hogges, and at present we have a little Pigg. . . .
>
> Many changes have taken place. . . . A big picnic at the Frog Pond or a small picnic in Bacon Hollow took the place of what later became a weekend trip to the college camp. [After Alumnae Hall was built] next year's freshmen were heard inquiring the way to the "aluminum" building. Young ladies had feet in those days, but ankles were invisible; the standard measured length of a graduation dress was four inches from the ground. . . . By 1921, ears were a secret, but ankles were not, and middies were in style. . . .
>
> Then they called girls "chicken" and later on "flappers"; now I believe they are "janes." Well, after a while ears appeared again and everyone bobbed her hair.
>
> But with all these changes . . . the attitude of the students has not changed from the high standard set at the beginning. . . . Our graduates have filled and are filling positions of trust and honor in the schools and colleges in the state, in hospitals, in county demonstration work, in supervisory positions, and in many commercial and industrial positions. Others are presiding with grace and dignity over happy homes.

> [They] have come from every county in the state, the District of Columbia, and from 25 other states, from Texas to Michigan and from California to Massachusetts, and from several foreign countries. These made an army of nearly 12,000 students, many of whom come back from time to time to bless their Alma Mater.

Twelve thousand—the number gave his listeners pause. If only half of those had entered the teaching profession—and more than half had—the ripple effect on generations of Virginians would have been clear. In fact, more than 1,900 graduates and former students either were teaching or serving as principal or supervisor in the public schools of Virginia in 1930–31. Harrisonburg Teachers College had become the wellspring for attitudes, values, knowledge, and decisions beyond any single class. The sheer numbers reminded all of the faculty of their awesome responsibility for the future, how their legacy extended beyond their lifetimes. Individually and collectively, they renewed their dedication to do more with less, as circumstances now demanded.

EFORE CAMPUS RADICALISM arrived in later decades, the State Teachers College at Harrisonburg was a hotbed of "normalcy" through the Duke years. Student days began with the wake-up bell at 6:45 A.M. and revolved around classes, meals, dates, and clubs. National and international politics drew scant attention, until the latter part of the 1930s. As alumnae Sue Quinn ('38) remarked looking back, "Family problems and situations that individually we thought about were augmented by our concern with the world, but on campus few students read daily newspapers. Getting our weekly copies of *The Breeze* was a necessary, vital time to all of us, and the weekly was as much a part of campus life as going to classes."

The Breeze, launched in 1922 with a biweekly, four-page edition, improved its format and increased its frequency through the years. Content progressed from English class compositions to more journalistic fare. Recognition of the improvement came in 1928 when the faculty voted to fund a $100 scholarship for the editor, in line with that offered for the yearbook. While the front page fully covered campus news, reports on national or international affairs bore a decided provincial slant. For example, on May 2, 1931, the lead story under "National News" headlined "$175,000 IS RAISED FOR [Richmond's] LEE MEMORIAL." The only other "national" article reported "HOOVER ASKS THE NATION TO KEEP BETTER HOMES WEEK."

Students often turned first to inside pages dominated by humor and social life. The humor column, "Campus Cat," depended on such quips as "Mary Watt thinks a scholarship is a floating university." And eyes quickly scanned the

THE BREEZE

HARRISONBURG, VIRGINIA, DECEMBER 2, 1922 — TEN CENTS PER COPY

(Reproduction of the first issue of The Breeze newspaper front page with columns headlined "...TING HOCKEY GAME / ...IORS PLAY SENIORS," "FORMAL OPENING OF OUR NEW AUDITORIUM," "Y. W. C. A. GIVES SERVICE OF LIGHTS," and "H. N. S. GETS SCHOOL PAPER, 'THE BREEZE'")

The first issue of *The Breeze* drew rave reviews. Students had decided the name by voting in a final run-off between "Campus Cat" and "The Breeze." It would remain the same into the next century, holding off a massive student push in 1942 to change it to "The Madisonian" or "Mad Cap." (Photo: *Images of James Madison University 1908–1983*)

Chapter Nine

The Final Parenthesis
of Peace
(1933–1940)

Basketball Varsity

First Row

MARY KATHERINE BOWEN	ELSIE QUISENBERRY
ANNA LYONS SULLIVAN	FRANCES ROLSTON
ESTHER SMITH	EVELYN BOWERS

Second Row

MRS. JOHNSTON *(Coach)*	JULIA DUKE
MARY FARINHOLT	SUE LEITH
MARY WATT *(Business Manager)*	

Basketball remained a crowd pleaser under the coaching of Mrs. Althea Loose Johnston. Undefeated seasons in 1929, 1930, 1934, and 1935 fulfilled dreams. Home games drew crowds brandishing gold and purple sticks from the stands and twisting into a snake dance at half-time. (Photo: *The Schoolma'am or* Special Collections)

popular listings of every student's "guests" or dates visiting the campus, plus any "Week-end Trips." "Aunt Abigail's Happy Wisdom"—witty answers to fictitious letters—rounded out the favorite features. Coverage of sports, entertainment, and creative writing filled the rest of the pages.

The paper reflected the conventional interests of sheltered, middle-class girls, conservative in manners and politics, with more emphasis on the former than the latter. Now that women could vote, polls were held for presidential elections. In 1928, the "straw vote" gave Hoover an expected victory over Al Smith. As during the earlier struggle for women's suffrage, however, issues sparked little campus discussion or allegiance. Four years after passage of the 19th Amendment (sans Virginia's ratification), the 1922 *Schoolma'am* honored President Woodrow Wilson "with one voice and one heart to him—revered leader in all they hold as the highest." The question of whether or not he had impeded women's voting rights carried no significance. No student, in these years, raised the irony of a women's college being dominated by Wilson Hall.

Acceptance of authority was the rule. In fact, the first "student rebellion" proved short-lived, having been prompted by an over-supply of lettuce. Florence Reese Moffett ('29) recalls the dietician had either been given or mistakenly ordered "a carload of lettuce served morning, noon, and night. The girls rebelled and started all sorts of rumors, pretty ugly at times." Moffett complained to the dean, who suggested she put her objection in writing. "I couldn't, so had to forget it—and I learned a lesson for life—if you can't put it in writing, forget it."

Food, of course, could always prompt gripes. Yet complaints were put aside as students scurried to be inside the dining room before the doors were locked each mealtime. For dinner at night, having donned the required stockings and dresses, early arrivals cheerfully milled around the lobby of Harrison Hall until the doors were opened. Breakfast, however, brought higher absenteeism, some wayward souls preferring to break their fasts with Coke and "Cheese-Its" in the college Tea Room rather than sacrifice sleep for the first meal of the day. Other sleepyheads could be discerned "going to early morning classes in overcoats that covered pajamas rolled up to the knees and carrying a bunch of grapes that some kind soul had brought to you from the dining hall," wrote Quinn.

Rules mandated wearing hose and a "nice" dress or suit for evening dinner as well as the one midday Sunday. The dreaded hosiery evoked the second student protest. Jean Bell Grandy ('43) remembers the strike of 1940: "How we hated so to put on those stockings for dinner at night and on Sundays. The freshman class, when I was a sophomore, had a strike to get rid of some of the restrictions. They marched up the middle of campus that night garbed in blankets and went right into the faculty meeting and told them what they wanted. It did help, too, because we took off those doggone stockings and a few other restrictions were lifted."

Mary Wright Thresher ('41) recalled the irate mass meeting but said, like most juniors, she kept out of it since they were soon to receive senior privileges. Stockings still had to be worn downtown and certainly under the formal gowns proscribed for the Lyceum programs.

Birthdays also meant formality. Marine Aleshire Modisett ('41) said, "Once a month we had birthday banquets at which we dressed formally. Those who had a birthday that month were seated together at a long table and walked in together. . . . The birthday table was always a little more festive and had something a little more special than the others. The meal was always delicious."

Formal dictates posed no problem. Each girl's wardrobe generally included two to four long gowns, new or carried over from high school dances. The total look demanded elbow-length evening gloves as well as the floor-sweeping gowns, not only on campus but also at off-campus affairs. Modisett confessed, "We loved going off to the college dances of the boys' colleges. Our escort had to write a letter to the Dean of Women and also our parents. However, we didn't require a chaperon, which I thought was quite generous."

Lexington, site of the two all-male bastions Washington and Lee University and Virginia Military Institute, proved a favorite destination. At either W & L or VMI, the long stag lines provided so many "breaks" that every girl could bask in popularity. Soon H.T.C. dances offered turn about. The twenty-fifth anniversary celebration in March 1933 introduced the coed or "girl-break" dance. According to Dingledine:

Mary Bryant Cox Rose, May Queen in 1937, stands with her Maid of Honor Katherine Stone Sutherland in front of Wilson Hall. Mary became president of the Student Body, May Queen, and Apple Blossom Princess. Such training served her well later as the first lady of Nepal where her husband Paul headed the Four-Point Farm Program there. Her five daughters grew up finding nothing unusual in their mother entertaining celebrities such as Lowell Thomas and Eleanor Roosevelt. (Photo: Courtesy Katherine Stone Sutherland)

For a decade and a half the girl-break dance would be characteristic of Harrisonburg dances—dances at which many a boy had his first acquaintance with feminine "stags" lining the walls, dances from which many a young man emerged nearly breathless as his date tried to give him a "rush" by having all her acquaintances dance with him. . . . They were dances not only enjoyed by the girls but also by many of the male faculty, who came not just to chaperon but to dance. Girl-break dances enabled them to receive a grand "rush."

The president as well as other faculty also received a rush. For students, any interaction with Duke formed a lasting impression. Moffett claims her most vivid memory was her freshman year's first formal dance with boys and the president whirling around the dance floor, Duke dancing not only with his wife, but also "with the girls." And for Virginia Heyl Crawley ('37) an outstanding recollection was "the annual hike to the top of Massanutten Peak with Dr. Duke as guide. It was a thrill to see him sit high on the Peak and cut a notch on the stick he carried yearly—a record of his climbs."

As the school had grown, its president's accessibility had lessened. Nevertheless, Duke drew enormous respect from faculty and students alike. Years later, Quinn wrote:

> Dr. Duke was known to us only when he appeared on the rostrum in Wilson Hall's auditorium. His sense of humor was readily perceived by all students in those moments. What stands out in my mind, however, was the accord given him by some dignitary from Richmond who stated to the student body convened there, "Your President is a financial wizard." We got to our feet in recognition of this acclaim. I think that Dr. Duke was more a symbol to most of us than a person. He represented authority, administrative ability to deal with the larger problems that we felt only vaguely concerned us, and we felt he was kind, though few of us were ever close enough to him to develop a more personal feeling about him.

And "financial wizard" he was; his appellation, "The Builder," well deserved. By the end of his tenure in 1949, the campus had increased in value from $400,000 to $4 million, with student enrollment expanded from 300 to just over 1,000, despite the Great Depression and world conflict.

A reading room in the new Madison Memorial Library, opened in December 1939 at a cost of $140,000. At the height of the Great Depression, Duke had obtained Public Works Administration funds from the federal government to underwrite the project. (Photo: *Images of James Madison University 1908–1983*)

A new club came to campus in 1939—the Granddaughters Club, whose mothers had been daughters of the college. Original faculty members, Miss Elizabeth Cleveland, Mrs. J. C. Johnston, and Dr. John Wayland, acted as club sponsors. Homecoming brought mothers, daughters, and faculty together to enjoy an informal tea and exchange memories. In the fall, the club presented the library a penknife with twenty blades formerly owned by President James Madison. (Photo: 1939 *Schoolma'am*)

During the late 1930s, before the nation entered World War II, life on campus in Harrisonburg remained insular and charmed. Beyond the classrooms, clubs and organizations flourished.

Frances "Bett" West Brewston ('36) cherished memories of College Lyceum programs where she heard national artists such as Cornelia Otis Skinner and the Boston Pops Orchestra. Crawley said, "I still get a thrill when I see Lowell Thomas on TV because he lectured once in Wilson Hall." Brewston saved copies of the inspirational talks and readings given at the YWCA programs on Thursday nights and Sunday afternoons. On the lighter side, she recalled, "Every girl gained weight her first year in school. One of the reducing tricks was to leave school at five in the afternoon, dash madly downtown for a Coke at Friddles, and dash back for dinner at six. The two-mile walk with no food was supposed to do the trick!"

Sue Quinn enjoyed extracurricular activities but recognized the potential pitfall of her studies taking a back seat. She confessed, "In my case this was often true, to be perfectly frank. Enthusiasm that often was lacking in the classroom was almost certainly felt in these student groups. Working on *The Breeze* staff was an exhilaration; planning and participating in the YWCA vesper programs was an inspiration; meeting together in the literary societies [no sororities in those days] was fun and gave a sense of 'belonging'."

Crowded three to a room her freshman year, Quinn lived out of a trunk so her roommates could use the two dressers provided, enthusiasms undampened by cramped conditions. She relished dorm bull sessions after hours, cupcakes from home to share with friends, nightly struggles between being hospitable and studying. She did admit, however, "I never quite got used to the 'public' bathrooms where three enclosed tubs served all students living on both sides of one end of the hall."

Her memories capsule a girlish innocence:

Campus life was walking across a wide lawn on perfectly straight sidewalks laid out in so geometrical an arrangement that it was tempting to break the pattern and cut across the sparse grass that Mr. Duke strived so desperately to let live; it was cool, starlit nights with a friend who shared interest in poetry; it meant running and watching on the hockey field while the autumn sun went down and the air became colder as the shadows of the lombardy poplar trees grew longer on the green; it meant ironing shirtwaists while laughter and giggles rang down the halls from other rooms; it meant personal kindnesses reciprocated and animosities ironed out and joke-telling and mimicking professors or repeating what they said in fun or in seriousness; it meant leaving campus to walk "downtown" to buy something; it meant a daily or more frequent visits to the row of mailboxes in Wilson Hall and often disappointingly finding it empty or finding the letter from home that contained the monthly spending

(L to R) Three freshmen in the spring of 1936, Katherine Stone Sutherland from Elk Creek, LaFayette Carr Crawford Richardson from Galax, and Dorothy Sears from Appomattox. LaFayette was later president of the Student Council and of the Glee Club. After graduation she served as assistant to the dean of women, Mrs. Cook. (Photo: Courtesy Katherine Stone Sutherland)

This hockey team (identities unknown) from the early 1930s never won the acclaim of basketball, but it laid the groundwork for the strong program of today that fields national winners. The hated black stockings remained a requirement until 1937, except for one bare-legged season in 1933. (Photo: JMU Special Collections)

allowance check; it meant doing your own laundry because the college laundry ruined your clothes and a midnight feast illegally in another student room after hours; it meant giving and taking, learning and playing; it meant we lived.

Quinn's graduation in 1938 came near the close of the parenthesis of peace. When President Franklin Delano Roosevelt broadcast his weekly "fireside chats" over radios into the dorms and homes, his words were comforting. At his first inauguration, he had cautioned, "The only thing we have to fear is fear itself."

And for "Duke's girls," fear had been faced down in the freshman year or was something to thrill to in a darkened movie house. Real fear was alien, although occasional images haunted from newsreel footage (often narrated by Lowell Thomas) shot overseas. Life on this side of the Atlantic generated optimism and excitement. A forty-hour work week was established in 1938 and the economy boomed with European orders of arms and equipment from those countries opposing fascism.

Movies had become more marvelous, more sweeping and grander than ever before imagined. In 1937, Walt Disney's first full-length animation, *Snow White and the Seven Dwarfs*, set girls swinging across campus in step to "Whistle While You Work." Two years later the tune was "Over the Rainbow" from that year's

Equestrians of 1934 brought their own mounts from home and stabled them on campus now that the school no longer had horses of its own. The stable eventually became a garage. Stableman Lee stands to the left of M. Chapman on Lollo, Anne Bond on Chief, Madaline Newvill on Lady, and Edith Todd on Nicky. (Photo: 1934 *Schoolma'am*)

The Wizard of Oz. In 1939, too, idealistic future teachers dreamed of Robert Donat in *Goodbye, Mr. Chips* or Leslie Howard's romantic, scholarly Ashley in *Gone With the Wind.*

If fear proved an alien emotion, romantic idealism did not. This generation had followed "the love story of the century" in 1936 when the Prince of Wales became Edward VIII and promptly stunned the world by abdicating his throne for "the woman I love," Wallis Simpson. Girls talked for days of "Edward and Wally."

They also broached more serious topics. The civil war in Spain had no analogy in U.S. history. A war of faction against faction, not division by region, was a new idea. Two black Americans also dramatically undermined notions of racial superiority that shaped the segregation policies of the Jim Crow South, including Virginia, and the ideology of Germany's Nazi party. In 1936 at the Berlin Olympics, with Adolph Hitler in attendance, Jesse Owens won four gold medals in track events, and in 1938 Joe Louis knocked out German Maxwell Schmeling in the first round of their championship fight for boxing's heavyweight title.

Quinn wrote of 1937: "In this year Amelia Earhart, in a round-the-world flight, disappeared somewhere in the Pacific area. We thought about the mortality and immortality of life, discussed in many 'bull' sessions in the dormitories. Amelia Earhart's success thrilled us—all women—at Madison. Her death was real to us."

Quinn and her senior classmates continued toward more reflection. Change marked their lives. They had matriculated at one school and left another. Harrisonburg Teachers College had become Madison College, the Class of '38 its first graduates. When the decade had opened, three of the original faculty—Elizabeth Cleveland, Althea Johnston, and John Wayland—were still on hand. By the decade's close, the turnover to the next generation was complete. The new, larger staff no longer focused solely on teacher preparation. Like the larger-sized

ᴇ ᴇ ⌐ ᴇ | **Tomorrow Night**

, March 8, 1935 — Number 22

East rg 31-30
2 Years cord Of :ats
n record of no games and two State Teachers returned Sun-

Harrisonburg Teachers College Authorized To Grant A. B. Degree

Library Spending $3,000 This Year
Over 750 New Books, Also Many Magazines And Pamphlets

All Virginia Teachers Schools Share In Privilege
CURRICULA CHANGES REQUIRED

While he won the right to grant an A.B. degree in 1935, President Duke could not persuade the General Assembly to grant the school liberal arts status. The Assembly pointed to its success at turning out teachers and argued that, if it became a liberal arts institution, the impact would be a massive teacher shortage statewide. He was too good at what he already did. (Photo: Headline from *The Breeze*, March 8, 1935)

Schoolma'am, for 1938, Madison College expanded its curricula to a full program of liberal arts. Yet its graduates carried cherished traditions into the new Madison, still to discover that change proves the only certainty in living.

WILLIAM HARRISON UNIVERSITY?

In 1938, when the State Teachers College at Harrisonburg was recast as Madison College, campus support was firm for President Samuel Duke's choice of the name. Off campus was a different story. Those local proponents urged that "Harrison College" would be more appropriate and would have advertising value for the city and county. Duke responded that advertising a community was not the function of a state institution. Furthermore, a school named for President James Madison had statewide appeal rather than simply local or sectional draw.

Townspeople countered that President William Henry Harrison, also a Virginian, was recognized statewide. They cited two other Harrisons who deserved honor: Dr. Gessner Harrison, a Harrisonburg native who taught Latin at the University of Virginia for twenty years (JMU's Harrison Hall carries his name); and, more locally significant, settler Thomas Harrison, who had been responsible for the General Assembly's selecting Harrisonburg as the county seat, after he had donated fifty acres to found the town, first known as Rocktown. His small stone house still stands on Bruce Street half a block west of Main.

But the 1938 faculty minutes and copies of the college newspaper indicate no interest in the counter-suggestion for the Harrison name. With Fredricksburg State Teachers College opting for "Mary Washington" and "The" University at Charlottesville historically bonded to Thomas Jefferson, Duke saw Madison as the logical choice. In addition to being "Father of the Constitution," he was Virginia's third native son among the nation's first four presidents. He had been a champion of public schools, higher education, and teacher training. And, perhaps due to Dolley's influence, he was a pioneer advocate of higher education for women. Why not "Dolley Madison College"? Dr. Duke saw the future, and the day of men on campus. According to Dr. Raymond Dingledine's history:

> Duke deemed the name appropriate for other reasons also. It had dignity, looked good in print and sounded good when referred to orally.... It was distinctive, used by no other college in the country—although shortly after the General Assembly passed its bill, the Nashville Agricultural Normal Institute at Madison, Tennessee, changed its name to Madison College....
>
> He reminded those who felt Madison had no connection with the area that Rockingham had originally been part of Madison's home county of Orange, and that Madison had been married and had honeymooned in the Shenandoah Valley.

And, of course, Duke mentioned the other James Madison born near Port Republic, first Episcopal bishop of Virginia and president of William and Mary College for more than three decades. But Duke's Madison College was named for President James Madison, and the college returned the favor by calling its teams the "Dukes."

O N December 7, 1941, before the historic announcement that shattered a crisp Sunday afternoon, Madison girls strolled lightly back to campus from downtown churches. Such excursions demanded feigning haughty indifference to the boys driving up and down the two-way flowing traffic of Main Street to ogle the passing parade, both strollers and drivers fully aware of one another.

Within hours, most of those same boys would turn sober thoughts to marching up and down the main streets in unknown towns overseas. A stunning announcement broke into radio's regularly scheduled programming at 2:30 P.M. (EST). A dawn attack by Japanese planes had destroyed the U.S. fleet based in Pearl Harbor, Hawaii. After church many girls had tuned to soft music to study by, with room radios having been approved just a year earlier, and the school itself on air as WMC, broadcasting from the old student government room. Earlier, radios on campus had been strongly opposed, although most girls came from one of the thirty million homes with

Chapter Ten

"A new birth
of freedom"
(1941–1943)

sets. Even dorm smoking, approved in 1936, was considered the lesser of two evils. To discourage radio's noisy distraction, the school set strict limitations. Rules demanded installation by the school electrician, payment of a "radio fee," observance of "quiet hours," and containing sound within the room.

But sound that Sunday penetrated walls and hearts. Broadcasts began the first nine hours of continuous radio coverage by NBC and CBS following the attack.

The 1941–42 session had the highest enrollment in the school's history with 1,344 students. Dorm overcrowding required three girls to share one room with some forced to find housing off campus. Duke leased the Shenandoah Apartments and bought the Carter and Lincoln houses on Main Street to accommodate the burgeoning population. The war years would bring a slight decrease in numbers but never below 1,000. (Photo: *Images of James Madison University 1908–1983*)

At Madison, girls clustered in hallways and rooms, often repeating the terse announcement as if needing the reality check of hearing one another say the same things. Seniors, whose main thoughts had centered on hope chests and teaching placements, suddenly shifted focus. Here and there, a few girls sat quietly crying.

On Monday, the president's call to Congress for a declaration of war to meet the "the date that will live in infamy forever" energized the nation. Only Montana's Congresswoman Jeanette Rankin failed to endorse Roosevelt's request. She won no praise at Madison where staff and students strongly supported their head of state. Yet the faculty meeting the next day came too soon for any real response to war and held to routine matters. Not until after the holidays did the focus center on responsibilities mandated by war.

That January, Duke warned his staff to expect a restless student body, and he optimistically predicted the conflict's end by 1944—with Russia and the U.S. delivering the knockout blow; Britain he deemed past its military prowess. Duke recapped points made by historian Douglas Southall Freeman in a recent address to state college presidents. Freeman had said that by January 1943 there would be five to ten million men under arms, and by September '43 we could expect conscription of both sexes for industry. He predicted that seventy-five percent of national manpower would be utilized for defense, and colleges as well would be requisitioned by the federal government. He warned against lowering academic standards to meet the needed acceleration of students through college.

Acknowledging the inevitable depletion of his faculty by the draft and/or by patriotic fervor, Duke assured that no one serving the country would lose his or her place on campus; those called to war would be granted leaves of absence. By September '42, Melvin Pittman, Argus Tresidder, and Glenn

After the government announced a possible call up of all typewriters, the 1942 staff of *The Breeze* tried to analyze what to do. (Photo: 1942 *Schoolma'am*)

Smith had become naval officers and Dr. Joseph Schnieder tapped for specialized war work. Next spring, the announcement that Dr. Leland Schubert had joined the Navy came with Governor Colgate Darden's request for one-fifth of the college's typewriters for the Army.

Upperclassmen nostalgically recalled their early years. The 1940 annual had preserved scenes of outdoor worship services at the school's camp. The year's photos and copy evoked other memories as well: "the shuddering organ on Sunday afternoon worship programs in Wilson, the candle-light services . . . cabinet meetings on Wednesday evenings, which we always closed with 'Blest Be the Tie That Binds'—our new blessing—the Christmas kid party—the thrill of visiting little folks at the hospital and at the children's home—the firelight picnics in Mr. Dingledine's back yard."

Now the college camp (currently JMU's farm) had closed, Dr. Dingledine had died in February of 1941, and summer would transform backyards into Victory Gardens. The students' world literally dimmed as blackouts prohibited candlelight on many evenings. The sixth of June brought the first trial blackout, and June 17 a dusk-to-dawn one—hailed by Duke as an oblique answer to his frequent plea for saving electricity. "Dollars for Defense" became a recurrent theme. Earlier in 1941, the federal government had initiated the sale of savings stamps and bonds. Madison's president no longer considered the program optional. He convened a special faculty meeting on April 21, 1942 to introduce the Payroll Deduction Plan and urge full participation. And by June the subsequent year he proudly boasted, "Except for three persons on the regular teaching staff, faculty members are paying . . . 2 percent to 30 percent of their earnings." That outlay plus the federal income tax—from which state employees had been exempt until March of 1940—proved a sizeable sacrifice to many faculty families. But the enforced frugality brought little complaint.

Students were no less diligent in helping fund the war. An editorial in the April 17, 1942 Breeze urged everyone to "Save . . . And Save America." The plea accompanied a quarter-page ad for the same goal. A soft sell might have worked as well for that first year of war. The media had pulled out all stops to promote patriotism. Films such as Mrs. Miniver, starring Greer Garson and Walter Pidgeon, brought to life the terror of air raids. John Steinbeck's best seller The Moon Is Down portrayed the horror of German occupation. The poignant popular song "The White Cliffs of Dover" promised peace, in counterpoint to "Praise the Lord and Pass the Ammunition," which was also played at dances that year.

A plug for U.S. Defense Stamps and Bonds from *The Breeze*

Save . . . And Save America

By last night the college sale of Defense Stamps and Bonds for the week had climbed to a total of $937.05 according to the officers of Pi Kappa Sigma sorority, present sponsor of the drive on campus. Students and faculty alike have for the moment shaken off their indifference to the call of minute-men posters and have invested their dimes and quarters wholeheartedly for defense.

The week's record speaks of an awakening of resolutions to give the boys more than written encouragement and spoken praise. It suggests that perhaps the "women behind the men" are willing to sacrifice a movie and a coke every now and then to do their part for the victory of democracy.

As campus post office records show, $401 of Defense Stamps were sold in January, following the outbreak of war in December. The sales fell to $245 in February, and to $274 in March.

We don't expect our American armies to fight for one week and then pitch camp for a rest. Neither would we allow munition factories to close shop for vacation-leave, after having completed a certain amount of armament production. We value America, her freedom, her ideals, too much for that.

We must not forget, on the other hand, that our dimes and quarters must be given just as continuously as fighting must be carried on. Otherwise our country can not remain the free, democratic one that it is now.

Start now to set aside part of your allowance *each week* to buy Defense Stamps! Buy them *regularly*. They are our big chance to help make V mean victory!

The tradition of the Old Girl–New Girl Wedding started in 1924 to welcome officially new girls into the student body. The "groom" was a sophomore; the "bride" was a freshman; and the minister was the student body president. Old girls were groomsmen; new girls the brides-maids. Often two faculty children served as ring bearer and flower girl. Continuing twenty-five years, the ceremonies were first held outdoors and later moved to Wilson auditorium. (Photo: 1943 *School-ma'am*)

Not even war, however, could curtail dances. Cotillions continued along with other traditions on campus—normalcy to balance uncertainty. The "Old Girl–New Girl Wedding" still carried the importance of binding classes together. Breakfast remained fifteen cents in the Tea Room. Nancy Gibson-Geiger ('44) cherishes her memory of "our graduation prom with the men consisting of 4-F's and dads. We were grateful to have them!"

One traditional rule gave way to the times—and blessedly so for most girls. The hateful stockings, mandated whenever girls left campus or went to dinner, were now so scarce they almost disappeared. Nylon and silk had "gone to war." Lena Ritchie ('44) recalls, "Sometimes these were 'made' by drawing a brown line down the back of our legs since we wore 'Bobby socks' over them anyway." And finally Bobby socks instead of hose were allowed for those who worked in the dining room.

Other changes marked the war years. National sororities supplanted the literary societies, once key to social life. Replacing Lee, Lanier, and Page were Tri-Sigma, Alpha Sigma Alpha, and Pi Kappa Sigma. Formal and informal parties filled rush week in February and filled the hearts of freshmen with hope for acceptance by at least one sorority. Friday ended the rush and sealed fates. Girls lucky enough to receive bids met in Mrs. Cook's office, then headed to the house chosen to be welcomed by their new "sisters."

Girls less smiled upon tried to pretend it didn't matter and banded together, heading downtown to commiserate over sodas at Friddles or Julias Restaurant, deliberately combating heartbreak with chocolate. If a sad movie were playing at the Virginia Theater, all the better. One girl confessed how good it was to cry and know those around her would think it was because of the movie, not her own despair.

Amazingly, wartime restriction on travel didn't curtail the continuing tradition of Lyceum programs. *The Breeze* staff still labored late into the evening.

Teas in Alumnae Hall still required white gloves. But girls also began knitting for the Red Cross—yarn provided by the YWCA, instruction by registrar Helen Frank. They took new courses in first aid, nutrition, and signaling, and "accepted the rationing of sugar and tires and the shortage of silk like true patriots and didn't quarrel about it"—according to one anonymous account.

At the start of hostilities, the national shortage of nurses had been deemed critical. One report called for an increase of 50,000 to 65,000 more students for nursing schools. Madison partnered with Rockingham Memorial Hospital to allow its trainees to take needed science courses on campus. The graduating nurses received their diplomas in Wilson Hall from Duke, who was also president of the hospital's board of trustees. The College Glee Club provided entertainment.

College-derived entertainment was commonplace, as were concerts by guest performers. Frequent community requests for campus groups reflected the

Top: Martha Graham and her company of modern dancers performed during the 1941 Homecoming. (Photo: 1942 *School-ma'am*)

Bottom: Dance classes freed students to interpretive movement to music. Popular through the decades, the program formed the base for today's renowned dance department. (Photos: *Madison College Guidance Bulletin*, March 1953)

popularity of the fine arts. The Madison College Concert Orchestra, under Clifford T. Marshall, presented a series of spring programs around Rockingham and Augusta counties. The School of Music opened to the public their student and faculty recitals in Wilson. The first "follies" took the stage in 1942 as the annual commencement play. The two-act revue, with lyrics by Dr. Argus Tresidder and music by Marshall, proved a hit. The Choral Club sang at various churches on

Sunday evenings. Many groups such as the French club, Le Cercle Français, performed plays on occasion.

The war raised another social question. At the first faculty meeting in September 1943, the staff went over the rules for their charges on campus. Disappointingly, enrollment had dropped by 321 from the all-time high of 1,344 the year before. Duke voiced two problems "giving great concern." As usual, noise headed his list. Then he asked, "What is the college attitude going to be to student participation in the entertainment of soldiers passing through Harrisonburg?" Faculty consensus that the troops represented a cross section of the general population led to a liberalized policy: "Under proper chaperonage and with a representative of student government present, students may attend entertainment approved by the college." Later, Duke would need to address the problem posed by relationships between college girls and high school boys. A popular song's lyric, "They're either too young or too old, either too gray or too grassy green," described the dilemma resulting from the exodus of desirable bachelors into the armed services.

That fall also led to a more liberal policy on student marriage. Senior Minnie Lee McLelland, who married Warren Branch on November 15, 1943, writes:

> We were married with Dr. Duke's permission to marry, to visit Warren in Texas (he was a cadet in the Air Corps), and return to Madison to graduate with my class after he left for England. I was in the Home Management House and Mrs. Moody invited Warren

Three unidentified sophomores and their guys who knew the meaning of "Saturday Night Is the Loneliest Night of the Week" when listening to The Hit Parade all alone. (Photo: 1946 *Schoolma'am*)

to dinner. What excitement for all the residents in the house! A man for dinner other than a teacher.

My roommate Barbara Jane Smith tutored me by the hour when I returned to school. All the girls gave me a bridal shower. Such lovely memories of 50 years ago. Yes, we celebrated our 50th anniversary with a party given by our two children.

Initially, in spite of war, Duke's building program appeared safe. In March of 1942, the state assembly appropriated $150,000 for an addition to Maury Hall, the science building, plus another $150,000 for a new dormitory, including an infirmary unit. Construction, however, was never federally approved. Like Americans everywhere, the Madison community had to make do with

The Tea Room in Harrison Hall was, according to *The Schoolma'am* in 1942, where "the nickels went and the pounds came, but somehow we couldn't stay away." Professors as well as students lingered there. (Photo: 1942 *Schoolma'am*)

The indoor swimming pool in Reed (Keezell) Hall led to a new requirement for graduation: one had to be able to swim the length of the pool. (Photo: *Madison College Bulletin*, 1953)

what it already had and sometimes even less. Ration books for distribution of meat, sugar, and gasoline became as much a part of the school scene as plaid skirts, cardigan sweaters worn backwards with single-strand pearls, long hair in pageboys or pompadours, and saddle shoes.

John Wayland (who was on leave to devote full time to research and write since 1931) and Elizabeth Cleveland (who was to retire in June) had witnessed immense social changes since 1909. Those two faculty members from the original staff were honored with a testimonial dinner on December 3, 1942. Also still teaching were Althea Johnston (health education), from 1909; Margaret Hoffman (English), 1911; Henry Converse (math), 1912; Mary Louise Seeger (education), 1913; and Edna T. Shaeffer (music), 1915.

Duke was grateful for the balance of long-termers during the wartime stress to keep faculty positions filled. In addition to the eight in military service, others left for new positions. Mrs. Cook moved from her post as Madison's dean of women to become personnel director at Arlington Farms near Washington, D.C. Alumna Dorothy Garber returned to take her place. Retirements and deaths brought further natural attrition.

Student absenteeism emerged as a major problem. With relatives or sweethearts home on last leaves before heading overseas, girls extended weekend trips and requested excused absences. Duke considered the matter so serious that in the spring of 1943 he issued a long letter to parents soliciting their cooperation to prevent unnecessary absences. It was the same spring his military drill corps fell through.

Dingledine's history details the rise and fall of military drill after appeals from the federal government for emphasis on physical fitness: "Every student was asked to enlist for four hours a week—two in military drill and calisthenics and two in forums and war projects. . . . At first there was much enthusiasm." Girls enlisted to form six companies under an elite officer cadre.

Dingledine continues, "Girls in sweaters and skirts and saddle shoes formed for close-order drill on the athletic field and the campus driveways. Governor Darden visited the College and the 'corps' passed in review. Then the enthusiasm began to wane. Jealousy of student officers appeared. In April, the program was called off."

Historian Dingledine cites other more successful projects, however:

> Girls volunteered for airplane spotting and were allowed to go on duty at the local aircraft spotting center as early as 6:00 in the morning. A surgical dressing center was established in Senior dining hall and students made thousands of bandages. A day nursery on campus freed area mothers for defense work. The Sesame Club [formerly the Granddaughter's Club] enlisted its members to help in Harrisonburg defense offices. Home Economics students planted a victory garden behind the Library. A Red Cross First Aid Detachment was formed on campus. The Civilian Defense Committee used a special bulletin board in Harrison Hall to keep stu-

Two-way traffic in front of Wilson Hall turned no heads in 1942. (Photo: 1945 *Schoolma'am*)

dents posted on defense announcements and the progress of the war. During the 1943–44 session, Madison students trooped to downtown churches to help entertain convoys of soldiers passing through the city—a "drafting system" being "worked out to stem the flow of willing volunteers, rather than to keep the number up to a certain quota." Then, of course, there were bond and war fund drives. . . .

Patriotism remained high. The 1942 *Schoolma'am* had been dedicated to "Those men everywhere who are fighting that democracy may live." The next volume dedicates itself "That we may enjoy a new birth of freedom."

The war had two more years to run.

Julias Restaurant on North Main Street in downtown was a popular place where town and gown met. (Photo: JMU Special Collections)

IN 1944, Dr. Ruth Phillips's and Miss Myrtle Wilson's Scottish terrier Bobby still bought defense stamps every week to fill his own book— ostensibly aiding the war effort by setting aside what he would have normally spent on meat. Two years earlier, President Roosevelt's own Scottie, Fala, had written to commend his effort. *The Breeze* had reported:

> A few days ago [Bobby] received a letter from the White House saying that Fala wished him to know how much his master appreciated his cooperation in our country's defense effort. Although the letter was signed by Grace Tully [the President's secretary], Bobby feels very sure that Fala himself dictated it.

But the times were serious. During the first war years, dispatches from European and Asian fronts did little to lift morale. Home-front spirits sank along with each report during the early months of 1942: seventy-nine merchant ships destroyed by German U-boats in the Atlantic; island after island in the Pacific fell to Japanese forces; moviegoers from Harrisonburg to Hawaii watched newsreels to memorize new names such as Corregidor and Bataan, where tens of thousands of Americans were butchered. April through May, newsreels followed General Douglas MacArthur's dramatic farewell to the Philippines, pledging "I shall return," and General "Vinegar Joe" Stillwell's overland retreat from Burma into India. Heroic Stillwell had refused air evacuation for himself to face capture with his men.

News clips also featured women in factories building planes and Henry Kaiser's remarkable Liberty ships. With four-and-a-half days from keel to delivery, they slid down the gangplanks at the rate of one a day by 1945. Soon "Rosie the Riveter" was added to the public's vocabulary and the safety hair net she wore evolved into the fashionable "snood" on campus. Movies were no longer simply for entertainment. Educators began to realize the impact films had on teaching and influencing viewers. Madison established a cooperative program with the University of Virginia to interchange films "of an educational nature."

Chapter Eleven

The Dawn of Peace, the
Final Days of Duke
(1943–1949)

Like the Tea Room, the Post Office drew daily visits. It held joys one day, disappointments another, and frequent surprises. It had been moved from Wilson to the basement of Harrison and roommates sometimes had to share boxes due to the ever-increasing numbers of students. (Photo: 1942 *Schoolma'am*)

Thus, on campus, war and normalcy continued to intertwine. Ellen Britton ('45) remembered first-person horror stories from a guest lecturer who had taught chemistry in Prague: "Dr. Snyder had escaped from Czechoslovakia and told us how the German soldiers made them line up in the snow in their pj's." On campus, however, snow brought frolic outdoors and swimming inside. The audience that could be moved to tears by war's horrors was also made up of girls provoked to a sit-down strike against the rule requiring a hat and gloves to go downtown. They commiserated with those starving overseas but fully enjoyed the local restaurants, "having toasted pound cake with ice cream after the movies," according to Jean Raup Grady ('45). And spring onions might flavor their milk, "but we'd put it on our 'pencil shavings' [breakfast cereal] anyway," Britton recalled.

In spite of war, freshman enrollment grew. Dr. Duke reported a thirty-five percent increase in freshmen between 1943 and 1944. He also managed to ensure that Madison received the largest financial increase of any state teachers college between those years. September of 1943 brought 815 students to dorms where every interior had been refinished except for Alumnae Hall, and the college received an additional $12,000 for capital outlay for the 1944–45 fiscal year.

Enhancing its prestige, Madison successfully sought membership in the American Association of Colleges and added a new department. Raus McDill Hanson came from Nebraska to establish the department of geography. In October 1944, however, faculty enthusiasms over growth were tempered by the loss of a favorite colleague, George Warren Chappelear. The '45 *Schoolma'am* carried a formal tribute:

> Fifty-five years—a span of life not long, but crowded with interests and activities, even after failing health had laid its hand upon him. Mr. Chappelear's cup seemed full to the brim all his days: In the college laboratories and classrooms, head of the biology department for more than a quarter of a century; on the campus, superintendent of buildings and grounds, planting shrubs and trees; in his home, the friendly host, dispensing a tireless hospitality that made the students feel very free there; in the town, a civic leader and a man whose understanding heart taught him how to be

a true neighbor; in his profession, a strong advocate of the advancement of science in our state and nation; in the field of genealogical research, an unwearying student and writer; in his rambles through woods and mountains, an eager explorer who cared about all wild life; in his church, a helper to be counted on, ready to serve as vestryman or to take hold of the lowliest, most inconspicuous tasks.

Alumna Mary Wright Thrasher ('41) caught the characteristic humor that won converts to his classes. She said, "One was not truly initiated into the Freshman class until she had Mr. Chappelear for biology and had seen his imitation of a frog!" President Duke liked to quote educator W. E. Hocking, who said, "Every great teacher must have two minds, one of what he knows and the other of what is in the student's mind." Chappelear always tried to bridge the gap.

Nineteen forty-four marked Dr. Duke's twenty-fifth anniversary at Madison's helm. The faculty honored both its president and his wife at a celebration in May. Faculty, alumnae, and students presented them a sterling silver tea and coffee service. Duke proudly noted the school now had an annual enrollment of 1,600 (including summer sessions) and a faculty of eighty. It offered both A.B. and B.S. degrees in Education and Liberal Arts, plus a two-year pre-nursing program. The prospectus mailed to potential students heralded the assets of a campus now worth more than $2 million. It cited "Both urban and rural training schools, athletic field and tennis courts, two gymnasiums, two swimming pools (indoor and outdoor), a college camp on the Shenandoah River, four-manual, two-manual and electric organs, modern equipment for sound-motion pictures, and modern recording and broadcasting equipment."

Students applied from an increasingly wider geographic sweep. Dr. Duke had announced in March that pre-enrollment was up fifty-five percent over the same date the year before, but bemoaned a heavy withdrawal of freshmen caused by "poor work, loss in value of the Friday Assembly, poor advisory, and demoralization due to young men going into the service." To welcome the students who arrived that fall, he suggested that each college teacher take a student from where she left off in high school and carry her on from there— yet not treat her as if still in high school. "Good will rather than hard-boiled teaching would bring better results."

However, "good will" did not always flow between the president and his staff. All of the faculty respected Duke, but not all liked him. Except for a small inner circle, Duke remained an aloof, austere administrator. Dingledine's history notes: "President Duke's life and interests were wrapped up in his college. His office was the nerve center of the institution. Active, vigorous and efficient, he kept a firm hand on every phase of its development. At the same

The six Home Management students invited guests to dinner as part of their training while living at the Practice House. Here special guest, President Duke, carefully carves under the eyes of his hostesses with Mrs. Duke at the foot of the table, Mrs. Varner to the far left. Varner, former dean of women, headed the Practice House after Mrs. Moody left. (Photo: JMU Special Collections)

time, his faculty found him approachable, frank, and absolutely honest." Yet Dingledine also acknowledges, "A department head might be brusquely denied a request, but he knew where he stood." Another former professor recalled, "You couldn't just walk in his office and call him by his first name. He was a stickler for order and bestowed no money for frills."

From another former faculty member came an anecdote to support the latter slant: "When I went in his office to let him know I planned to be married, his only response was 'I expect you'll be staying on. Now I won't have to advance you any more.'"

Certainly the stress of maintaining a staff during wartime, handling the day-to-day exigencies in housing and education for almost a thousand girls, meeting civic responsibilities, and planning for continued growth and postwar demands were sufficient to curb geniality. Duke's focus was clear. The good of the school was his first priority. Not one of the assembled faculty doubted his sincerity when he said that beyond education his most important considerations were "First, that the students be fed properly; second, that the faculty be paid properly; third, that the library be cared for properly."

The importance he accorded teacher education grew from his voracious reading in the field. He closed many faculty meetings with specific suggestions for faculty readings. In February 1945, for instance, he called attention to an article in *Harper's* by Dr. Joseph Schneider, member of the chemistry staff on leave for government work, plus a book titled *Teachers for Our Time*.

Duke fought for higher faculty salaries, not only funds for capital improvements. As the war ground toward what seemed an eventual Allied triumph with General Eisenhower's victorious armies racing across Europe and General MacArthur's recapturing American outposts in the Pacific, Duke mounted an assault of his own. That April he appealed to the State Board of Education and General Assembly members for *all* professional staff members to be included in an annual salary schedule. He appealed for paying assistant professors $2,500, associate professors $3,200, and full professors a grand $4,000. He also suggested that provisions be set for increases, planned promotions, and standards of evaluation.

Ammunition for Duke's appeal seemed self-evident. June's enrollment increased by 100. Regular sessions brought 200 applications more than the available dormitory space. He readily set about implementing new standards for both scholarship and citizenship, and refused all applicants in the lowest third of their graduating classes. He also prioritized in-state students over those out-of-state.

The end of World War II in August of 1945 brought new challenges to college campuses. A grateful U.S. Congress enacted the "GI Bill" offering a college education free to every returning serviceman who desired it. Nothing could counter the national mood of optimism. High spirits infected young and old, and Duke was no exception. Governor Colgate Darden with his lieutenant governor, budget director, state engineer, and seven members of the General Assembly descended on Madison for a hearing of budget problems. Duke ordered the faculty to attend the program in full academic regalia and stepped out of character to instruct Miss Gladin to "furnish lunch for the visitors—all budgetary limitations to be disregarded for the occasion."

Duke never desired an enrollment beyond a thousand. He had 1,076 by that September, with forty-six boarding in town. "We have turned away several hundred . . . some daughters of mothers who attended Madison . . . some sisters of Madison students; and some of whom are even upperclassmen who have been here before. Since all Virginia colleges are filled to capacity, there is nowhere else within the state for these students to go. There are students on our waiting list who will come to Madison whenever there is a vacancy, whether it be at the beginning of the first, second, or third quarters." The business manager was reminded that all veterans attending under the GI bill paid in-state tuition, regardless of home residence.

The GI Bill covered tuition and housing as Uncle Sam's thank-you to the millions of servicemen and women who returned after the war. An article in the *Daily News-Record* alerted local veterans to Madison's compliance. Local veteran Walter Eye ('49) had been accepted at the University of Virginia, but the only housing offered him was in Fishersville. He applied to Madison. "I switched from law to teaching and I've been glad ever since," Eye, a retired high school counselor, remarked fifty years later.

Top: In 1947 Claude Warren, coach at Harrisonburg High School, started Madison's first men's basketball team: BACK: David Turner, Walter Eye, Tom Driver, Raymond Showalter, Bill Wolfe, Beryl Snellings; CENTER: R. T. Bruce, Dick Spangler, Alvin Carter, Dale Sumption, Ronald Burton; FRONT: Tom Garner, Bill Nash, J. B. Figgatt, Pete Corbin, D. J. Driver. They named themselves "Dukes" hoping President Duke would fund uniforms and equipment. It didn't work for the uniforms—they bought their own.

Bottom: They played home games in Reed (Keezell) Hall, and furnished their own transportation to away games. (Photos: 1947 *Schoolma'am*)

In the fall of 1946, thirty-nine men enrolled full time. Madison College, Harrisonburg, Virginia, was still officially termed "A State College for Women" in all publications. But the times were changing. Sophomore D. J. Driver's photo was the first male face to break the all-female, alphabetized bevy of sophomore girls in the 1947 *Schoolma'am*. Fifteen more male faces interspersed the freshmen section. By the year's close, part- and full-time men totaled 101; not all were pictured in the yearbook, which retained its feminine name.

The Sesame Club (for day students) welcomed men. Other clubs remained strictly female, and more than two decades would pass before males invaded dormitories, but athletics gave way quickly. In the winter of 1946–47, the first male athletic team in the history of the college arrived with men's basketball and dubbed itself the "Madison Dukes," which had a grander ring than "Madison Boys"—and a practical purpose. "We nicknamed ourselves for Dr. Duke hoping he'd fork over some money to buy balls and equipment—and he did," related Eye, who played forward on that first team.

The girls cheered Coach Claude Warren's squad of fifteen to a 4-3 season. They beat the Mary Washington Boys 31-24 in the season opener, then took the Shenandoah Boys and Bridgewater Freshmen.

The school motto still read, "That our daughters may be as cornerstones, polished after the similitude of a palace," but "sons" were being polished as well. The 1948 yearbook pictures sophomore Andrew Beryl Snellings from Fredricksburg as the first male class officer. He also headed Sigma Delta Rho, the first fraternity, organized in the spring of '47.

The school opened in the fall of 1948 for its fortieth session with an enrollment of over 1,300, including 125 men. Duke held to routine matters, conducting the initial faculty meeting on September 18. That meeting would prove his

Another banner event marked 1947—fifteen seniors became the first Madison students included in *Who's Who s in American Colleges and Universities*. Pictured here: BACK: June Sterling, Shirley Williams: Laura Virginia Foltz, Jane Hartman, Carolyn Woodfield, Claire Bennett; CENTER: Emily Leitner, Margaret Ritchie, Marguerite Coffman, Alice Agnor; FRONT: Betty Jo Stretchberry, Hilda Davis, Mary Jane Fulton, Jeanette Pickrel.

In 1948, Beryl Snellings, pictured here with fellow sophomores (left to right) Shirley Jones, Jean Parker, and Peggy Shomo, became the first male class officer. He was also president of the first men's fraternity (bottom photo), Sigma Delta Rho, formed in the spring of 1947. (Photos: 1948 *Schoolma'am*)

last. On Monday, September 27, the *Daily News-Record* led with a front-page headline, "Dr. Duke Stricken At University/Suffers Cerebral Hemorrhage While At Football Game."

The paper informed readers that, while attending a game between Miami University and the University of Virginia, Duke had slumped over shortly into the second half and was rushed to the hospital. It was his second stroke, following a slight one in May from which he had felt fully recovered. During the summer, Duke had occasionally complained about feeling tired, and had rested more than usual. At sixty-three years, he attributed his fatigue to age, and pressed on with his duties. The Friday night before the game, the paper reported, "Dr. and Mrs. Duke were hosts at the President's reception to freshmen at their home, 'Hillcrest.' He shook hands with each of the 400 students and visibly did not appear fatigued."

Tuesday's front page reported "Dr. Duke Unchanged"; on Wednesday, "Dr. Duke Reported Some Improved." Then there was no further word until a October 13 headline read, "Committee Will Direct Affairs Of Madison College." Blake Newton, president of the State Board of Education, called a special faculty meeting to announce he had appointed an executive committee to administer the affairs of the college "until Dr. Duke is able to resume his duties."

From the 1949 *Schoolma'am* are pictured three of the first male graduates in regular session: (left to right) Nicholas Thomas Passcaretti, David Harold Turner, and William Nelson Nash. Men still couldn't live on campus, but the GI Bill gave them rights to the classrooms.

To the public there appeared no question of Duke's returning, but in the interim Dr. Walter Gifford, dean of the college, would chair an administrative committee made up of Howard K. Gibbons, business manager; Hope Vandever, dean of women; Percy Warren, dean of Summer School; and Clyde P. Shorts, secretary of the faculty.

The transition proved seamless. The committee carried through into graduation exercises for the Class of 1949—with the first male graduates of a regular session.

Part Three

Miller:
Years of Change,
1949–1970

Art students found "the Rock" a favorite
place to perch for sketching out-of-
doors—and much less crowded than
the art department on the third floor
of Wilson, where classrooms were
crammed and the corridor lined with
easels displaying student work. Benches
had been installed at the Rock for more
ladylike seating—but the limestone always
attracted a few. (Photo: 1946
Schoolma'am)

SAMUEL PAGE DUKE never returned to office. Reluctantly facing the reality of his resignation in the summer of 1949, Madison College elected him President Emeritus and refurbished the recently purchased Zirkle House across Main Street to be the Dukes' final home. In thirty years of dedication to the college, Duke had made no arrangements for his own future. So, although they departed "Hillcrest," the couple resided comfortably in college housing until his death in 1955.

However grateful he must have been for the school's generosity, Duke also must have struggled with mixed emotions as he peered across Main Street each day at the institution in which he no longer played a part. Any loneliness, however, could be countered by a justified pride in how far he had brought the life of that campus. More students strode the walks than he had once imagined. Under his leadership, enrollment had quadrupled from 310 in 1919 to 1,264 in 1949. Students also had broader choices. The one-time teachers college had expanded into a multipurpose liberal arts institution. Courses as diverse as geology, physics, foreign languages, commercial subjects, premed and prenursing augmented teacher training, leading to Bachelor of Science as well as Bachelor of Arts degrees.

Duke drew pleasure watching from his window as students crisscrossed the campus, the grounds resplendent under the changing seasons. He could count fourteen buildings, eight erected on his watch, including the grand Wilson Hall and the modern library clearly visible from his new home. And the grounds had become a rolling landscape of sixty-nine acres, twenty more than what he began with in 1919. Total plant value had grown from $400,000 to $2 million. His thirty years had left an imprint worth any personal cost.

Prodded by Governor William Tuck, the State Board of Education urgently cast about for Duke's replacement. Prospects soon centered on George Tyler Miller, the current state superintendent of Public Instruction. Miller, however, was a reluctant candidate. Decades later, in an interview with Ray Sonner, Miller explained:

> I did not possess a Master's Degree or a Doctorate, although I
> had completed many hours beyond the requirements for a Master's
> . . . and had taught classes at the University of Virginia. Also, I had

been state superintendent . . . for little more than three years and felt that there was a lot to be done in this post. When one adds these to the fact that my entire life had been spent in public education, I did not consider myself a prime candidate for a post in higher education.

Certainly there were faculty members at Madison who agreed with his self-assessment, wondering at the selection of a president with neither an advanced degree nor experience in higher education. But the governor was confident he had the right man. He assured Miller that, if the appointment fell short of public approval, he would "take full responsibility for any and all criticism." In setting forth his candidate, Tuck had described him as "endowed with sterling virtues and qualities . . . a man of integrity and courage . . . [possessing] a natural aptitude for leadership and . . . all of the qualities so vital, if not indeed indispensable, in a successful executive."

The general public agreed—based on Miller's record. He had been an outspoken advocate for strengthening the teaching profession, first as a high school principal, then as superintendent of schools in Rappahannock and Warren counties and in Charlottesville. He had also headed the Virginia Education Association. Tuck had elevated him to state superintendent from the post in Charlottesville.

In three short years in Richmond, Miller had made his mark, conceiving or sponsoring important changes at a critical juncture for Virginia's educational system. Statewide, teachers were leaving the profession in droves, buildings were obsolete, and curricula enrichment at a standstill. He countered the problems with a nine-prong attack. He successfully:

- Reorganized the state Department of Education into more sharply defined areas of responsibility and authority.

- Developed Woodrow Wilson Educational Center, a rehabilitation program that received national acclaim.

- Acquired nearly $6 million of surplus government property for school use.

- Established scholarship plans to enhance the professional skills of current and future teachers.

- Established a statewide plan for sick leave.

- Increased state appropriations for teachers' salaries.

- Clarified the goals and objectives of elementary and secondary education.

- Developed an eighth-grade course of study.

- Issued teacher handbooks with specific teaching strategies.

Top: Through the years, the routine of signing out and signing in to leave the campus remained in force.

Bottom: Pin curls and a last hand of bridge were also routine before lights out at eleven o'clock. (Photos: 1949 *Schoolma'am*)

Tuck recognized Miller as a man of action, and action was the cardinal need for higher education to succeed in this postwar era. Tuck also knew that Miller, perhaps more than any other man, understood the pressing demand for turning out new teachers, especially for elementary schools. Virginia faced a critical shortfall as the postwar baby boom impacted public schools.

When the new president arrived on campus, the faculty set all misgivings aside and rose to the occasion to welcome him. Dorothy Garber, who would continue as his dean of women, concealed her misgivings about his academic shortcomings as she bustled about to see that his opening reception at "Hillcrest" would show "her girls" to their best advantage. Shirley Morris Kappes ('51) reported how Garber instructed them to "Go stand around, look at each other, and

smile. If you can't think of anything to say—as if a bunch of girls couldn't think of anything to say—look like you're having a good time. You can even look at each other, just say your ABCs and smile." But they managed more than their alphabet, charmed by the genuine warmth Miller displayed to all. He accorded no less cordiality to students than he bestowed on faculty and dignitaries.

Dr. Ray Sonner, who closed his illustrious career on campus as president of the JMU Foundation, illustrates—in a later doctoral thesis—the new president's combination of drive and daring on his immediate arrival in town, when the local paper happened to carry an obituary for one George T. Miller:

> That the deceased and the new president were not even remotely related might have been of little comfort to a superstitious man, but Tyler Miller was undaunted as he went about the first few days of his new responsibilities. Possessing a flair for the dramatic, Miller moved quickly to attract attention to his position. . . . He prevailed upon his longtime friend Governor Tuck to release needed money from state surplus funds to enable Miller to announce the awarding of a contract to build the first dormitory [constructed] in more than ten years. The dramatic announcement attracted attention in Harrisonburg and on campus. The new president had wasted little time in getting a project underway and seemed to have performed miracles in financing it.

In his inaugural address on December 10, 1949, Miller was equally dramatic and specific, leaving no doubt about his optimism for the future. He favorably impressed citizens locally and beyond. Initiating a personal crusade to improve teacher preparation, he presented a nine-point program of goals for his administration that gave educators something to talk about.

One of the educators at Miller's inaugural was early graduate M'ledge Moffett ('11), a dean at Radford College. She wished the new president well but had praised his predecessor's administration as rendering Madison "the pace setter for the other colleges. It laid the groundwork for the standards and interpretation of teacher education on the college level." Miller determined that no less would be said of his time. That December day, he outlined his plan for several changes.

One innovation was to provide more common curricula for secondary and elementary teachers, to allow future teachers more job flexibility. Secondary graduates often couldn't find jobs, while elementary schools were understaffed.

Miller also promoted expansion of practice teaching opportunities plus the construction of a campus training school. He touted the idea of postgraduate programs, of college and public school staffs working together on curricula, and of revising admission standards. He urged "Full legal authorization for the admission of men students and the establishment of the College as a coeducational institute," a move that would allow men who were not pursuing a teacher-training degree to remain at the school beyond their sophomore year and free them from their restrictive day-student only status.

His teacher preparation options were soon implemented. Coeducation would have to wait, as it proved a thorny issue for segregationists. Madison was a southern school in a southern town. Racial integration threatened the status quo, and most Virginia lawmakers feared that arguments for allowing men on campus might be used as precedents for allowing blacks into white schools. Men, under special status, had been part of the Madison scene since the GI Bill brought veterans to the campus. But the numbers were decreasing.

The voice for racial justice, however, was increasing. Black veterans, returned from World War II battlefields, demanded those same rights in post-war, segregated America for which they had put their own lives on the line. In 1954, after the Supreme Court in a landmark decision ruled that "separate but equal" was unconstitutional, Miller's old province of Warren County became the first county in Virginia to circumvent the law. In Front Royal, white parents set up private schools for white students, abandoning the public system to "Negroes" and the few sons and daughters of what they considered

Crowds gathered to witness regal May Queen Ebie Copley preside over the May Day proceedings in 1949 with a male attendant as well as the usual female ones. In 1953, Alumni Homecoming was added to the May Day celebration and included a parade through downtown with student floats. (Photo: 1949 *Schoolma'am*)

Echoing genteel southern ways, Virginia Military Institute cadets in traditional gray uniforms offered a romantic contrast to the equally dashing men in black tuxes. For the girls, however, long formals, with or without straps, could be any color, but the short gloves that had replaced the elbow-length ones of the 1940s were always white. In 1966 the first student of African American descent enrolled at Madison College. (Photo: *Images of James Madison University 1908–1983*)

"misguided liberal" citizens. Miller followed the news accounts with dismay at the setback for public education, but he had little time to dwell on problems in his old stomping grounds. The current welfare and future of Madison College demanded his full attention.

M iller's successes during the first decade of his presidency quickly dispelled faculty doubts about his fitness for the position. The reluctant candidate proved an aggressive president. After the initial dramatic proof that he could move the General Assembly to act by getting funds to execute an already-awarded contract for Logan Hall, he continued to champion building, renovation, and expansion. In 1952, his negotiation to buy 240 acres extended the campus the farthest since the school's founding. It also laid the groundwork for future growth.

Dingledine's history of the first fifty years underscores the achievement: "If the College became fully coeducational, dormitories for men could be located in the addition. Athletic and recreational areas might be developed. The damming of the creek running through the property could provide a lake for swimming and boating." All would come to pass.

Chapter Thirteen

"We give thee, Alma Mater, dear, Our Love and Loyalty" (1952–1958)

An aerial photo from 1951 shows room for both campus and community growth. Fast forward only a few decades and land east of the campus will be divided by I-81 and filled in with large-scale commercial development (including Valley Mall), new housing, and the future CISAT campus. (Photo: 1951 *Schoolma'am*)

But for college students, the future is always now. Madison students' excitement over the college's growth waxed in direct proportion to personal impact. Girls of the classes of '51 and '52 were thrilled to move into Logan on November 19, 1950. Its completion had been delayed by a local shortage of stonemasons plus a national steelworkers strike. Named for beloved English professor Conrad Travis Logan, who died in 1947, the new dormitory was the first built in twelve years. To the girls, more important than its enhancement of Miller's public image was its ultramodern comfort—though the bathtubs were as hard as ever when one studied there after lights out.

Betty Morgan Matthews ('55) recalls the lights-out difficulties for a "night person" like herself who needed to study or finish a book: "Now one can only wonder how many flashlight batteries were worn out while reading under the covers or on pillows in the bathtub. . . . Someone always had to be on guard for the housemother making her rounds seeking a ray of light beaming from beneath the door."

After Logan's completion, the next September brought groundbreaking for a new science building that would be two years under construction but worth the wait. No more in Maury's cramped quarters would the bitter odor of hydrogen sulfide from the single chemistry lab—which had to accommodate 282 students—fight tantalizing smells from home economics. The new Burruss Science Hall (named to honor the first president) housed the departments of biology, chemistry, geography, geology, mathematics, and physics. Thus, a renovated Maury afforded a full floor for home economics, and the second for business classes and audio-visual needs.

And so it went through the 1950s. "Such was the remarkable program of physical expansion that Tyler Miller was able to carry out in less than a decade," Dingledine assessed. "Grounds and buildings valued at about $4 million in 1949 had been developed into a plant estimated as worth $7.2 million in 1958. The number of buildings had grown to 32, including 21 of limestone with red tiled roofs."

As the president prepared for the future, the students turned to cherished traditions and established new ones. Each year the *Schoolma'am* photos preserved ceremonial rites of passage. "Out" went the New Girl–Old Girl Wedding. In its place the YWCA held a Big Sister–Little Sister Party to help ease first-month jitters. Still "in," however, was the formal reception to welcome students at "Hillcrest" by the president and his wife. A formal ceremony in November officially installed freshmen as part of the student body when upperclassmen pinned purple and gold ribbons over their hearts.

Floor-length formals remained *de rigueur* for teas at "Hillcrest," worn by both students and female faculty. Dean Garber's class on "white glove" behavior proved memorable for its precise dictates, if not its practicality. Garber cautioned the girls never to sit when an elder is standing; never to wear white

before May 31 or after September 1; and to eat ice cream served in a bowl with a spoon, but with a fork when served on a plate. Hose, gloves, and a hat were mandatory on Sunday. Dresses or skirts were still required for classes, as were raincoats to conceal shorts and jeans worn on campus. Matthews recalled "the many times we all struggled to roll up those jeans legs so they wouldn't hang down below a raincoat long enough to return a book to the library on the other side of campus, or to go to Doc's for a milkshake. No one wanted a 'call down' for improper dressing."

Loretta Koch Copperthite ('54) found it "galling to be required to wear a raincoat over jeans or gym suits. There were very few male students in 1954, and those wonderfully baggy suits would not have titillated a gorilla! Besides, the school laundry starched them so heavily that they would literally stand alone. We looked like little tin soldiers until physical activity cracked the starch."

Sorority rushes each fall were followed by Halloween parties, candlelight services, the Christmas Kid Party for needy children and the YWCA-sponsored Christmas pageant, now with actual males taking parts as Joseph and the Wise Men. The pageant's yearly casting of beautiful girls as Madonna, First Angel, and four additional angels "inspires us anew as the Christmas story, accompanied by Christmas music, is retold," describes the '51 *Schoolma'am*.

Certainly the copies of the yearly *Schoolma'am* and the weekly *Breeze* were "in," as were evening dresses or tuxes at dances. Highest honors included not only being chosen by the combined faculty and student body for *Who's Who in American Colleges and Universities*, but also being selected by popular vote as Miss Madison or elected to represent Madison as a princess at the annual Apple Blossom Festival in Winchester. Class Days continued full force, each class working the day around its chosen theme. But next to graduation, the most spectacular tradition came in May.

Left: When new questions arose in 1952, Chairman Peggy Turner Johnson and the committee took its "never-ending duties" seriously and so did the students.

Right: The Standards Committee's effort to "promote the very highest standards of social conduct and appearance" led them to include dance rules, dining hall etiquette, campus behavior, proper dress, and assembly conduct in a section of the *Handbook* issued every student. FRONT: F. Pettyjohn, B. Crosby, G Johnson., H. Watkins; BACK: J. Thompson, M. Miller, B. Staples, N. Walker, M. Groseclose, L. Jefferson. (Photo: 1952 *Schoolma'am*)

Sorority houses of the day, as shown in the 1958 *Schoolma'am*. Zirkle House and Shenandoah Hall on Main Street still stand. The others were razed for campus expansion. Sororities came to Madison in the spring of 1939, Sigma Sigma Sigma and Alpha Sigma Alpha the first. They soon replaced literary societies in prestige and importance. Before housing a sorority, Zirkle House became home for President Emeritus Duke and his wife after two strokes led to Duke's resignation as president in 1949. They remained until his death in 1955. (Photo: *Images of James Madison University 1908–1983*)

Carter   Zirkle

Shenandoah   Sprinkle

Messick   Dingledine

The traditional May Day celebration on the back-campus lawn became a royal coronation for a white-gowned queen in the center of maids of honor and attendants. The regalia brought out dancers winding ribbons around the May pole, a moment, according to Helen Warren Tuttle ('59), that "always provided a bit of suspense on whether all the weaving would end up right or not." Grace and dignity marked May Days. One daring break within the tradition came in 1954 when the maids and attendants all wore strapless evening dresses. The next year they returned to more circumspect attire. The audience included family and friends from across the nation as well as locally.

Perhaps the 1954 belles felt more daring that year under new dean of women Ruth Jones Wilkins, who had gradually allowed rules to relax. Mid-

No matter the season, certain things were a part of everyday life at Madison—keeping off the grass and standing for grace before meals in the dining halls. (Photo: 1955 *Schoolma'am*)

night had become the deadline for lights out. Trips downtown with other girls no longer required "signing out." Men could call for their dates at sorority houses and dating centers in the new dorms, not the single meeting room at Alumnae Hall. Upperclassmen could "ride at any free time by signing out according to parental approval." Even freshmen could ride with dates at specified times.

Dean Wilkins, however, expected the girls to toe the line, and they obeyed and revered her. Kay Alderman King ('59) counted her "a no-nonsense woman with great good humor—a winning combination." Years later, King contrasted dining on campus then and now: "I remember well the ending to the blessing Dean Wilkins always said in the dining hall, '. . . and Lord make us ever mindful of the needs of others. Amen.' I was surprised at the tears that sprang to my eyes when at the reunion dinner we paused for a 'moment of silence' instead of having a blessing. Dean Wilkins was a very special presence at Madison."

For many students, both male and female, the faculty exerted influence far beyond the classroom. Yearly annuals were dedicated to respected and popular professors. A. E. "Pete" Corbin ('54) said, "When I enrolled at Madison in June 1946, Dr. Glenn Smith was my advisor. When I completed my M.A. degree in August 1958, he was not only still my advisor, but a close personal friend. He instilled in me a love of American history that I still have today. It is difficult to describe the warmth that existed between the students in the '50s, but you can feel it when we return and meet at reunions."

Housemothers, officially titled social directors, endeared themselves as indelibly as professors. Copperthite never forgot her freshman days at

SCHOOLMA'AM DEDICATIONS, 1910–1958:

1910–Adolph H. Snyder, Editor of *Harrisonburg Daily News*

1911–Julian Ashby Burruss, first college president

1912–Sen. George Bernard Keezell, "Farmer, Citizen, Friend of Education"

1913–Elizabeth P. Cleveland, English

1914–Prof. Ormond Stone, Board of Trustees, Manassas, Virginia

1915–Annie Vergilia Cleveland, French

1916–Spirit of Shakespeare on the 300th Anniversary of his Death

1917–Dr. John Walter Wayland, History

1918–James Chapman Johnston, Science

1919–Natalie Lancaster, Mathmatics

1920–Julian A. Burruss & Samuel Page Duke, "Our presidents"

1921–Mary I. Bell, Psychology & Hygiene

1922–Woodrow Wilson, "Son of the Valley, World Patriot"

1923–Frances Isabel Mackey, Household & Industrial Arts (Alumna, '13)

1924–Walter John Gifford, Education, Dean

1925–none

1926–Elizabeth Cleveland, English (repeat)

1927–Samuel Page Duke, President (repeat)

1928–Memory of James Chapman Johnston, Science (repeat)

1929–Bernice Reaney Varner, Dean

1930–"Our Mothers"

1931–Ann Virginia Harnsberger, Librarian

1932–"Our Fathers"

1933–"Our Builders" with photo of Keezell

1934–Katherine Miner Anthony, Director, Training School

1935–Walter John Gifford, Dean (repeat)

1936–Edna Trout Shaeffer, Director, School of Music

1937–Grace Margaret Palmer, Fine Arts

1938–Dr. Edna Tutt Frederikson, English

1939–Adele Raymond Blackwell, Home Economics

1940–"Our Roommates"

1941–"Our Parents"

1942–"Those men everywhere who are fighting that democracy may live."

1943–"The hope that a new and better world may rise from the ashes of this war."

1944–"The students and faculty of Madison College"

1945–"The Future Teachers of America"

1946–"Children of the Post-War Years"

1947–William Hampton Keister, Harrisonburg Superintendent of Schools

1948–Memory of Conrad Travis Logan, English

1949–"Our Faculty"

1950–Samuel Page Duke & George Tyler Miller, President Emeritus & President

1951–Margaret V. Hoffman, English

1952–Howard K. Gibbons, Business Manager

1953–Dr. Raymond C. Dingledine, History/Social Science

1954–Dr. & Mrs. Raymond Poindexter, Education

1955–Alfred K. Eagle, Director of Student Guidance & Placement

1956–Dr. Paul Hounchell, Education

1957–Stephen C. Bocskey, Education

1958–Dr. William L. Mengebier, Biology

Spotswood under Mrs. Anna B. Beasley's probing eye and the exclamation, "I see little fuzzy-wuzzies," as she peered under beds during room inspection. Anne Southworth ('54) spent her junior and senior years at Sprinkle House (Sigma Sigma Sigma) under Agnes Dingledine. She remembered, "Mama Ding was a guardian angel. She was the housemother and taught us social graces and a strong faith through her actions." Wailes Darby ('50) echoed the praise, "Mama Ding cared for each of us as if we were her own daughters."

Southworth also recalls her sophomore year in Johnston dorm with open porches at each end, where one evening the girls braved administrative wrath by dragging mattresses onto them to sleep outside. "I think we were watching for the UVA boys who were having 'Panty Raids' at girls' schools." Their hopes were dashed when social director Pearl S. Hoover showed up and the boys didn't.

Sunday's brown-bag suppers held over a less popular tradition from the earliest days of the college, and sit-down meals continued to be served family style in Harrison's Dining Hall. Faculty and students settled themselves by eights around the cloth-draped tables with cloth napkins. Individual napkin rings designated places and allowed the napkins reuse. The food brought few

The Blue Stone Dining Hall on the second floor of Harrison Hall accommodated freshmen and sophomores. Juniors dined on the first floor, seniors in the basement. Linens were standard with each student furnishing her own napkin ring—often simply a clothespin inked with her name. Napkins were reused, laundered midweek and before Sunday dinner. Madison fried chicken was a favorite entrée. Prominently placed center tables were reserved for faculty and housemothers, who kept an ever-watchful eye on behavior. (Photo: JMU Special Collections)

Doc's Tea Room, at 1007 South Main Street, served no alcohol but was as close as students legally could get to a bar atmosphere. Jukebox songs—five cents a play, six for a quarter—blared in the background, while Cokes, smokes, and hamburgers fueled easy conversation and inexpensive date time for guys on a budget—who in the 1950s were expected to pick up the tab. (Photo: From a 1950s brochure sent to prospective students)

complaints, but Copperthite recalls, "On '*liver nights*' the dining halls would be half empty. Menus were not published, but you could get information from girls who worked in the dining halls, then dine on peanut butter and crackers."

No one counted grams of fat or worked out in those days, though physical appearance was important. While no one wanted to be fat, muscle-building and toning were left to men. The nearly universal goal of Madison women was marriage, and few coeds planned a career beyond the home. Most Madison grads expected their college education to be used in the work force for a few years before marriage and to raise their market value on the dating scene. A homemaker's worth was always a reflection of her husband and children's accomplishments. Also, education helped prepare one for useful voluntary service after marriage.

The 1958 *Bulletin Madison College, Vol. XVI, No. 1* clearly stated the institution's values to include strength of character and "willingness to sacrifice oneself for worthy and useful purposes." Also "sound scholarship and a broad understanding of mankind" were necessary for success in teaching, where one's goal was for a "complete, happy, and useful life."

The *Bulletin* reflected national yearnings. Fulfilling a national longing for Warren G. Harding's slogan "a return to normalcy," President Dwight David Eisenhower won an overwhelming victory in the 1952 campaign, winning 442 of 531 Electoral College votes against his Democratic opponent Adlai Stevenson. "Normalcy" encapsulated Americans' desires, even as news stories through the decade headlined events destined to revolutionize that "normalcy." Nevertheless, on campus they evoked little comment at Coke parties and rare mention in *The Breeze*.

In addition to forming various sports teams, the Men's Student Organization held an annual Men's Smoker for students and faculty, hoping refreshments, entertainment, and a few good Cuban cigars would stimulate better student-faculty relations. President Ed Grandle led the 122 members and made *Who's Who in American Colleges and Universities*. (Photo: 1951 *Schoolma'am*)

The campus paper ignored the 1951 advent of UNIVAC (Universal Automatic Computer), which injected the words *transistor* and *semiconductor* into vocabularies but was met with little understanding of the coming technological revolution that would penetrate every area of everyday life. In 1952, the U.S. detonated the first hydrogen bomb to enter a new age of military might. Two

years later the Supreme Court exploded a bomb of its own, ruling that race-based segregation in public schools violated the Constitution. School districts had four years to comply. Four years later, Arkansas Governor Orval Faubus defied the order, and forced a reluctant President to dispatch federal troops. Martin Luther King Jr., too, had gained public attention as a civil rights leader, organizing the 1955 bus boycott in Montgomery, Alabama. Virginians, black and white, watched and waited.

Nineteen fifty-four introduced Senator Joseph McCarthy's "witch-hunts" that played on Cold War hysteria and guilt by association. In anticipation of nuclear war, student teachers nationwide added "duck and cover" air-raid drills to the more routine fire drills. And backyard bomb shelters dotted some neighborhoods and towns. Fears heightened when a nation used to being number one was dramatically displaced in 1957, after the U.S.S.R. sent Sputnik skyward to beep its mocking signal back to Earth. Ignominy was compounded that September when the U.S. satellite *Vangard* blew up at launch before a horrified audience. School boards across the nation geared up to emphasize science and mathematics at every grade level.

"We were fairly serious and aware of what was going on in the outside world," said Judy Shreckhise Strickler, forty years later, recalling her class of 1960 that also included Marcia Angell. Both went on to graduate school. "We had bulletin boards littered with corsages, dances, crazy class night hats, and dance cards. And we sang the silly 'nun, nun, nuns of Madison,' but we were more aware of circumstances and social issues we would face. Student teaching had broken through the cloistered state on campus. We met students from

Before e-mail there were activity boards to keep everyone up to date on forthcoming meetings and events. This one in Harrison Hall drew daily scrutiny from passersby. (Photo: JMU Special Collections)

broken homes, students who faced sexual abuse, situations we had never encountered before.

"We wanted to graduate, get a job, settle down, and contribute to the community. We wanted to make a difference."

Every dorm now had a TV, a washer, and a dryer. Occupants enjoyed satisfaction with their dreams and the world. No one yet could fully grasp the importance of UNIVAC and Sputnik; however, the administration and faculty paid attention. Madison's two-day Fiftieth Anniversary celebrated the theme "Emerging Horizons in an Age of Science." The March 13–14, 1959 program included two national figures from the field of science: Dr. Robert Charpie, an assistant research director at Oak Ridge National Laboratory, home of the atomic and hydrogen bombs, and Dr. Ashley Montagu, anthropologist, social biologist, and author. Another guest speaker was Dr. Joseph C. Robert, president of Hampton-Sydney College.

Left: Even if there were no physics applications required, physics students would
have enjoyed an afternoon tour of Grand
Caverns. But here they're collecting data
with a Gieger tube. The young man in the
center holds the battery and electronics,
listening for the audible clicks at a rate
proportional to the radiation being measured. The other two have probes to take
the readings. (Photo: 1951 *Schoolma'am*)

Right: President Miller, history professor
Raymond Dingledine, and Dean of the
college Percy Warren in 1958 at the
Founders' Day Convocation at the Fiftieth
Anniversary Celebration. Today each man
is remembered by a campus building
named in his honor. (Photo: *Images of
James Madison University 1908–1983*)

The Founders' Day observance marked a triple celebration: "first, it ends
the year-long commemoration of the Fiftieth Anniversary . . . next, to give
appropriate recognition to the impact of science and the behavioral sciences
upon contemporary American life . . . Finally, . . . the dedication of six new
buildings erected in the last several years: Burruss Hall (science building),
Logan, Wayland, and Gifford Halls (residences), the Anthony-Seeger Campus
School, and the College Infirmary."

HARRISONBURG AT THE START OF THE 1950S still ran two-way traffic on Main and Liberty streets with parking allowed on both sides. With I-81 not yet conceived, travelers threaded U.S. Route 11 bound north and south, and U.S. Route 33 east and west. Madison girls' parents on overnight visits had their choice of seven downtown hotels in which to stay. Shopping centered in downtown as well, with stores clustered near Court Square—Alfred or Joseph Ney's, J. C. Penney or Leggetts for clothing, McCrory's or W. T. Grant for variety, and Barth Garber's for shoes.

Faculty housing was concentrated within walking distance of faculty offices. In 1952, of the 110 listings in the faculty directory twenty-three lived on South Main Street, ten on Campbell, nine on South Mason, and most of the rest resided along streets nearby. Only six listed out-of-Harrisonburg addresses, with Mrs. Georgia Brown of Mt. Solon the most distant, at fifteen miles. The faculty that taught together played together. One former professor confessed, "The bridge clubs wielded real power, were the real decision-making groups for a lot of hiring and firing and other campus policies."

Chapter Fourteen

"Polished its daughters"
becomes *Passé*
(1950s)

For Madisonians in the mid-1950s, downtown Harrisonburg was still the happening place for shopping, movies, dining out, and greeting friends. To the regret of many, little of this architectural heritage remains today. (Photo: *Images of James Madison University 1908–1983*)

New buildings paralleled administrative and program changes. Beginning in 1954 the school had its first full-time dean in Percy Warren, after the retirement of Dr. Gifford, who had served part-time as dean of the college. Prior to his appointment, Warren had directed the summer sessions to make them as accommodating as possible for mature students returning to upgrade their certificates. He made dormitory rooms available for men and opened housing for mothers who wanted to bring their children with them, implementing activities for the youngsters during the day. Thus, his appointment as dean proved a popular choice.

Another change accrued as an outgrowth of faculty input when Miller reorganized departments into divisions in 1954. His July report to the state board cited the advantages as more effective administration and curriculum planning, and enhancement of staff cooperation through greater understanding of the total picture. Four divisions arose—humanities, natural sciences, social sciences, and teacher education.

English department head Dr. C. H. Huffman guided humanities until his retirement in 1957, when Louis Locke assumed both roles. The division drew together the departments of art, English, foreign languages, music, and philosophy. Next, the division of natural sciences under Dr. J. E. Ikenberry encompassed biology, chemistry, geology, mathematics, physics, and physical and health education. For the third division, David Hatch, already a groundbreaker as the school's first professor of sociology, directed social sciences until his retirement in 1957, when Elmer L. Smith took over. Their charge for social sciences carried business education, geography, history, home economics, library science, and social science. The final division—and the one usually drawing eighty percent of the student body—was teacher education. Dr. Charles G. Caldwell accepted the challenging position as director to oversee the education and psychology departments plus student teaching.

Caldwell had arrived in 1951 from the University of Maryland, having chosen Madison despite offers from William and Mary, the universities of Virginia and of Alabama, and a promising future as dean at Maryland. He chose Madison for its potential, with full confidence in his own contributions to that potential. Twenty-five years later, he wrote of satisfying achievements. He had spearheaded a revitalized curriculum in human growth and development, and required it of all education graduates. He felt this led to "a teacher preparation program whose products were in demand throughout the state and region and which served as a model. . . . Not only were Madison . . . graduates sought, but also its program was emulated by other institutions across the state." One national conference of the American Association of College Teachers of Education based its theme on the same diagnostic-prescriptive-remediation approach Madison had instituted a decade earlier.

Student teaching was an essential component of Madison's success. Placing students in real-world situations off campus harked back to Burruss. Contracting a master teacher to supervise each for all-day practice began in 1951. Caldwell broadened classroom opportunities to include practice in school systems both in and beyond Harrisonburg and Rockingham County. By the 1958–59 session, sixty-eight percent of the student teachers had been placed in fifty-seven schools across seven county systems, including Albemarle, Arlington, Augusta, Clarke, Culpeper, Fairfax, and Frederick, plus the cities of Charlottesville, Falls Church, Waynesboro, and Winchester. Caldwell directed their experience toward making each teacher become an agent of change, "a vital, contributing member of the *total* community, with certain specialized skills: a knowledge of how people grow and develop and the ability to interpret this growth and development into learning patterns both formal and informal."

Students learned outside the classroom as well as within—though not always as expected. Betty Morgan Matthews ('55) traversed the Blue Ridge: "How we all looked forward to being 'away' from campus for this half of a semester, yet longed to be there, participating in the usual senior activities. Each experience was different, but for those of us who went to Albemarle High in Charlottesville, those boarding-house dinners contrasted greatly with

Falling snow cancelled all rules of fair play to pit one photographer against Madisonians hurling snowballs. (Photo: JMU Special Collections)

the wonderful supervision we received at the school." Newly found freedom proved a heady experience — and an introduction to a different side of humanity.

Professor Martha Sieg drove Mathews and another student to Charlottesville to find them lodging and dining facilities for the nine-week period. She situated them in a comfortable private home where the owners allocated a little refrigerator space so they could make their own breakfast. Lunch, of course, was eaten at school. Dinner had to be elsewhere. So Sieg found a nearby boardinghouse, a gracious picturesque colonial with a large front porch. Mathews, however, recalls the interior did not live up to its outer promise: "It always smelled musty. The dining room was large with one long table. The furnishings were a mix of colonial and Victorian and all curtains, draperies and upholstery that we ever saw were dingy, faded, and appearing in need of a good cleaning. The food was put on the table in bowls and platters and we passed it around family style."

At their meals, Mathews describes the boarders they found to match the setting:

> The cast of characters who ate there could have been straight out of an old English novel. It was a totally new experience for both of us who had grown up on a Virginia farm. There were times we could hardly eat . . . [and we] spent most of the dinner hour stifling giggles at some of the antics of the others at our table.
>
> Looking back, we must have been young and foolish [unable] to understand the problems with which some . . . were trying to cope. There were young and old boarders, some could not hear, others did not talk but shouted every word. They were male and female, stooped and wobbly, some with good minds, others forgetful to the point of repeating every word over and over during the dinner hour. Most of the elderly had been eating there for some time. . . . they held their discussions, sometimes political and not very polite with each other, and we were only bystanders. Occasionally, one of the women would get so angry with one of the men that she would jump up and march out, slamming the door and leaving without eating. There were no assigned seats and I seldom remember having the opportunity to sit near any of the few younger people. At any rate, none seemed to have much to say. Perhaps they were like the two of us, always wondering what would happen next among the older crowd. It was certainly a different experience for us.

In spite of the dissonance at dinner, Mathews enjoyed her student teaching: "We were fortunate we had two very capable home economics teachers for our supervisors. It was a good experience in living in the real world before we actually graduated. We had to solve our own problems and live within our financial means. We had lesson plans to prepare and be approved as well as papers to grade, so we had plenty to do in the evenings. . . . it was a very positive experience."

Caldwell felt teachers needed continuous exposure to new learning. His enthusiastic proposal for a graduate program in early childhood education led to a $55,000 award to establish one. Other programs followed. In June 1956, the college bestowed its first master's degrees: Everett E. Wilfong, principal of Keezletown Elementary School, had fulfilled his requirements in February for a Master of Arts in education. The second M.A. went to Mrs. Vivian Berry Fauver, a seventh-grade teacher at Harrisonburg Junior High School, who had just completed her orals the prior Tuesday.

Once underway, the graduate program numbers signified its success. By the end of the 1959–60 session, the school had conferred a total of eighty master's degrees. "In time, it became a model and was observed, emulated, and praised not only in the State, but also region-ally and nationally," wrote Caldwell.

National praise also ensued for the campus school, Anthony-Seeger, which opened in 1958. Planned by a cross-departmental committee, the building itself was awarded a prize for architectural excellence by the American Institute of Architects. In addition, the National Conference of American Association of School Administrators viewed a model on exhibit at its national conference in Atlantic City, New Jersey.

But the real satisfaction for the school rose from within its walls. Evelyn Watkins, who taught first grade, recalled, "I loved teaching with people who had the same philosophy. It was one of those interesting schools where everyone was working for children. The director, Dr. Henry L. Sublett Jr., all the teachers, the janitor reflected the same philosophy."

Dingledine House was razed to allow erection of Anthony-Seeger Campus School, which opened in the fall of 1958. Fronting Main and Grace Streets, its class-rooms served grades K through 6. In addi-tion, the building held an auditorium, cafeteria, and facilities for reading, speech and hearing, and child guidance centers, a major benefit for education majors and for community children who enrolled. (Photo: JMU Special Collections)

Creativity and flexibility were essential. Parents and Madison faculty were in evidence daily. Watkins again recalled:

People were so cooperative, I always had a piano, had materi-als—didn't have to buy them ourselves. Parents volunteered to help you make bread or churn butter or take you on a trip. And the professors were so helpful. Dr. Wells took us to the observatory, Margaret Gordon would bring her skeletons and things over, Dr. Diller and Mr. Gill would let you invade their studio and make things. When I had the Beer children, we made up sculptures. Dr. Zinger, of course, taught us geography. One year we had Spanish—we learned Spanish dances, Spanish songs. There were maybe a few weak spots but for the most part a good community school for the area and for students to observe.

Watkins gave another example of the easy rapport. One group of her first graders engineered a surprise party totally without her knowledge or input. "Imagine six- and seven-year olds being able to carry it off!" she said. "Parents, of course, were in cahoots with the children. But imagine—a surprise party for the fun of it!"

Teacher training, however, was not the only area eliciting national notice. Both the Madison College Glee Club and the Concert Choir toured the eastern seaboard. Kay Alderman King ('59) still counts such trips as "special times," though not every moment was perfect. She vividly recounts her freshman experience of "an exciting road trip for the Concert Choir with Miss Shaeffer to the Naval Academy to sing with the National Symphony Orchestra. This busload of girls, dressed in their Sunday best, gets off the bus in the

Every Tuesday night and Wednesday afternoon, the Concert Band rehearsed under the direction of Mr. C.T. Marshall. (Photo: *The Schoolma'am*)

From 1916 (top) to 1956 (bottom), Miss Edna T. Shaeffer headed the school's Glee Club. Often on tour, her final year she flew the group to Iceland, Bermuda, and the Azores to entertain servicemen and civilians there. (Photos: 1916 and 1956 *Schoolma'am*)

pouring down rain for a 'rest stop' somewhere near Annapolis. When we got back on our way once more, we are overwhelmed by the smell of fifty or so Mouton coats—a very wet, smelly sheep smell." Their sound, however, was unaffected. The group won accolades.

In 1954, the Glee Club sang in Miami before the National Federation of Music Clubs. Afterward, it received a special invitation to make an Easter concert tour of selected U.S. military bases. In the spring of 1956, the club's twenty-nine girls boarded military C-54s for Iceland, Bermuda, and the Azores—a wonderful finale for Edna Shaeffer's forty years as a member of the music faculty and choral director. She had started the Glee Club in 1916.

At the close of his first decade, President Miller's inaugural goals were well on the way to attainment—except for the admission of men as regular, full-time students. Dingledine's history capsules the controversy:

> [Miller] emphasized various reasons for having men students. . . . They were an asset to the College, doing satisfactory academic work, adding to extracurricular activities, and contributing needed income. Nearly half of the men thus far graduated had completed teaching curricula . . . a number . . . for elementary teaching, in which there was a particular shortage of men. Miller stressed the support that leaders in Harrisonburg and Rockingham County gave to the policy of boys attending . . . boys who would thus be encouraged to remain in the community after college. . . . without Madison, many of these young men would not be able to go to college. The acceptance of male high school graduates from surrounding areas . . . helped relieve the pressure for more dormitory facilities at the men's colleges.

Yet, in spite of his valid reasons and in spite of a strong citizen delegation supporting his request, the state board voted that men could only be accepted as day students, and even then could not remain beyond a second year unless enrolled in a teacher training program. Nevertheless, Madison discarded the traditional motto "polished its daughters" and published a new creed two pages long. The *Alumnae* Association became *Alumni* and the Men's Student Government Association prospered. But the state board, like the General Assembly, had succumbed to fear that the idea of coeducation might set a precedent for college desegregation. Madison symbolized a southern school in a southern state.

MADISON GIRLS strode with confidence into the 1960s, most by evolving from student to teacher in classrooms across the Commonwealth. Miller strode with satisfaction from "Hillcrest" to his office each morning. The school had survived the enrollment decline of the early 1950s, a decline he'd predicted, and had countered its financial losses first with fiscal conservatism and then with a reluctant series of tuition increases. Yet by the new decade, the numbers reversed, with an upward swing he had also predicted. In an address to the Virginia Association of Colleges at Hotel Roanoke in 1955, he had warned of "a tidal wave of students approaching," stressing the need to plan for the 1970s.

Still primarily a college to prepare teachers, annual evaluations of Madison graduates teaching in Virginia validated the school's program. Since 1951, Richard Haydon, Director of In-service Education, had visited each alumna teaching in Virginia at least once during the initial two years on the job. Miller had mandated this policy to discover both strengths and deficiencies in teacher preparation. Administrators' responses indicated their satisfaction never fell below ninety percent, and by 1963–64 the percentages exceeded ninety-seven year after year.

In his doctoral dissertation, Dr. Ray Sonner, former JMU Foundation president, cites an interview with Miller that reveals how the college responded successfully to a recurrent problem:

> [Haydon] found that many of our teachers were simply finding it difficult to adjust to the community. They had no experience in community relationships during their student teaching, and it was a problem for them. We made certain that this topic received a great deal of attention in appropriate classes. Finally, we added a course in school and community relationship techniques to compensate for the lack of experience in the area.

One area not covered was salary negotiation. Graduates were on their own and often in for a shock. In numerous school systems the superintendent set the salary for each teacher "according to whim," said one graduate claiming

Students in the 1950s and '60s continued to hone their teaching skills through classroom practice. Classroom teachers sought student-teaching placements and graduates easily found jobs. Between 1943 and 1958, JMU supplied 2,636 teachers to the Commonwealth, more than any other school in the state. Teaching graduates also crossed state boundaries, heading classrooms in nearby and distant states. (Photos: 1964 *Bluestone*)

anonymity. She reported being offered $1,800 a year in 1952 by a superintendent who explained, "I don't think you'll need more since you can live at home." But a fellow beginning-teacher reported that, in his interview, the same superintendent tendered him $2,400 "since men expect and need more." The female graduate crossed county lines to join a system "burdened with the new-fangled idea of a set salary scale."

In spite of a 1946 state law passed after the Denny Commission report that suggested each school division adopt a minimum salary schedule, system after system continued traditions of salary inequity. Divisions adopted a minimum, but allowed superintendents to embellish it at will. Since the pattern had been the same for professors on campus, little questioning of this practice occurred. Gradually, however, differing points of view soon divided along gender lines on campus. Department heads and deans submitted faculty names and suggested salaries. Disparity between male and female professors rankled the latter, yet continued. Change came first to the public school sector.

For example, in Rockingham County, where so many of Madison's future teachers trained, the first salary scale appeared on February 16, 1954, when the school board approved the following steps:

Years Experience	Salary
0	$2,200
1	$2,300
2	$2,400
3	$2,500
4	$2,600
5	$2,700
6	$2,800
7	$2,900
8	$3,000
9	$3,100
10 Plus	$3,200

"The Masters degree would be $200.00 above the B.S. and A.B. degree scale and Normal Professional Certificates would be paid $200 below the scale for B.S. and A. B. degrees," the school board decreed.

The school board minutes also indicated that military service merited an additional "$100.00 for each year or major fraction there of . . . for those below the maximum on the scale." Yet even that proved inadequate for one ex-GI from the Korean war, who left not only the county, but also the state. Future state senator Kevin Miller signed a contract in 1957 to teach in the San Diego city school system in California for a whopping $5,100. Miller said, "According to Mr. Haydon, the Director of Placement, this was the highest starting teaching salary ever for a Madison graduate." In 1969, Miller returned to his alma mater to teach accounting.

In Harrisonburg, which on May 27, 1946, had followed and improved on the Denny Commission's suggestion for salaries, Superintendent M. H. Bell retained final authority over support staff pay. Administrative secretary Bonnie Miller recalled sitting across from Bell in a silent salary negotiation in the late '50s. He wrote down figures on a sheet of paper, passing them to her until she agreed to accept one. Happily, this agonizing power play soon disappeared. By the early '60s most public school systems, if not colleges, set varying scales across the Commonwealth for both teachers and support personnel.

Yet salaries, however important to faculty members, may have ranked less prominently in the minds of Madison's seniors. Students centered on the immediate—the day-to-day balancing acts to juggle study and play. They relished each year's traditional series of "special days" as Class Day, Senior Capping Day, Moving-Up Day, Convocations, and May Day punctuated the semesters with formal rites of recognition. Class Days focused on fun and frolic. Patterned by the school's earliest decade, each class took responsibility for a theme and entertainment on a set day. Moving-up Day gave recognition

In 1957, new graduate Kevin Miller accepted a contract to teach in San Diego, California, at the highest annual salary yet reported for a new Madison graduate, $5,100. Two years later he returned to his alma mater to teach accounting. From 1980 to 1984, Miller served as a delegate to the Virginia General Assembly, then as state senator from 1984 to 2003, always a friend of education. (Photo: 1957 *Bluestone*)

Senior Capping Day was the day seniors first wore their robes to march into Wilson. For the capping ceremony, each senior chose one underclassman to place the mortarboard on her head, a significant honor accompanied by hugs, smiles, and tears. Begun as a pre-breakfast, robe-gowning ceremony in 1933, it moved to Wilson in 1947 on the evening before Class Day. (Photo: 1964 *Bluestone*)

to rising classes with minimal pomp. Capping Day carried heavier formality. Each senior asked one underclassman to "cap" her. On that spring day, seniors filed into Wilson Hall wearing graduation robes for the first time. During the invocation and speeches, the assembled "cappers" filled the rows behind the seniors, cradling the coveted mortar boards. Then the moment arrived. Amid nervous laughter and even tears, seniors were formally capped.

In 1962, the first *Bluestone* replaced the *Schoolma'am*, the new name reflective of a coed college. It recorded the profusion of activities beyond classes. A student with journalistic talents might join publication staffs of *The Bluestone* or *The Breeze*. Popular students were elected to Men's or Women's Student Governments, or named to the Honor Council, the Standards Committee, or the Social Committee. Even appointment to such seemingly less important groups as the Recreation Council, Fire Safety Committee, Junior Marshalls, Ushers and Handbook Committee were esteemed.

Honor societies merged academic and social life. A 3.0 average entitled students to membership in Sigma Phi Lambda. Pi Omega Pi, a national honor fraternity in business education, and Kappa Delta Pi, a national honor society in education, recognized outstanding students in their respective areas. In 1958, Dr. David Diller and Dr. Crystal Theodore brought the art fraternity, Kappa Pi, to campus, the first chapter of an international honorary fraternity in Virginia. Sigma Alpha Iota, a second international fraternity, honored music and music education majors.

The 1962 *Bluestone* featured eight intermural sports teams plus intramural teams. Greek life consisted of seven sororities and one fraternity, plus the Pan-Hellenic Council. Ten religious organizations, fourteen departmental clubs, and six creative groups—five in music and one for drama—offered variety. Additional social clubs for day students and for each geographic area, plus the prestigious German and Cotillion clubs, meant students had more than seventy-two choices for spare-time activity.

Yet one campus dream, the Chapel Building Fund, faded away almost unnoticed by the end of the 1960s. Started in 1956, the fund alternately had stalled and revived over the years. Early donors steadily gave small sums. Class

Campus chapters of national and international honor societies evoked enthusiastic participation from students invited to join. Left: Kappa Pi, an international organization to encourage potential artists established the state's first chapter at Madison in 1964. Right: Judi Burkholder headed the local chapter. Also on campus were the national organizations Sigma Alpha Iota, which encouraged professional woman's music, and Kappa Delta Pi, which honored outstanding students in education. (Photos: 1964 *Bluestone*)

An architect's rendition of the school's proposed chapel is as far as the project got. Although a popular idea beginning in the late 1950s, fundraising never took off. The last recorded gift was $175 from the Class of 1967, after which the money raised was presumably dispersed into other funds, although no one knows exactly where. (Photo: JMU Special Collections)

A CHAPEL DREAMED OF LONG AGO

Reflecting a statewide controversy over invoking any deity at public school graduation ceremonies, James Madison University now omits prayer from its formal commencement. Phillip B. Reed issued the last invocation on July 31, 1992, for his fellow summer graduates. Yet Christian worship played a strong role in campus traditions during JMU's earlier decades.

Edna T. Shaeffer, instructor and director of the school of music from 1915 to 1956, said: "The school hymn, 'Praise to God, Immortal Praise,' the commencement recessional, 'On Our Way Rejoicing,' the blessing sung in the dining hall, the music of our chapel services as we pause in the midst of our busy days for a brief period of worship, carols around our campus Christmas tree—all voice a spirit of reverence, one of the ideals of this college from its beginning."

The 1950s SGA campaigned in that spirit. It petitioned President G. Tyler Miller for a chapel. In his letter of April 2, 1954, to Norma Proctor, SGA President, Dr. Miller said, "At the meeting of the State Board of Education . . . I presented the request from the Student Government Association for authorization to proceed with the proposed plans . . . for erection of a chapel on the Madison College campus. I am pleased to advise that by unanimous vote the Board approved . . . provided the Attorney General should rule that it is not in conflict with the constitution and laws of the United States and the State of Virginia which require separation of church and state."

The ruling came in their favor and *The Breeze* ran a banner headline on Monday, May 1, 1961, "Almond Permits Chapel Drive." Governor J. Lindsay Almond authorized a statewide finance campaign. Illustrating the story was an architect's drawing of the proposed nondenominational chapel, which called for a traditional gray limestone exterior housing a sanctuary on the main floor to seat 210 and auxiliary rooms below.

Architect J. Binford Walford of Richmond estimated the total cost, based on Harrisonburg's Nielsen Construction Co. preliminary figures, at $70,000 to $75,000. That figure included construction, architect's fee, and equipment—a most reasonable total.

Local committees agreed the goal was reasonable. There were six divisions of the Chapel Committee. Nine members came from the student body; six from the faculty, with Dean Percy Warren chairing the whole. Six members of the Alumni Association included Mrs. Marian Stickley, president of the local chapter. And three local ministers—Reverand Robert L. Sherfy, Reverand Albert G. Edwards, and Reverand Ward McCabe—gave backing.

Episcopal Rector McCabe had originally expressed reservations "that it might become a substitute for church—in effect a one-congregation denomination . . . students 'converted' to the buildings and its services and then on leaving college, might feel stranded and without a real church affiliation. . . . I would hope that this chapel would never develop a Sunday morning service of its own, a college chaplain, or even a special college choir."

The heavy hitters backing the chapel, however, came from the business and professional community. C. Grattan Price, Dr. Noland Canter, R. L. Jeffries, Samuel Shrum, Senator George Aldhizer II, J. A. Willett, Dr. Galen Craun, Walter Zirkle, S. B. Hoover, Hon. Charles W. Wampler Jr., Mr. Edgar Wine, and E. C. Tutwiler Jr. remain family names known to the area today. They had been persuaded by President Miller's statement: "When our forefathers came to these shores, almost their first act was to build a house of worship. Religion has played an important part in the development of our American way of life. It is important, therefore, that our colleges emphasize and encourage the spiritual growth of their students since religion must occupy an important place in the lives of our future leaders if they are to function effectively as constructive citizens. . . ."

The campaign was underway. But somewhere along the way, it foundered. When Dr. Ray Sonner, former executive assistant to President Miller, arrived in 1963, he recalls no push for a chapel. "I remember Raymond Dingledine once said he thought they'd raised about $14,000 before it died. No one seems to know which alumni program the money was funneled into. I couldn't find it."

Former president Ronald E. Carrier recalls hearing it mentioned when he visited the campus in 1970, but he, too, attributes its death to lack of funding. Dr. Sonner, for whom Sonner Hall is named, suggested there were also questions over the propriety of a chapel at a state school—the University of Virginia, VMI, and others notwithstanding.

checks proved larger. For example, freshman president Lee Tumlinson handed President Miller a check for $100 from the Class of 1960 to purchase a Bible for the proposed chapel. That June, Richard Haydon began designing a brochure "to be used . . . for the purpose of securing funds to erect a Chapel. . . ." Business Manager Gibbons approved between $1,500 and $2,000 for promotional costs of fundraising in a letter to Dean Warren, but the campaign never took off.

Gifts trickled in—Miller thanked senior class president Ann Shotwell for $25, and various dorms for similar donations in 1959. In 1960, after receiving a contribution from the department of education and psychology in memory of Mr. Clyde P. Shorts, Miller solicited advice from Winston McCellan Co., of Durham, North Carolina, on fundraising and establishing a foundation. Through the Corporate Alumnus Program, companies such as General Electric gave matching grants for employees. But the building remained on paper—the architect's sketch. The fund's final donation for $175 came from the Class of 1967. Miller thanked Miss Brenda Lacks and closed his letter with "Later on this year, it is our plan to have a campaign to raise funds for the Chapel. . . ." That "later on" never arrived.

New buildings stoked student enthusiasm during the 1960s. Left: The lights from Shorts Hall, the first high-rise dorm and the first dorm for men, illuminated the campus at night. Right: Duke Fine Arts Center and its Latimer-Shaeffer Theatre added panache to the campus for the visual and performing arts. (Photos: JMU Special Collections and 1969 *Bluestone*)

HOW THE ART DEPARTMENT GOT SHORTCHANGED

Excerpts from a taped interview with Tyler Miller on July 14, 1982, by Raymond Dingledine and Martha Caldwell, faculty members:

MILLER: . . . while Governor Harrison was governor, he was greatly disturbed over
the closing of Frederick College down in Portsmouth—because of the financial situation, they had to close—and he wanted to get the men who were in that institution
placed in a higher education institution in Virginia. There were about 300 men and he
asked me if we could take [them] and I told him I didn't see how we could because
we already were crowded in our dormitories. But he said if you will double up,
you've done it before—if you will double up the occupancy in the women' dormitories putting three to a room. . . . So we opened the doors to the Frederick College
students. They still had to meet our admission requirements. . . . The biggest nucleus
of men students, boarding students, came to us in [the] early beginning from Frederick College as transfers. . . .

DINGLEDINE: I was thinking back, with the Frederick College situation—Harrison
was governor from '62 to '66. . . . So it must have been there, around '65 or '66.

MILLER: I would guess. And you know what I did? I made a deal with him. We were
having trouble getting enough money to finish the Fine Arts Center. We had built the
section for the music department and the auditorium, but the other half—we had
used up all the money for the whole building just to build that building in segments,
and in the contract we had agreed to build the art section for the art department at
the same bid price that we had. And I made a deal with Governor Harrison that we
would take these transfer students from Frederick College if he would guarantee
that we'd get the money to build the rest of the Duke Fine Arts Center. And he said
he would put it at the top of his list of priorities, and he did. We finished it. Of
course, that was built too small, but so was everything else in those days, including
the library addition that we provided before I retired. And I knew it was too small.
But it was all the money we had.

Yet other new buildings marked the landscape, including Duke Fine Arts
Center in 1967 and Madison's first high-rise dorm in 1968, Shorts Hall. Students were excited over both. Shorts housed men that first year, Duke housed
the music and art departments, an art gallery, and a theater. The music side
seemed fine, but the art department felt shortchanged, though any improvement over their past quarters was welcomed.

Prior to the move, the art professors had shuttled between a supply room
on the fourth floor of Wilson and classrooms and offices on the third. Former
department head Theodore recalled, "I ran up and down those darn stairs for
ten years before Duke finally materialized. I had been told during my interview
that an art building was top priority—unfortunately, top position on the list
was subject to frequent change." Theodore also pointed out deficiencies in the
newly completed building: "We wound up with too-few offices—each had to
house two staff members—and had to cut off footage from a couple of stu-

dios/classrooms to accommodate the faculty at that time. No provision was made for growth."

Disappointment with the new quarters didn't dissipate the quality of the art program. All studio teachers were practicing artists who exhibited regularly. The department initiated a master of education in art. Theodore continued writing scripts for the weekly public TV show "Viewpoint," working with Kappa Pi, and teaching. Each member of the department carried fifteen semester hours, served on committees, met "art" requests (i.e., posters) from other colleagues, as well as having to order, distribute, and inventory all supplies.

"No one expected—or received—remuneration or time release for any of the foregoing. It took real strength of character to persevere at the job *and* to do our own art work," Theodore recalled.

Such pride and enthusiasm permeated departments across campus. Music, too, continued extending opportunities beyond the required six hours for all students. Outside the classroom, music honor students joined Sigma Alpha Iota. Band director Charles Smith attracted between thirty and fifty members to practice twice a week for their three yearly concerts. The college orchestra met daily under Clifford Marshall's baton.

Dr. John Lyon directed the Chorale, a large mixed choral group, while Wayne Nelson led the Concert Choir into its second decade. As the largest touring choral group at Madison, the Chorale attracted kudos for the college and for the department. In addition, the Madison Singers, formed in 1968, performed different styles of music, including popular songs. The Music Educators National Conference had opened a chapter on campus. The department truly embodied its goals to help "the student to realize the essential nature of music and his capacity for participation," plus "provide adequate stimulus and background for . . . later life."

Three departments combined to produce a stellar arts festival each spring. Infused with enthusiasm by English department head Louis Locke, both art and music departments contributed to a the week-long celebration with exhibits in the [Sawhill] Gallery, notable speakers in Wilson Hall, and musical performances. Locke's widow Jeanette recalled the production of the musical *Oliver!* and a talk by writer Katherine Anne Porter as two of the outstanding memories. "Wilson Hall was always filled for the speakers and the musicals, open to the public for free so that they were well attended by students and the community," Mrs. Locke said.

As enrollment continued to grow, faculty size increased. From fifty members when Miller assumed the presidency, the number soared to 300, counting full- and part-time. Early on, Miller had often called in department heads for conferences "at noon so as to catch everybody" to make major announcements or to seek input. He also frequently invited entire departments on a rotating basis to lunch in the president's dining hall in Gibbons. These lunches were "pretty well attended," according to past participants. But faculty growth lessened intimacy. Long-time staff members seemed aware that a subtle erosion was taking place, a distancing between administration and faculty and between departments—except in grief.

On November 22, 1963, the initial announcement that President John F. Kennedy had been shot came during class following lunch. Confusion ensued, little more. Then soon thereafter, CBS anchorman Walter Cronkite's familiar voice, choked with emotion, told the nation: "Ladies and gentlemen, the flash apparently official, President Kennedy died at one o'clock."

Janet Pfoutz ('65) remembers moving to her next class, and a vast silence behind everyone's crying. "Someone had a radio on and we listened in disbelief. Classes were cancelled, and I went home and we were glued to the TV. The next day it was all we talked about." The memory remained vivid decades later.

Kennedy was the president who had fueled the idealism of the times. At his inaugural, he had called on the nation "to bear the burden of a long darkness against the common enemies of man—tyranny, poverty, disease and war itself." His rich Massachusetts accent had urged, "Ask not what your country can do for you, ask what you can do for your country."

Expanding the space program in 1962, Kennedy had echoed Thomas Paine's emphasis on the value of adversity, saying, "We choose to go to the moon and other things not because they are easy but because they are hard. We set sail on this new sea because there is new knowledge to be gained and new rights to be won, and they must be won and used for the progress of all people." He had raised the hope for a better world and inspired the young especially to exert themselves toward that fulfillment. For so many students, the loss seemed personal and their first encounter with mortality.

A second death came just as unexpectedly, and devastated those who knew and loved Dean Percy Warren—almost everyone on campus. A violent tornado hit Toledo, Ohio, where Warren was visiting his daughter during Easter break in 1965. He and his mother-in-law were killed; his wife Alberta sustained a broken arm and multiple compound fractures of her right leg. Daughter Mary, her husband Reverend William H. Jones, and their baby miraculously survived, the latter protected by a heavy beam felled at an angle above the crib.

The 1965 *Bluestone* wrote: "With sorrow in our hearts, we pause to remember . . . to honor . . . to pay tribute . . . to one we have loved and lost. . . . a man who truly walked among us. We cherish the memory of twinkling eyes . . . a cheery smile . . . the word of greeting . . . which were part of his frequent walks across campus. . . ." Students and faculty mourned, but none more than Miller. He had lost not only a friend, but also a capable administrator whose abilities he'd recognized early.

In 1953, when Miller discovered that Dean Gifford planned to retire, he urged Warren to complete his doctorate. "I cut his classes—he was then head of the biology department—to three days a week, and he completed his dissertation without being on the campus of Columbia," said Miller in 1982. And he recalled Warren's unanimous support from the faculty and his appointment as dean as "a turning point."

Yet the dark days following Warren's death prefaced an equally unexpected but happier turning point on Miller's personal horizon. A chance meeting with the lovely widow Betty Thaxton Mauzy came at a party at Russell

Dr. Miller's new bride in 1968, the former Betty Mauzy of Winston-Salem, enjoyed social gatherings—even the reception for 1,100 who came only her second week at "Hillcrest." She said of the students, "They were the cutest things you ever saw, all dressed up, so polite." However, she would also witness another side of student gatherings in the campus unrest that led to demonstrations on the lawn and a case in the U.S. Supreme Court. (Photo: JMU Special Collections)

"Buck" Weaver's home in Harrisonburg. Weaver, an attorney and new member of the Madison College Board of Visitors, was a longtime friend of both. Since Mauzy lived in Winston-Salem, North Carolina, Miller began quietly conducting a long-distance courtship. Several years later, they married. The simple ceremony in August 1968 in Southern Pines, North Carolina, ended Miller's lonely years as a widower. It brought the president's daughter, young Elise Miller, a new mother and three additional brothers, Charles, John, and Bill Mauzy. And it brought "Hillcrest" an official hostess who charmed her constituency. "She was a marvelous hostess, absolutely delightful, who took over where he needed her," said Mrs. Locke.

Madison's new first lady assumed her role with grace and enthusiasm. She said, "Before we married, Tyler told me he would retire in 1970, so I came knowing it was a two-year period. I thought it was important to open the President's home for social gatherings." She did just that—with the first occasion being to greet more than 1,100 guests at the new students' reception. "They were the cutest things you ever saw, all dressed up, so polite. Of course they were curious, too, about the president's wife," she said in a later interview.

The next two years seemed to promise a happy close to a distinguished career. But not all student gatherings would prove as congenial.

ON THE NATIONAL SCENE, just as World War II had drawn Americans together, the '60s drove them apart. Nothing prepared those in authority for the coming challenge to that authority. The students of Madison College, however, reflected little of the national mood swing until President Miller faced an initial challenge in 1964. That summer's riots in Rochester, New York, a "kneel-in" in Lynchburg, Virginia, murders of Civil Rights workers in Mississippi, and cumulating deaths of American soldiers in Vietnam had evoked discussion but few outcries at Madison. Movie star Basil Rathbone's appearance in Wilson Hall that summer generated more interest.

Yet Miller's report in December to the newly installed Board of Visitors on the state of the college did mention the first portent of future unrest:

Chapter Sixteen

"In the vortex of
a changing world"
(1968–1971)

Until recently snow didn't warrant any closings. Ten inches of new snow across the Valley on February 6, 1961 saw Mrs. W.W. Bird, the film librarian, arrive in an antique one-horse sleigh her husband had restored and kept on hand for such occasions. (Photo: '69 *Bluestone*)

Unfortunately, during the summer session some disciplinary problems developed, requiring the suspension of several men students. As a result of this situation, there was a demonstration on the campus. . . . This resulted in some unrest among a small group of undergraduate men and women students. Some of the newspapers in the State carried distorted and incorrect articles about it, which over-emphasized the seriousness of the situation. . . .

The local *Daily News-Record* had not been one of the papers distorting the story, according to its own editors. The paper's single headline on July 27 indicated "MC Campus Quiet After Demonstration." The story said the school "weathered an uneasy but quiet night Thursday after a torch-light demonstration by a small group of boys late Wednesday night" and reported that Thursday's follow-up consisted of about fifty students sitting on a dormitory's steps singing "We Shall Overcome," the protest anthem of the day. When five suspensions followed, prompting questions elsewhere, the *News-Record* editorialized over "distortions" from other newspapers: "There is some reason to suspect that it is part of an ill-conceived plan to discredit the College because it acted firmly—and rightly so—in the suspensions."

The Wednesday "protest" appeared to be a spontaneous response to Miller's suspension of a male student that afternoon. The suspension triggered a march by about a dozen sympathetic students, carrying torches around the flagpole in front of Wilson. They then paraded to "Hillcrest," shouting, "Make Miller resign." Harrisonburg Police Chief Julius Ritchie made no move to intervene, since the protesters were neither disorderly nor destructive.

Miller responded with calm confidence—and added suspensions. The *News-Record*'s endorsement of his decision reflected local opinion: "Neither the College nor the public (which puts up 40 cents of every dollar spent on Madison students) should be expected to tolerate irresponsible acts by students who purposely damage the College's good name."

The Board of Visitors concurred. Furthermore, it approved the president's revising the student catalog to carry the following warning:

> Good citizenship, as well as satisfactory scholastic achievement, is required of all students at all times, and students who conduct themselves in such manner as to injure the good name of Madison College may be required by the President to withdraw from the College.
>
> Any student who causes the College to receive unfavorable publicity may be required by the President to withdraw from the College or may be subject to other disciplinary action, including indefinite suspension.

> The Governing Board has assigned responsibility for the administration of the College to the President. . . . Therefore, the President has full authority to make final decisions in all matters governing the conduct of students.

The Board of Visitors and president felt that would be the end of it. The school's "good name" was clearly being enhanced year after year. From the Fine Arts Festival each spring to the annual Regional Science Fair begun by the physics department in 1961, accolades mounted for special programs. In 1963, an annual "Home Economics Day" had been instituted; the following year brought an annual "Business Education Day." Lectures by distinguished visiting scientists and scholars attracted wide audiences. Throughout the decade, graduate programs increased and more professors published nationally. Dr. Raymond Dingledine had three biographical sketches of famous Virginians in the 1965 edition of *World Book Encyclopedia*; he also proofed its Virginia pages. Professor R. F. Hursey, Jr. completed a major algebra textbook. Professor Caroline Sinclair contributed to *International Sports Medicine Encyclopedia*. Each year, Miller's report to the Board of Visitors contained page after page listing professors' publications.

As salaries advanced so did the number of graduate degrees held by the faculty. By 1965, only ten had less than a master's ranking. Of 139 teaching faculty, forty-eight held doctorates, while ten were on leave to attain that degree. The doctorate had become almost mandatory for the rank of professor, with twenty-eight of Madison's thirty-one full professors holding one. The "Salary Scale for 1966–67" reflects the value of rank as well as longevity.

The president was proud of, and respected, his faculty. He loyally protected them in any controversy. Retired English professor Dr. Frank Adams recalled one incident in the late '60s:

> I had two male students who appeared the first day, appeared next for the first hour test, then the second, then the final. They didn't do well on any of the three. In addition, they had no quiz grades but plenty of unexcused absences. So on a number of grounds, they got the F's they deserved. Because the F's made them eligible for the draft, they were concerned. One of the two was on close terms with a U.S. Senator. Soon Tyler Miller got a telephone call from the Senator's office asking that the two F's be raised. Then he got a letter. Then he got a telephone call from the Senator himself. Miller did not budge. The F's stood. And Miller never told me any of this until years later.

The escalating conflict in Vietnam had brought a new pressure to bear on grades. Too often professors were torn between holding to academic standards and extending leniency toward a potential draftee. Nightly newscasts of this first televised war graphically projected its gruesome reality into living rooms. Wilfred Owen's admonition from World War I rang vividly true against "The old Lie: *Dulce et decorum est/Pro patria mori*"—that it is sweet and fitting to die for one's country.

Not that patriotism had fled: it was split. Passions divided the nation into those who claimed that true patriots supported the Vietnam War, and those who countered that true patriots questioned or opposed it. Yet however heated the growing dialogue became on campus, a surface civility reigned. October 15, 1969 was declared "Vietnam Moratorium Day" nationally. Miller instructed the faculty:

> Classes will be held as scheduled. Faculty members will be expected to teach their classes to fulfill their contracts to the College and the students.
>
> We feel that it is more appropriate for students and/or faculty to have peaceful meetings and discussions on that day in regard to the Vietnam situation, if they desire to do so.

Most students attended classes as well as discussions in Wilson Hall. The auditorium was opened for panel discussions by faculty members and students arguing both sides of the issue from ten o'clock in the morning until the afternoon. Attendance throughout the day ranged from about fifty to 200 at any given time, all orderly. On the events of that evening, Dean James W. Fox later reported:

> [There] was a registered event scheduled to be held on the quad between 10 and 11 P.M., consisting of the reading of the Vietnam dead from Virginia and a prayer. This activity drew approximately 100-150 students and was completed within approximately 15-20 minutes. It was followed by a silent walk of the 150 students from one end of the campus . . . to the other. . . . The demonstration broke up immediately thereafter with no incident whatsoever. Constant surveillance was made of the activities by the security staff and the student personnel deans. . . . Chief Monger was able to maintain *constant contact* with his security staff by using a *walkie-talkie*, and the Dean of Student Services [Fox] was with Chief Monger at all times. . . .

Dean Fox's report subsequently became part of the president's report to the Board of Visitors in November 1969. And close scrutiny of students became an accepted part of staff duties, with professors on the watch for potential

troublemakers. Social surveillance had always been a duty augmented by housemothers—designated "dormitory hostesses"—at the women's dorms. They eyed dates and checked students signing in and out for appropriate attire and destination.

Strict codes of conduct continued through the '60s as though the institution were still for women only. Johanna "Jo" Fisher Atkinson ('64) recalled thirty years later, "We were all to be 'Madison Ladies.' Slacks were not allowed except on back campus on Saturdays and hats and gloves [had to be worn] to church—any Sunday morning date was a church date. Weekends [away] were allowed only at 'approved' homes and questionnaires always followed to check up on us."

Protest occupies no place in Atkinson's memories. She reels off a litany of innocence:

Hair freezing at night returning to dorms after swimming.
Hockey on back campus—and the huge calf muscles that resulted.
Swim meets, watching the 'Dukes' from the balcony. Sorority Walk

Even as late as 1969, dormitory hostesses or housemothers provided a matronly presence to enforce the rules and watch for signs of danger. "Their girls" might turn to them in times of need or deride their old-fashioned ways in times of anger, but they held boys at bay and calmed parental angst about daughters away from home. SEATED: Lois Zirkle, Carolyn Pendleton, Althea Manley, Helen Layman; STANDING: Anne Lincoln, Doris Mulvanity, Neola Behrens, Marie Gardner, Mary Rusmiselle. (Photo: '69 *Bluestone*)

Attendants for the May Court in 1967 reflected the residual influence of former First Lady Jacqueline Kennedy. Left to right: Pat Griffin, Becky Strauser, Diane Strauser, Barbara Mauzy, Candy Ford, Sandy Leathers, Jackie Weeks, Sue Harvey, and Nancy Franklin. (Photo: '67 *Bluestone*)

on the day of decision . . . Dr. Warren and his plans for the University—changes in the curriculum of Home Economics . . . the new Arts building & gallery . . . my white rat experiment in nutrition . . . the 4-inch snow that allowed us to wear slacks on campus . . . living in home management house, gaining weight to keep from hurting someone's feelings by not eating food they prepared.

In '69, approximately seventy-six percent of Madison's students enrollment of 3,800 lived on campus—2,500 of the 3,100 women, and 400 of the 700 men. Shorts, Ashby, and Jackson were men's residences; two new women's dorms, Dorothy Garber and Agnes Dingledine halls, opened in September 1969. Total tuition, board, and fees for in-state students ran $1,320 for the year, with $1,680 charged for out-of-state students. The payment, expected to rise the next year, included housing, food, and laundry, plus an infirmary fee in the miscellany.

Dr. Walter Green, III, coordinated an infirmary as part of health services. As Miller's personal physician, Green was appointed when Miller was asked to place a physician on call for the school. In addition to nurses, the staff included Dr. Dick Ramser and Dr. Irvin Hess in orthopedics and Dr. Walter

Zirkle in gynecology. A typical year recorded between 7,000 and 9,000 visits, "mostly upper respiratory infections, mono, pneumonia's, and strep throats," according to Green. There were also rare pregnancies. "When we delivered babies [at Rockingham Memorial Hospital], they were put up for adoption—private adoptions in those days. An unplanned pregnancy could destroy a girl's life, so secrecy was paramount in such situations," Green recalled.

The decade ended with few rule changes. Most "marches" were in line with what Bronwyn Garbee Cowell remembers from her freshman year when her class circled the campus in one body shouting "Fine, fine, mighty fine—we're the Class of '69!" Snowball fights on the quad allowed exception to the "Keep off the grass" rule. Yet keeping off the grass became so ingrained that Emily McCeney Boots ('69) says, "I'm still unable to walk on grass if there's a sidewalk anywhere nearby!" Not that Boots went strictly by the book in her student days. She also confesses to "going to early classes with my PJs on under my raincoat and letting friends in the fire escape door after room check in Cleveland Hall."

Kate Coates Woodworth of that same Class of '69 wonders about the value of such rigid rules. Describing her conversation with a friend at a '90s reunion, she wrote, "As we gazed out at the quad, perched on the steps of Wilson Hall, we remarked about all the fun activities going on. When I asked her why I don't remember anything similar going on during our time, she replied, 'Kate, we weren't even allowed to walk on the grass!'" Woodworth generally applauds the later changes.

Those changes would not come under Miller. His last years were shadowed by the disharmony of the era. As the decade unfolded, the guidelines he had added to the catalog after the student demonstration in July of 1964 only impeded for a while the growing dissent against the status quo, directed at all levels of society, that many Americans, especially the young, voiced. And even as Miller maintained an open-door policy and initiated frequent "open meetings" with students with the intention of avoiding disruptive dissent on campus, he and the school ultimately collided in court with one student who directly challenged the college's admission policy. That student—Jay Rainey—became an anathema to the school administration.

As bizarre as it may sound to young readers now, the length of a male's hair created shock waves at that time. During the '60s and '70s, boys were kicked out of schools and even their homes for wearing long hair. When Jay Rainey attended Madison in 1967–68, he wore—à la "hippie" fashion—blue jeans, blanket ponchos, and sandals, and he let his locks grow. President Miller and Dean Fox both counseled him to change his appearance. He refused.

After Rainey's contentious first year, the young man from Alexandria was refused readmission for 1968–69. The refusal precipitated a suit filed by the American Civil Liberties Union of Virginia on Rainey's behalf in February.

The Sixties proved a time of mixed messages. Right: In the '69 *Bluestone*, fraternity sweethearts kept to tradition and fluttered hearts. Opposite page: Senior pictures from the same *Bluestone* reflected a changing society, traditional formal portraits now passé. (Photos: '69 *Bluestone*)

FRATERNITY SWEETHEARTS

PHI ALPHA PI: Linda Griffith

SIGMA PHI EPSILON: Gerri Savage

TAU KAPPA EPSILON: Sue Anne Harkins

PHI KAPPA BETA: Betty Perry

The ACLU charged Miller and the Board of Visitors with violating the student's constitutional rights. In court, Miller justified the college's refusal on the grounds that Rainey was "unclean and unkempt," wore "bizarre apparel," and "had attempted to organize a class boycott to disrupt the educational activities of the institution. It was an administrative action, not subject to due process review." Professors James Poindexter, Horace Burr, and Robin McNallie testified that, although Rainey's dress was "unusual, bizarre and unorthodox," he was clean and his beard was neat.

The suit dragged on until September of 1969. After a seven-hour session of the U.S. District Court, Rainey gained permission to register for the 1969–70 term with the stipulation that he obey all the established rules regarding conduct and dress. Judge Ted Dalton instructed the youth be a loyal student, avoid agitation, and refrain from activities reflecting unfavorably on the college.

Zan O'Brien

Vickie Lynn O'Dell

Marion Mack Orebaugh

Dorothy Olinger

Nancy Gale Overpeck

Sharon Rae Orling

"A spirit of cooperation must be established between Rainey and college officials. If complaints persist, the case will be re-docketed," Dalton said. He continued, "I am not in sympathy with bizarre or hippie dress, but here is a taxpayer due protection. What bothers me is that no formal hearing was provided in the college."

Miller had felt an administrative action required no explanation. In his report to the faculty on September 29, 1969, he wrote:

> For many years Madison College has had dual goals and pur-
> poses . . . (1) for intellectual development and academic success;
> and (2) for developing the students socially and emotionally,
> including standards of appearance and conduct, so that they may
> be ready to assume responsibilities as good citizens and profes-

sional persons. . . . Because Mr. Jay Rainey did not live up to these standards . . . it was recommended by the Dean of Men . . . that consideration be given to not readmitting him. . . . Accordingly, this action was taken . . . consistent with previous actions in regard to women students. . . .

For that fall semester Rainey and the school managed a wary truce, but February of 1970 brought a run-in. Three English faculty members—Jack Adkins, Jim McClung, and Houston Rodgers—all in the second year of a four-year probationary period, were notified they would not be reappointed. Adkins had planned to leave for graduate work; so, had he notified Miller in time, his resignation would have been accepted and no notice of non-appointment sent. The other two professors were "not being re-appointed," Miller explained in a February memo to the faculty, "because the basic education requirements . . . were changed with the approval of the faculty and the Board of Visitors. There was a resultant reduction in the English courses required for sophomore students. . . . [and] a reduction in the number of freshmen to be admitted for the 1970–71 session [due to] the increased number of returning students and an increase in . . . transfer students above the sophomore class level."

Many students and faculty didn't buy Miller's excuse. Recalling the incident decades later, one former English faculty pointed out, "These English profs were quickly replaced, which casts doubt on Miller's spin." Harambee, a campus underground organization of protesters, also didn't buy Miller's explanation. It scheduled a meeting for February 18 at 9:00 P.M. in Wilson Hall, which got underway with a mock "President's Open Meeting"—based on the semi-

Vietnam protester and movie star Jane Fonda appeared on campus to encourage students to join the antiwar activists. Here she fields questions from the audience in an open assembly with ACLU lawyer John Lowe, who represented the students against Madison College at the U. S. District Court of Appeals. (Photo: '71 *Bluestone*)

monthly meetings Miller held with students to answer questions on policies and procedures. Initially informative and relaxed, those dialogues began to deteriorate in late fall of '69 when Rainey led a group of students who attended solely to ask Miller questions to which there were no answers. The group then claimed Miller failed to communicate. Following Harambee's mock "open meeting" convened by the dissenting students, the three professors spoke. McClung indicated he had appealed to the Faculty Grievance Committee, the American Association of University Professors, and the American Civil Liberties Union for help. The audience of between 400 and 500 students voiced support and then followed Harambee leader Lee Hammond's call to march around the campus.

Campus patrolman Wilson reported:

> At 9:30 the demonstration moved outside between Gibbons Hall and the President's house, where the main speaker was Dennis Gregory. A lot of foul language was used at this time by Gregory. He stated, 'Don't be afraid of the faculty for all they can do is ball [*sic*] you out, don't be afraid of the campus police for all they can do is lock you out of a building and we can have a damn good time out here. . . . we have contacted the leaders who led the demonstrations in Boston, Maryland, and several other large colleges, who will be here within 48 hours to give us legal advice and lead us. . . . now who will follow me. . . . as the damn President is gone when something happens.'

As the group paraded by each dormitory, new students joined until there were "800 to 1000" according to Wilson's estimate. His report also stated that the marchers pelted people on the side lines with ice and called out foul names. Plans for a follow-up demonstration fell through, but the underground campus paper *The Fixer* continued fueling the fires of rebellion with an array of tinder beyond the cause of the three professors. "Issues," McNallie later recalled, "were tangled in both academic politics and outside politics involving views on the Vietnam War." Rainey wrote a series of articles calling for the appointment of a new president and urging students to violate current rules. However, there was no major confrontation until April.

The first demonstration, on April 23, proved fairly "low key" according to Dean James Fox's five-page summary to Miller. The second, on April 29, led to student arrests. Food Service Manager Robert Griffin was officially assigned to photograph and observe along with Dean Fox. Griffin began his photographic record with Dean Fox addressing the students on the illegality of sit-ins. Then both men left to wait for students to disperse. It didn't happen. Griffin made an official report afterward:

I was outside, back of the building [Wilson Hall], while Bob Plummer entertained the crowd, and I listened for several minutes to Les Hammond asking others to join the sit-in. I specifically heard him say, 'They won't arrest us if enough people come inside. . . . There are ways to get in—the windows are open.' I walked around immediately and photographed Bruce King assisting someone in through the window at the end of the auditorium. Some time later, I photographed Jay Rainey and Les Hammond assisting others into the building. . . .

I heard Jay Rainey . . . specifically say, 'We may all go to jail.' He continued talking, particularly to the girls who were faced with the decision of returning for curfew [a school policy that didn't apply to male students]. He urged them to stay, but made clear that the consequences could be severe.

I was outside the building when the police van arrived . . . standing in the crowd to the south of Wilson loading platform and heard Les Hammond protest . . . 'I want my rights!' . . . struggling with two policemen, who threw him into the truck after he resisted. . . .

I saw Professor McClung and photographed him several times actively participating in the demonstration. I conversed with Professor Adkins on several occasions, and until he was arrested, did not know who he was. He was so completely dissociated [*sic*] from the demonstration that I thought him a reporter or some other interested party . . . [did] not even see him talking to the demonstrators. I was there when he was arrested. He very quietly said, 'You don't have to read the warrant to me.' . . .

Certainly, the demonstrations and arrest of twenty-eight Madison students disturbed others beyond those directly involved. Dean Fox was besieged by "students sympathetic to their cause and by many faculty members also sympathetic to encourage me to drop charges and to intercede in their behalf." Many people also claimed the protesting students had been locked in Wilson Hall, making it difficult for them to leave. Dean Fox, however, was intransigent. He answered all appeals saying, "Just as the students felt they had an obligation and were willing to meet that obligation in true civil disobedience style, so I had an obligation to the preservation of order on this campus and I intended to meet my obligation."

His position, supported by Miller and the Board of Visitors, led them through another long judicial process from lower courts to the U.S. District Court of Appeals for the Fourth Circuit. In 1971, the Court overturned an earlier ruling by Judge Robert Merhige that Madison's demonstration rules violated

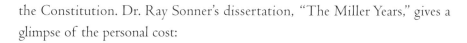

the Constitution. Dr. Ray Sonner's dissertation, "The Miller Years," gives a glimpse of the personal cost:

It is rather ironic that the one thing Tyler Miller fought so hard and long to accomplish, the admission of men on a full-time basis, probably led to his early retirement. The confrontation with students and the long court battles wore heavily upon him. He had served as Madison's President for two decades. He had directed its growth to a major institution of higher learning in Virginia. As he prepared to retire, an atmosphere of unrest was present on the Madison College campus. . . .

The final months of Tyler Miller's tenure . . . were the most trying for the man who had served forty years in education. There were students and faculty who believed his age precluded his understanding the issues on the American college campus in the late '60s and early '70s. There were those who believed that Madison College had never really accepted men . . . that Miller knew nothing of the problems faced by men on a college campus. Whatever the reason might have been, Miller faced diffidence and militancy with firm resolve. . . . The insults and criticisms Miller suffered in the waning days of his administration were hardly an appropriate end to a distinguished career.

WMCL-FM, Madison's first radio station, became a reality in 1969. The station was owned by the college and operated by students under direction of the Speech and Drama Department. It paved the way for WMRA-FM, the National Public Radio station that followed. (Photo: *Blue-stone* '69)

Front Row: G. Martin; B. Liddle; B. Snelson. *Second Row:* J. Chumney, Secretary and Record Librarian; B. Perry; B. Lebbon; J. Gu *Third Row:* J. Hoskins, Chief Announcer; B. Sutton; T. O'Dell; J. Shelton; J. Ramsey; C. Rothgeb; G. Hart; B. Smith. *Fourth Row:* I Moulton, Sponsor; B. Hawkinson, Secretary and Record Librarian; G. Watkins; D. Talaber; A. Medlin; C. Ballard; S. Alatary; J. Mueller, Stiles. *Fifth Row:* B. Crum; B. Pollard, Director of News and Special Events; J. Stanley, Program Director and Student Engineer; V. Mart Station Manager; F. Harrison; D. Mulligan; J. Turney; F. Wiggins; B. Musser; L. Harding.

WMCL-FM, Madison's first radio station, became a reality this year. The station broadcasts informative and entertaining programs over the ten-watt station. "The Information Station for the Shenandoah Valley" depicts the fact that WMCL-FM is the information media for the students of Madison College and the residents of Harrisonburg and surrounding communities. The station is owned by Madison College and is operated by students of the college, under the direction of the Speech and Drama Department.

FM RADIO STATION

Miller's tenure at Madison rang with major accomplishments, but he left to the sounds of dissonance and doubts. Years later Ronald E. Carrier, who followed Miller, would candidly assess:

> Tyler Miller had been a good president, was a very fine man. But the world was changing—dramatically changing. You'd had the assassination of John F. Kennedy, the assassination of Robert Kennedy, of Martin Luther King. You'd had the Berkeley free-speech movement, you'd had Civil Rights issues in Selma, Alabama, and Birmingham. You had the Vietnam War, had just had Cambodia, plus we had Kent State. You had some trouble here [at Madison] which was really minor but turned into more of an issue than

it probably should have been. Dr. Miller was caught in the vortex of a changing world. He really didn't want to go into that changing world yet didn't know how to get out of it. So he was whipped around—yet he got out in time, before it damaged him personally, no one asked him to quit, and—and before the institution paid the price.

President G. Tyler Miller announced his resignation for 1971, marveling that so many candidates sought his job.

NEW BUILDINGS FROM 1951–1969

1951-Logan (Conrad T. Logan, Head English), Residence

1953-Burruss (Julian A. Burruss, First President), Mathematics

1953-Greenhouse, adjacent to Burruss, used to grow and supply plants for biology and botany classes

1957-Nicholas House (Dr. C. E. Nicholas family), circa 1909, acquired house and property on South Main Street. Various administrative uses.

1958-Gifford (Walter J. Gifford, Dean & Head Education), Residence

1958-Wayland Hall (John W. Wayland, Head of History, Social Science), Residence

1958-Anthony-Seeger Hall (Katherine M. Anthony and Mary Louise Seeger, former Training School Directors), WMRA public radio

1959-Health Center

1961-Moody Hall (Pearl P. Moody, Head of Home Economics), College of Arts and Letters

1962-Frye Building (Lucius C. Frye, Physical Plant Operations Supervisor), Computer Sciences and Help Desk

1964-Hoffman Hall (Margaret Vance Hoffman, English), Residence

1964-Gibbons Hall (Howard K. Gibbons, Business Manager), Dining Hall

1966-Huffman Hall (Dr. Charles H. Huffman, English), Residence

1967-Frederikson Hall (Dr. Otto F. Frederikson, History), Residence

1967-Duke Hall (Dr. Samuel Page Duke, Second President), houses the Latimer-Shaeffer Theatre and Sawhill Gallery

1968-Shorts Hall (Clyde P. Shorts, Education), Residence

1968-Chappelear Hall (George W. Chappelear, Head Biology), Residence

1968-Hanson Hall (Raus M. Hanson, Geography), Residence

1969-Garber Hall (Dorothy Garber, Dean of Women), Residence

1969-Dingledine Hall (Mrs. Agnes Dingledine, former Alumni Association Secretary and Housemother), Residence

Part Four

Carrier:
Shaping a University,
1971–1998

Soon after Dr. Carrier's arrival as Madison College's president, everything changed—from the name of the school, to the growth of the student body, to the expanding campus. (Photos: JMU Special Collections)

T he Madison College Board of Visitors found no dearth of applicants for the position of president to be vacated by Miller. Nearly fifty hopefuls tendered resumes. But the board was also interested in one who didn't apply but who had been suggested by an outsider. Felix Robb, executive director of the Southern Association of Colleges and Universities, touted the name of a young Ph.D. serving as vice president of Memphis State University. Board members invited Ronald E. Carrier to the campus. Two Carriers, husband and wife, arrived one cold January day, sat for interviews, toured the campus, had tea with the Millers, and decided they weren't the least bit interested—especially wife Edith.

"We didn't want to move to begin with—we lived in Memphis in a nice neighborhood, had a new house. The children were young and involved in all kinds of things. They could walk to school—and I was happy where I was. And Ron hadn't applied for the job; they invited him. So he'd said, 'Let's just go, see what it's like. It'll be fun—we'll get a trip out of it.' So we came! We didn't care whether we got the job or not," she recalled with a laugh years later.

They returned to Memphis agreeing they didn't want to make the move. But board rector Russell "Buck" Weaver refused to accept their refusal. Edith reminisced, "That dear, sweet man called Ron and said in his deep, southern drawl, 'We don't think we asked the right questions. Would you come back again?'

"Ron said, 'Well, you know Edith and I decided

Polite applause at Dr. Ronald E. Carrier's introduction on December 4, 1970, followed by rousing applause after his inaugural remarks indicated the positive mindset of his audience. An excitement permeated the campus. Carrier is shown here with future Governor Mills Godwin to his left and Senator Harry F. Byrd. (Photo: JMU Special Collections)

Students held a welcome of their own on February 20, 1971, with the SCA Inaugural Ball. There the past and new presidents and their wives danced into the night. Then student accolades continued with the '71 *Bluestone's* dedication to both men. (Photo: JMU Special Collections)

we weren't interested, so it would probably be unfair to you if I came back—I know she doesn't want to come again.' Buck said: 'Well, just do it for me—just do that for me—just come one more time and let us show you a few more things, let you find out a little more that maybe you didn't find out.' So Ron went."

The February visit altered Dr. Carrier's opinion. He became convinced he'd found a school ready for change, with the potential for greatness. He recognized that the board was made up of good people directing an institution that "was like an island that had been kept from all of the turmoil that existed in the world. And it was very comfortable for those people who didn't want to recognize that changes were taking place—marvelous people, people you really loved in the '40s and '50s. But the board was ready for change, they knew the institution had to—but they didn't have a master plan."

Carrier not only formulated a plan, but also energized its implementation. He envisioned a regional, multipurpose college. He realized, however, that changing the culture of Madison to embrace and enhance a diversity of gender, race, and ideas would not be easy. He said: "I had different ideas about things like whether parents had to approve your dates, whether you could wear

shorts on campus—that culture still prevailed when I arrived here. And that was one of the first things I had to deal with, one of the most difficult. It's easy to build a building; it's hard to change peoples' attitudes and culture."

So he implemented changes gradually. Little by little, student rules relaxed. First, they could walk on the grass—visiting alumni could hardly imagine it when they returned. "No more call downs for cutting across the lawn," said Bev Noel, student government president in 1971 when Carrier came. She scarcely got to work with him, since Carrier took the reins in January of her senior year and she left for student teaching in Arlington soon after.

In 1970–71, Noel's presidency served the first combined male and female student government. In prior years, parallel governments operated based on gender. She assessed, "It made for more diversity plus an acceptance of what the school would become—fully coed. We could pool the efforts of both men and women for a more effective student government. I think that was the beginning of the coed factor of the school, and it was time." Her experience with Miller had been positive. She said, "I remember how supportive he was. And I have fond memories of working very closely with Fay Reubush, who was dean of women. She was there at whatever point we needed assistance and it was wonderful working with them."

Student government and students in general that year were more excited about the new campus center than they were about the new administration.

Evelyn Watkins ('26), pictured here with her students, retired from teaching in 1972, the same year she was named Outstanding Elementary Teacher of America. Since 1936, she had taught first grade in Madison's training schools (first Main Street, then Anthony-Seeger). She was loved by parents and students alike for her warmth and creativity. (Photo: JMU Special Collections)

Named for former Dean Warren, the center would house a bookstore, dining facilities, post office, meeting rooms—and student support services. Noel and the SGA pulled out all stops to hold an inaugural ball there, welcoming the Carriers and bidding farewell to the Millers.

While the succession of presidents moved seamlessly for the students, the faculty rippled with an undercurrent of excitement. Dr. Dorothy Rowe, who chaired the faculty-student committee for interviews, recalled that they had seen "some real jerks but were very impressed with the Carriers." For most faculty members, just as Dr. Miller looked like sunshine at the close of the Duke years, so Carrier did now.

Dr. Nancy O'Hare missed the interviews, off on sabbatical for her doctorate, but had returned when Carrier settled into his office on the second floor

The Anthony-Seeger faculty continued offering topnotch teachers to mentor education majors. Top, left to right: Mildred Dickerson, Dr. Charles Caldwell, Dr. Angela Reeke, Dr. Carrier, Mary Funkhouser, Marguerite Wampler, a visitor; and Peter Pederson. Bottom: Marguerite Wampler and students. (Photos: JMU Special Collections)

of Wilson. She said, "The faculty was very supportive—we were small then. Tyler Miller had been a good president for his time. He was forward thinking, had purchased land for the school so that we didn't have to grow vertically as most universities did. But, I think all of us felt we needed somebody who was dynamic, who was ready to take us a step further, expand our reputation—we were pretty much still a state teachers college. We had an excellent reputation in preparing teachers but were at the cusp, ready to explode in other directions."

The late English professor Tom Leigh earlier recalled the time a colleague from Memphis wrote and included a clipping about Carrier that praised his abilities. Tom said, "We felt lucky to have attracted such an outstanding fellow." Carrier's charisma, charm, and accessibility won over the faculty and students.

That accessibility also impressed O'Hare. She said, "His desire was to find out about every facet of the university. He was everywhere—the students

As shown here in 1972, Dr. Carrier's gregarious style received a warm reception from students. He made himself easily accessible to staff and faculty. (Photo: JMU Archives)

knew him personally, the faculty knew him personally." He ate with students in the dining hall, bought two tickets to the first outdoor Greek party, rode his minibike on the soccer field, stopped to talk midstride across campus, looked in on classes, pigeonholed staff in the halls and offices—"meddled everywhere," as one former professor affectionately charged. He also addressed the faculty council with new ideas for their input.

One idea was to replace the old administrative council with a college council composed of students, faculty, and administrators. Another was to form a faculty senate. Carrier had served on such a body when he was a professor and recognized the value. Next year the school replaced the old council with the more powerful senate. Dr. Max Bilsky served as speaker—and as translator of faculty concerns to the president. So Carrier often joined the senate on Saturday mornings to listen and learn from them as well as to address them. He had suggested

Saturday morning meetings because he knew any meeting on their own time would be as brief as possible.

Carrier also traveled the state. Television interviews, newspaper interviews, club speeches—wherever Betty Jolly, director of alumni relations, sent him. He sought publicity, not for himself but for the school. He understood that increased name recognition would boost the applicant pool and raise the quality and diversity of applicants. In 1970–71, men made up 25.1 percent of the student body. By 1974–75, they were 40.5 percent of the total enrollment. And that enrollment soared from 4,041 students in '70–'71 to almost 7,000 in '74–'75.

By 1971, May Day, shown here from 1950, seemed an outmoded vestige of an all-girls school rather than a reflection of the changing times. The tradition ended in 1971, leaving behind a romantic memory. (Photos and list of May Queens: *Montpelier*, Spring '98)

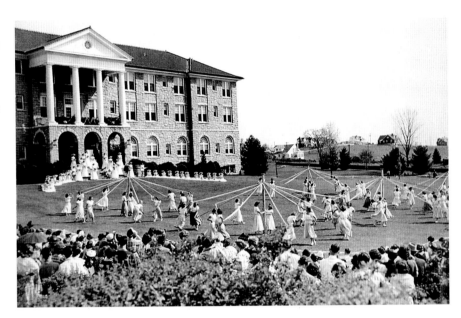

May Queen
1924–1970

While May celebrations were a continuing tradition from the early days, May queens' names weren't listed in the annuals until a full-page photo appeared beginning in 1924 with expanded coverage of the event. As attendant Evelyn Dickinson Dowling ('49) remembered, "Being in the May Court was very special — beautiful dresses and wide-brimmed hats to match. We went to a store in downtown Harrisonburg to be fitted for our dresses and bought them there. My parents didn't have much extra money, but this was one item for which they gladly paid."

1924 Mary Sturtevant, Portsmouth
1925 Alene Alphin, Lexington
1926 Mary Greene, Greenville

1927 Ruth Nickell, Herndon
1928 Lucy Davis, Norfolk
1929 Elizabeth Miller, Smedley
1930 Harriet Pearson, Winchester
1931 Grace Dalgety-Kerr, Lynchburg
1932 Margaret Beck, Winchester
1933 Elizabeth Carson, Lynchburg
1934 Lois Bishop, Norfolk
1935 Kathleen Carpenter, Norfolk
1936 Frances Wells, Suffolk
1937 Mary Bryant Cox, Independence
1938 Virginia Blain, Clifton Forge
1939 Lafayette Carr, Galax
1940 Marguerite Bell, Suffolk
1941 Gwendolyn Trueheart, Brandon
1942 Mildred Alley, Hopewell
1943 Jean Bell, Norfolk
1944 Marjorie Fitzpatrick, Lexington

1945 Sarah Overton, Sanford, N.C.
1946 Irene Rieder, Lynnhaven
1947 Ruth Davis, Agricola
1948 Anne Myers, Norfolk
1949 Ebie Copley, Oley, Pa.
1950 Elise Bellenot, Richmond
1951 Jeanette Cocke, Gretna
1952 Rosalyn Scarborough, Carson
1953 Peggy Armsworthy, Reedville
1954 Anitamae Snead, Warwick
1955 Gwendolyn McCormick, Arlington
1956 Martha Ann Morgan, Lynchburg
1957 Nancy Gardner
1958 Dorothy Ray Dawson, Richmond
1959 Charlotte Gush, Norfolk
1960 Suzanne Snedegar, Roanoke
1961 Susan Moyar, Colonial Heights
1962 Brenda Pipicelle, Meriden, Conn.
1963 Nicola Beverage, Newport News
1964 Sallie Ann Mahaney, Kenbridge
1965 Nancy Catlett, Portsmouth
1966 Mary Wood, Norfolk
1967 Linda Dashiell, Portsmouth
1968 Gayle Aydelotte, Winchester
1969 Lila Soler, Fort Eustis
1970 Carolyn Cook, Newsoms

In the beginning, the shift in the atmosphere on campus went almost unnoticed by students. But as their insularity from national politics diminished, students grew more vocal. A new stridency reflected the outside events that polarized feelings nationwide. In 1971, as the Vietnam War escalated with U.S. planes bombing Vietcong supply routes in Cambodia, nightly news on television penetrated complacency. When Lieutenant William Calley, Jr., was found guilty of premeditated murder of helpless children and women in the Mylai massacre in Vietnam, the news stunned Americans everywhere. How could one of their own become one of the bad guys—brutal, immoral, un-American?

At home, politics disillusioned old and young, but especially the young. In 1972, Richard M. Nixon was reelected president in a near-record landslide over Democratic rival Senator George S. McGovern. Vietnam's ceasefire was signed on January 23. Then the scandal of a White House-authorized break-in of Democratic party offices at the Watergate building complex in Washington, D.C., led to Nixon's resignation in the face of impeachment proceedings. Gerald Ford, newly named vice president to replace the disgraced Spiro Agnew, became president of the United States on August 6, 1974, and subsequently pardoned Nixon. Feeling honor had been betrayed, many youth discarded the moral compasses of prior generations and rebelled in new directions. By the mid-decade, as Westerns faded from all three TV channels, life no longer so cleanly delineated into good guys versus bad, TV reflected social change. James Garner exchanged his cleanly heroic, however roguish, Brett Maverick for an acerbic Rockford. Bumbling Columbo embodied the perfect hero, disdaining money, prestige, and fashion in his successful detective pursuits. TV sitcoms such as M*A*S*H and All in the Family prodded sacred cows—and provoked laughter along with questions on mores of the times.

Music, as an early portent of that youth rebellion, beginning in the 1950s with rock-and-roll, continued its decibel creep, growing louder and harder as students rejected the bands and popular singers of their parents' day. First Wilson Hall, then Godwin, rocked to the amplified sounds of groups such as America, Badfinger, Little Feat, Joe Cocker, the Doobie Brothers, and the Charlie Daniels Band. Lyrics voiced the idealism and despair of the decade: John Lennon invited people to "imagine all the world living life as one," and even Coca-Cola wanted to "teach the world to sing in perfect harmony," while Marvin Gaye pleaded "What's Going On?" and Edwin Starr averred war was good for "absolutely nothin'." Solo performers, including many students, and local bands, such as Happy the Man, played venues such as downtown's Elbow Room, often taking center stage. New albums by the Allman Brothers, Bob Dylan, Earth, Wind & Fire, Elton John, the Grateful Dead, Led Zeppelin, Ohio Players, the Rolling Stones, The Who, the Eagles, Poco, Joni Mitchell, Bonnie Raitt, and the four former Beatles spun through the dorms.

WMRA brought National Public Radio to the area in 1971 and kept Dr. Carrier at home. With the stronger signal, he no longer had to park at Anthony-Seeger to hear broadcasts of Madison's away ball games. The station's hours on air were limited, but students loved their involvement. (Photo: JMU Special Collections)

Clothes, too, signified rebellion. Turtleneck sweaters replaced shirts and ties for a few professors, although most men still wore ties—if not jackets. But many of their female counterparts donned pants suits. Flannel shirts, bell-bottom jeans, and pants with "Earth shoes" were worn by students of either gender. An international flavor carried over into loose dashikis. Long hair and earrings crossed gender barriers.

In at least one aspect, however, when the new clashed with the Greek tradition, the latter won. Most fraternities and sororities still sat for formal portraits in the yearbook. But little else on the pages of the *Bluestone* was formal—certainly not department photos or senior portraits. Formal dances had disappeared in favor of concerts. Social life had become casual, frequently well lubricated by alcohol, the legal drinking age having been lowered to eighteen. Beer was available by the glass or pitcher in Warren Campus Center and a few bars downtown, plus by the keg in dorms. Drinking marked an ordinary part of life after dark, and the president himself might drift by to lift a mug.

Yet, however casual Carrier appeared as he surfaced here, there, and everywhere, his appearances were calculated. His style was to take the pulse of the school for himself, with little escaping his notice or his memory. Shortly after his inauguration, he formulated an agenda for the next five years. His first annual report to the Board of Visitors stated the need "to continue its transition from a women's college to a co-educational, multi-purpose regional institution"—and the board readily endorsed his vision. Focus centered on the students, with the first step being expansion of the size and diversity of the student body. Looking at the figures projected for high school graduates both state and nationwide, Carrier pledged an enrollment growth to 8,000 by 1980, with forty percent male. He exceeded his goal. Male enrollment reached 40.5 percent by 1974–75 and enrollment totaled 8,073 in 1978–79.

To Carrier, diversity meant more than male and female ratios. The school moved toward attracting other races and cultures. The first African American at Madison, Sheary Darcus Johnson, had enrolled in 1966 and graduated in 1970. She received her M.S. from Madison in 1974, and later earned her Ph.D. from UVA in 1988. In Carrier's second year enough African Americans had enrolled on campus to form a Black Student Alliance. Its stated purpose was "to articulate the problems of black students at Madison College; to promote interaction and involvement in school activities; to foster continuous Afro-American pride and responsibility; and to foster black awareness among ourselves and the student body." A few American Indians, Asians, and Hispanics also appeared. But any real measure of success would have to wait two more decades.

Diversity also meant expanding the curriculum, which won favor with the faculty, and introducing football, which did not. The outcry against football was vociferous. Few in the academic chairs agreed with their president's reasoning. The majority opposed the creation of a football team fearing that "our standards would decrease; we would be letting in people whose IQ's weren't even at room temperature," said Dr. O'Hare. "It was awful, awful, awful. People said all the resources will be poured into football and athletics; academics will never get a thing."

Diversity on campus increased during the 1970s—from seventy-two African Americans in September 1972 to 169 by fall 1976. The first black student, Sheary Dorcus Johnson, had entered in 1966, won her B.S. degree in 1970, and added her M.A. in 1972. She later continued her education with a Ph.D. from UVA in 1984. The Black Student Alliance reflected the more inclusive campus and aired a popular weekly radio show called "Ebony in Perspective." (Photo: '77 *Bluestone*)

When other schools were cutting the sport as too expensive, Carrier started it. "My former boss at Memphis State, [president] C. C. Humphreys, told me I was crazy," said Carrier. "But there were three reasons why we did it: One, in training teachers, we thought it might be helpful to train them as coaches, too, to improve their chances of getting a job. To learn to coach, they needed to play. Two, we wanted to give our students something to do on fall weekends here rather than have them go down to VMI or UVA or VPI or home. Three, I thought it would be fun."

The school was the first in the state to lay an Astro-Turf field—in the summer of 1974 before football began that fall. Initial preconference football seasons had brought ignominious defeats. But the first full varsity season in 1974 ended with a surprising 6-4 record. Furthermore, head coach Challace McMillin was named as co-Virginia College Athletic Association Coach of the Year and two players, quarterback Leslie Branich and tailback Bernard Slayton, made the VCAA All-Star first team. Soon football kept students on campus during weekends of home games—one of the reasons stated for the program.

It was fun. But more importantly it accomplished other ends. Football pleased students and enhanced school visibility—a visibility that increased applications even as it added challenges. Earlier in 1971, Madison College had offered fifty majors at the undergraduate level and nearly twenty beyond. No small school could continue to operate that many. Carrier had sought input from both the faculty and the Board of Visitors on the options: "Either cut offerings and stay at 4,000 or increase enrollment to justify diversity." Both groups had opted for growth.

So Carrier turned to admissions director Frances Turner and asked, "Do we have 400 more applicants qualified for Madison?" "Yes," said Turner. Carrier

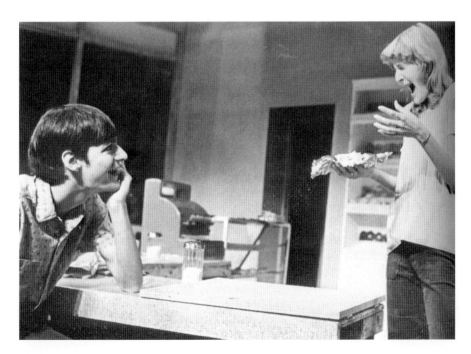

Roger Hall's production of *Fancies* presented a world premiere of an original play by JMU graduate Andrea Fisher ('78). It showcased another star, Phoef Sutton—future writer/producer of TV's hit sitcom *Cheers*—who played Emmet in this scene with Holly MacFarland as Ceecee. (Photo: '79 *Bluestone*)

On March 22, 1977, Governor Mills E. Godwin signed a bill to change the name of Madison College to James Madison University. Seated are Governor Godwin and Mrs. Althea Loose Johnston, a member of the original faculty in 1909. The Board of Visitors stands behind. Left to right: Robert L. Dolbeare, J. Leonard Mauck, Francis Bell, James B. Spurlock Jr., Nellie L. Long, President Carrier, and Inez G. Roop. (Photo: JMU Special Collections)

said, "Let's take 'em. It's going to be crowded but we're not going to have our foundation for the '80s unless we pick up the pace."

The pace picked up in construction as well, and structures soon accommodated enrollment. Constantly thinking ahead, watching timing and funding, Carrier persuaded the board and the legislature to fund additional acreage, new buildings, and expanded programs. State delegates and senators respected him. His common sense impressed them all—farmers, attorneys, and businessmen. He could talk the talk with legislators of any background, at any level of experience. He anticipated their questions and always backed his requests with hard facts. Annual reports to the Board of Visitors reflected results. For his first report, the General Assembly approved $28.4 million for operating expenses during the 1972–74 biennium and another $3.8 million for capital outlay. The next year ground was broken for $3.3 million Miller Hall. In 1973–74, the school gained an additional $900,000 to renovate Maury Hall and plan a new school of education building.

Ever aware of the need to sell the school to the public, Carrier soon reminded local business leaders that Madison contributed $25 million a year to the local economy. But the earlier bond between "town and gown" had eroded. Harrisonburg no longer exhibited the paternal closeness of early days of the school. Many local citizens abhorred the growth and opposed Madison's quest for university status. They were not among the pleased 41,200 faculty, staff, and alumni cited in newspaper headlines for March 25, 1977, after Governor Mills Godwin signed the bill to change the name to James Madison University. Godwin wrote his signature and handed the pen to Althea Loose Johnston, who witnessed the ceremony as the sole surviving member of the original faculty.

As Carrier closed his first decade at the college, as its fourth president, he felt confident he had made sound choices both for himself and for the school. Two other colleges had wooed him to be their top administrator. In the mid-'70s, Memphis State University and Florida State publicly announced their offers. Flattered by each proposal, he weighed his choices and stayed in Harrisonburg. He pledged to lead JMU "to become the finest undergraduate public university."

By 1980 James Madison University was no longer the "suitcase college" about which Penelope Hopkins Fergerson ('74) said students fled "as soon as possible on Friday afternoons." Social life now happened on campus. To the casual observer, the new name and campus expansion defined the fourth president's first decade; but to insightful watchers the real shift was toward a diverse, student-centered university. The small, one-time teachers college for women had disappeared. The 1970s brought a dramatic change in character and direction. Unlike many college presidents, Carrier's central concern was not budgets or faculty or buildings; it was students.

He told faculty and board, "All students should excel to do more than they think they can." And he had no qualms about challenging them with responsibility plus handing them the necessary funds to implement the solutions. "We turn over the entire one-half-million-dollar budget of the student program board to the students. And we give them a check for $250,000 to run the Student Government Association." While other schools clung to traditional

Chapter Eighteen

"A hard act to follow"

1978–1983

The "Hillside Gang" (left) and head football coach Challace McMillin (right) cheered JMU to an impressive 21-17 victory over the University of Virginia on September 18, 1982. (Photos: *Images of James Madison University 1908–1983*)

administration-student relationships, he broke with tradition to make students partners in the university.

As his student partners met those challenges of new freedom and responsibility, they accorded "Uncle Ron" their affection and respect. At the start of the school's Diamond Anniversary, the 1983 *Bluestone* revived a custom, abandoned in 1969, dedicating the yearbook to the college president. The '83 *Bluestone*, dedicated to President Ronald E. Carrier, describes him as:

> The steering instrument . . . [who] has more than doubled JMU's enrollment, faculty, bachelor degree programs and departments. Under his term we have seen our athletic program grow from little more than men's club sports and women's in-state competition to scholarship programs and nationally ranked teams. Carrier is responsible for more than $50 million in construction including 20 buildings and Newman Lake. . . .

Regardless of his administrative responsibilities and accomplishments, Carrier has always had his hand on the pulse of the student body which has earned him the affectionate title, "Uncle Ron." [He] is not just a name sitting in Wilson Hall; he is a familiar face on campus . . . always friendly, always encouraging. . . . "Thank you, Uncle Ron, this one's for you!"

With a shovel or without, Carrier knew groundbreaking. His first decade in office brought new buildings to front and back campus—Godwin, Miller, and Chandler halls, Greek Row, Madison Stadium, Grafton-Stovall Theatre, and the library addition. At the latter groundbreaking, Board of Visitors member Dick Strauss watched member Nell Long and Director of Libraries Mary Haban indent the ground while Carrier offered support. (Photo: JMU Special Collections)

"Uncle Ron" credited the staff and faculty for the success of a decade in which yearly applications had soared to 12,000, enrollment had boomed, faculty numbers had risen to more than 500, and budget allocations had increased from $9 million to $42 million. Yet he cautioned them not to rest on their laurels. At the opening of the 1980–81 school session, the president urged them to continue striving to make "James Madison University the top undergraduate institution in the country by the close of the decade." *The Breeze* for September 9, 1980, reported his challenge to establish "a community of scholars . . . [to] fine tune the achievements of the 'Seventies.'"

An article by Fred Hilton, head of public relations, cited the most prominent achievements:

- Enrollment has more than doubled from 4,000 to 8,800. Males increased from 29 percent to 45 percent; minority enrollment from 1.7 to 3.7 percent.

- Some 20 new buildings have been constructed or are now under construction, at a total cost of $50 million.

- Student rules and regulations have changed dramatically.

- An intensive program has been created for private support of JMU from alumni, corporations, foundations, and friends of the University.

- The institution's long-held reputation for academic excellence has been maintained and increased. The faculty has grown qualitatively and quantitatively; many new academic programs have been developed. The College Board scores of students have increased.

- The men's athletic program has moved to Division 1 of the NCAA, including the formation of a football team, and the women's program has maintained its traditional level of excellence.

At the close of the decade, the forty-eight-year-old Carrier had moved from being the youngest college head in Virginia in 1971 to being the senior man in terms of service among the state's public four-year schools. Yet he remained a catalyst for change. Wallace Chandler, former rector (1972–74) and member of the Board of Visitors when Carrier was hired, told a reporter, "At that time we saw Madison at a critical crossroads, as a school with tremendous opportunity. And we were looking for a dynamic leader." Like subsequent board members, Chandler was pleased with Carrier's special blend of talents. He had proved himself the dynamic leader they had sought.

For some longtime faculty members, however, change proved unsettling. Ruth Wilkins had been dean of women since 1953—when dates were "called for" in Alumnae Hall and had to be on a parent-approved list, when girls signed in and out, and curfews were rigidly enforced. Suddenly, it seemed, her world turned inside out. Carrier recalled the night they voted to build coeducational dormitories: "I remember Ruth Wilkins, I mean she was the pillar of southern womanhood—I loved to go to her home, she was so charming. But she got up and, as she went out the door, she lofted her hand high and shook a limp wrist, saying, 'Cast my vote NO.'"

Nevertheless, the university handbook for 1981 offered students seven different lifestyle options. Students could choose from dorms with:

- No visitation/no alcohol permitted.

- Weekend visitation/no alcohol permitted.

- Weekend visitation.

• Five-day visitation.

• Seven-day visitation, single-sex hall.

• Seven-day visitation, coeducational hall.

• Apartment living—Presidential Apartments.

The use of alcohol—at least beer—was taken for granted, unless noted otherwise. In the Diamond Anniversary yearbook, Dr. Raymond Dingledine, head of the history department and professor for thirty-five years, recalled a

Beloved by students and respected by colleagues, Raymond Dingledine, author of *Madison College: The First Fifty Years*, and his wife Agnes had been honored by a dedication in the 1964 *Bluestone*. He was one of the twenty-five-year professors featured in the '83 *Bluestone* along with (opposite page, top to bottom): Dr. Charles Blair, Dr. Mildred Dickerson, Dr. Thomas Leigh, Dr. Cornell Watkins, Dr. Z. S. Dickerson. (Photos: 1983 *Bluestone*)

(1) Dr. Raymond Dingledine, author of *Madison College: The First Fifty Years*, today and . . . (2) . . . as he appeared in the 1949 *Schoolma'am*.
(3) The Class of 1964 dedicated their volume of the *Bluestone* to Dr. and Mrs. Raymond Dingledine.

different campus: "I remember serving on a judiciary committee one summer and two girls were accused of having a can of beer in their room. Their answer was that they were using it to wash their hair. They may well have been telling the truth, but the rules were you did not have beer in your dormitory. So, we had to put them on 'strict campus,' which meant they couldn't leave campus for a whole summer."

Business administration department head Dr. Z. S. Dickerson, another of six faculty members who had twenty-five years or more of service, also remembered the earlier restrictions: "You couldn't go to certain places off campus. You certainly didn't go spend the night with your boyfriend. One night the dean of women called and told me to go with her down to a motel to get one of my juniors who was spending the night with her boyfriend. That wouldn't happen today. We went and got her and the next morning her parents came after her. She was kicked out of school."

His wife, Mildred Dickerson, had served an equal tenure as a professor of elementary and early childhood education, raising her own children along the way. She cherished memories of how close faculty families and students had been in the fifties and sixties. She said, "When we first came here, the freshman class elected a faculty sponsor that followed them through the whole four years and so you got rather close to a group of students in that way."

Two other twenty-five-year professors, Tom Leigh in English and Dr. Lowell Watkins in music, looked back with satisfaction over their quarter century. And elementary and early childhood department head Dr. Charles Blair was struck by "the tremendous amount of change that has occurred not only on this campus, but also in the community over twenty-five years, and at the same time you realize that things in some fundamental ways do not change."

One fundamental that didn't change was the camaraderie generated in four years of living on campus. Details might differ but friendships always flourished. Hula-hoops of the fifties were replaced by frisbees on the quad. Crowded dorm rooms still existed, but constructing loft beds or importing trailers became modern solutions to creating more space. Greeks still congregated in separate houses, but no longer in picturesque Victorians along Harrisonburg's streets. Newman Lake bordered the new brick housing for fraternities and sororities brought on campus by the university to allow it better control over social events. Music events still drew couples to concerts, but fewer formal dances under soft lights and mirror balls. In Levis and tee shirts, they shouted and gyrated to hard-driving rock bands at the Convo Center.

"Hillcrest" no longer housed the president and his family. In 1977, the University purchased a new residence on nearby Oak Hill Drive, complete with swimming pool and tennis courts. For the Carriers, privacy was at last an option—except when entertaining student and faculty groups on an increasingly demanding schedule. Historic "Hillcrest" housed the offices of the

Above: "Disc jock" Rick Mutzabaugh played ultimate frisbee with teams on the quad any sunny afternoon. It took concentration, timing, skillful execution, and endurance to win. Mother Nature provided boundaries—a little bush, an oak tree—or a student like Susan Mayberry studying as though totally oblivious to the action around her. (Photo: JMU Special Collections)

Right: Maxim's—or the Coffee House—hosted talented students every two or three weeks in the ballroom of Warren Campus Center. Performers such as Cliff Hoyt (right) strummed and sang songs while (bottom left) Annetta Clark, Kenny Giordano, and Frank Graviano won "Best of Maxim's" with their classic pop renditions. (Photos: '83 Bluestone)

(1) The audience can't help tapping their feet to the music when Cliff Hoyt performs his folk songs and popular fiddle tunes on his guitar.
(2) Their performances of classic pop music made Annetta Clark, Kenny Giordano, and Frank Graviano favorites with the crowd, winning them first place at the "Best of Maxim's."
(3) Maxim's packs a full house of entertainment-seekers and beer-drinkers.

BOSTON
January 22
Godwin Hall

From the mid-'70s on, the Campus Program Board under Jerry Weaver knew what sounds students wanted to hear. It brought major acts to campus venues from Wilson and Godwin halls to the Convocation Center. Here *Boston* heats up a winter night at Godwin Hall in January 1979. (Photo: '79 *Bluestone*)

alumnae association and University Relations. The new hotel/restaurant management classes could practice skills by preparing and serving faculty lunches there.

New programs—or reinstituted and expanded ones such as nursing—filled up the catalog. As if to prove the old saying, "The third time's a charm," Dr. Marcia Dake met the challenge to establish a B.S. degree for nurses. In 1997 she recalled, "A whole variety of things weren't ready with the first two [nursing program directors] hired—it wasn't time to go. But when I came in 1979, the time was right." Her background had spanned fourteen years at the University of Kentucky, where she had established that school's nursing program, plus stints with the American Nurses Association in Kansas City and at the national headquarters of the American Red Cross in Washington, D.C.

"Neither of those [latter two] were fun. I was attracted to higher education and looking for a place out in academia." In response to her curriculum vitae, JMU invited her to come for an interview that left no doubt about her strengths. She said, "The history of nursing education here had been involved with the hospital, so Ron said that my office would be in the hospital. I didn't think so. When vice president [Thomas] Stanton walked me out to the car, I said, 'Dr. Stanton, I have to tell you that I do not agree with the university's

faculty having an office in the hospital. And I would not accept the position under those circumstances. This is going to be a university program or it is not. If it's a university program, faculty has to be in the university, not isolated in the hospital.'"

A subsequent offer arrived with an office on the third floor of Wilson Hall. Then she provided the school with its next lesson: "My first priority was finding faculty—and convincing the administration of how many we needed. They simply were not attuned to nursing education, that a pediatric nurse did not teach surgical nursing and a surgical nurse did not teach psychiatric nursing, et cetera. We had to have all the specialties covered, and that surprised them a little bit," she laughed.

The university learned. By the time Dake retired in 1988, the nursing program was solid. Graduation sent men and women into well-paid positions across the Commonwealth and beyond. The nursing faculty was accepted by, and contributed to, the general academic structure of the university.

In the early '80s, innovative extracurricular choices increased, too. Carrier encouraged consideration of what to offer beyond the classroom and how an activity contributed to a sense of pride and involvement. In a '90s interview, he said, "Sports, for example, were never an end in themselves, but a way to strengthen individuals as well as the school." He seemed to apply Tom Paine's adage: "That which we acquire too easily, we esteem too lightly." Not only winning counted, but also competing at the highest level, whether intervarsity or intramural, team or individual.

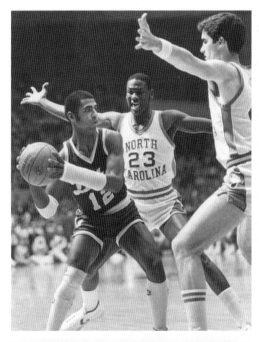

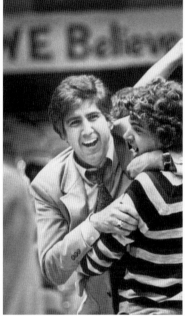

Top left: JMU's Charles Fisher works against North Carolina's Michael Jordan and Matt Doherty, in a NCAA tournament game.

Top right: JMU Coach Lou Campanelli enjoys a victory.

Left: JMU's David Dupont in play against Ohio State during March Madness.

(Photos: JMU Sports Media)

From 1981–83 JMU's men's basketball program enjoyed a period that will always be remembered as a special time in university athletics history. The Dukes during that period made three straight NCAA tournament appearances, advanced to the tournament's second round each season, and basked in the national television spotlight on several occasions.

JMU in 1981 and 1983 won the Eastern College Athletic Conference (ECAC) Southern Division Tournament, and the 1982 Dukes were at-large invitees to NCAA play. The 1981 team beat Georgetown 61-55 in the post-season event's first round; the 1982 squad advanced by defeating Ohio State 55-48; and the 1983 team reached the second round with a 57-50 victory over West Virginia.

Under coach Lou Campanelli, JMU in 1981 faced Notre Dame in second-round play, and the 1982 and 1983 teams faced impressive North Carolina squads. North Carolina's 1982 team went on to win the NCAA championship after edging JMU 52-50 with a lineup that included future NBA first-round draft choices Michael Jordan, James Worthy, and Sam Perkins.

JMU was 21-9 in 1980–81, 24-6 in 1981–82, and 20-11 in 1982–83. Center Dan Ruland and David Dupont and Charles Fisher were starters on each of the NCAA teams for JMU. Linton Townes, a 1982 senior, was conference player of the year in 1981–82, and Ruland earned the award in 1982–83.

For the March 14, 1983, post-season rally in Godwin—after the Dukes had nearly upset top-ranked University of North Carolina in an outstanding NCAA performance—the team plane was late, but the fans weren't—including (left) President Carrier and his wife, Edith, with Duke Dog. During the event, Coach Campanelli's speech and the appearance of the nationally ranked team brought the crowd to its feet, and senior Linton Townes (right) gave a warm farewell to JMU before his hello to the Portland Trailblazers. (Photos: '83 *Bluestone*)

Women's lacrosse, started in 1969, gained state and national recognition in the late '70s. In 1981, the team was ranked seventh in the nation, and in 1983 co-captain Heidi Rogers was named to the U.S. Lacrosse Squad. Dukes archers won regional and national championships and produced two national archery champions: Bob Ryder in 1973 and Janet McCullough in 1982. The baseball program captured repeated NCAA tournament berths and placed second in the Division II Regionals in '76 and third in the Division I Eastern Regional in '80 and '81. The 1983 baseball team made the College World Series in Omaha, Nebraska, the first Virginia college to achieve that distinction.

JMU moved to Division I-AA in 1980 and football seasons were studded with new highs—and lows. The Richmond Touchdown Club honored Coach Challace McMillin as the Virginia College Coach of the Year in 1980. The Associated Press praised future NFL stars Gary Clark and Charles Haley, alongside stellar performances by Jon Craver, John Kent, and Mike Thurman. But, after close wins against JMU, the "Wahoos" cancelled UVA's football series with the Dukes, and the "Hillside Gang" reluctantly was moved to new bleachers yet lost no enthusiasm.

JMU's 1983 baseball team did something no Virginia or Colonial Athletic Association team had done before, nor has any team since—advance to the College World Series in Omaha, Nebraska.

The Dukes, who were making their third NCAA Tournament appearance in four seasons, won four straight games to finish first in the Eastern Regional in Chapel Hill, North Carolina. They then met two of the top teams in the nation in Texas and Stanford while being among the final eight Division I teams in the nation playing that season. Top-seeded Texas, the eventual national champion, scored eight runs in the eighth inning and beat JMU 12-0, and Stanford edged the Dukes 3-1. Texas's roster that season included future professional standouts Roger Clemens and Calvin Schiraldi.

JMU finished 1983 with a 37-13 record after being 32-9 in regular-season play. Its top performers included Dennis Knight (top left), who batted .280 with nine homers and had a 7-4 pitching record; Tom Estepp, who batted .336; Steve Cullers and Jeff Kidd (middle left), who batted .326 and .322, respectively; Jack Munley and Justin Gannon (below), who had pitching records of 8-1 and 6-2, respectively; and Jim Knicely, Tony Morant, Jeff Urban, Phil Fritz and Mike Reeves, who had batting averages of .291, .288, .270, .263, and .262, respectively.

(Photos: JMU Sports Media)

Coaching counted. In golf, for example, Martha O'Donnell's Dukes won more state championships than any other women's sport at the university. They held the state title in '73, '74, '78, '81, and '82. Men on the links fared nearly as well, placing second in Division I for '76–77, '77–78, and '80–81. But soccer, under Coach Bob Vanderwarker, was the sport that brought men's athletics its first championship trophy, its first All-American, its first NCAA post-season bid, and its first move to Division I. The soccer team won more championships than any other men's team, and produced three pro players: Alan Mayer, Carl Strong, and Hal Partenheimer.

During games in the early 1980s, Godwin Hall was known as Electric Zoo. Rolls of toilet paper were smuggled in to electrify fans with a paper blitz at the first score by JMU. Cheerleaders and Dukettes then quickly cleared the court of the contra-band streamers. But the electricity never waned. (Photos: '81 *Bluestone*)

One of the oldest sports at the university, intercollegiate field hockey, begun in 1924, hosted the first national collegiate championship in the fall of 1975. By the mid-'80s, JMU's team was ranked nationally in the top twenty, year after year. Continuing across the spectrum of sports—cross-country, fencing, swimming, wrestling, gymnastics, and basketball—teams and individuals brought reflected glory to the school.

Some events created wild hoopla, some brought quieter acclaim. Coach Lou Campanelli's nationally ranked basketball teams brought out the "Electric Zoo," which finally had to be held in check with an administrative ruling against the tradition of throwing toilet paper on court after JMU's first score. Logan's Run concentrated greater energy but quieter success. Every October approximately forty students drove to Washington, D.C., disembarked at the U.S. Capitol steps, and ran back to Harrisonburg. The run had been initiated in 1976 by the all-male residents of Logan Hall as a fundraiser for Rockingham Memorial Hospital. Soon sponsorship expanded through the Bluestone residence halls. Runners began on Friday evening and ran through the night in

two-mile stretches, finishing at the steps of RMH late Saturday afternoon. The first seven years of Logan's Run reaped $19,000 and national praise.

The nation's capital bounded Logan's Run, but other enterprises stretched further. In 1979, English professor Ralph Cohen extended the campus abroad with a semester in London. Between twenty and thirty JMU students annually moved into the Arran House Hotel near the University of London and took classes twice a week, plus field trips. As one participant put it, "It's formal education, living education, and travel education—all in a completely affordable package."

Instructors from the University of London taught in the program, as well as a JMU professor accompanying the group. The more than thirty field outings included tours of Parliament, museums, pubs, and theaters, as well as the unexpected—such as a visit to Highgate Cemetery, the most "haunted" cemetery in the world and the burial place of Karl Marx.

For those who couldn't travel abroad, the chance to learn from internationally respected scholars was not denied. The Fall Arts and Sciences Symposium drew a stellar gallery of speakers such as Michael Harrington, who discussed "The Other America in the '80s," and human sexuality researcher Shere Hite, who riveted audience attention with her opening question: "How do men feel about clitoral stimulation?"

The incomparable Vincent Price made return visits based on popular response. As part of the Fine Art Series in 1983, he lectured in Latimer-Shaeffer

The new Convocation Center opened in July 1984, a necessary addition to accommodate JMU's expanding sports and entertainment programs. The architectural firm was Wright, Jones & Wilkerson. Creative Contractor of Roanoke built the shell, and Nielson Construction, continuing its long tradition with the school, completed the interior. (Photo: JMU Special Collections)

PIONEERS ABROAD: THE FIRST LONDON SEMESTER

by Dwayne Yancey

Now the truth can be told. It was the eggs that almost did us in.

A month or so into the inaugural semester in London program, the novelty had worn off and homesickness was beginning to set in—along with a severe case of cabin fever. Ralph Cohen, the program's founder, guiding spirit, and professor-in-residence, called us together so we could air our gripes. Ralph always called the twenty-plus students on that first JMU semester abroad "pioneers" and warned us we'd be "roughing it," paving the way for legions of future JMU students—assuming, of course, the fledgling program worked.

So he was eager to hear the things that were bugging us.

That night, we muttered and sputtered and went 'round and 'round.

Being cooped up in a bed-and-breakfast within strolling distance of the British Museum, well, once we talked about it, that didn't seem so bad after all.

Spending night after night at the theater—if not the Royal Shakespeare Company's productions, then the latest premieres at the National Theatre, or maybe some highly acclaimed "underground" performance in the West End—you know, put that way, maybe we did have it pretty good.

So why were we feeling so grumpy?

Finally, someone hit upon the one thing that was really grating on our nerves—the eggs! Every morning, the same thing—fried eggs staring up at us from our breakfast plates. At first, the hearty English breakfast that Major Dick Richards, the retired British army officer and proprietor of the Arran House, served up seemed a wondrous treat. Certainly an improvement on D-Hall food back on campus. But after the first four or five weeks, the virtues of a hearty English breakfast were losing their appeal.

Someone—I've long since forgotten who—timidly suggested an alternative. Maybe Major Richards could SCRAMBLE the eggs instead. Did he and his staff know how?

No, but Ralph was willing to show him. Within days, we had scrambled eggs and so the first semester program was saved.

Or something like that.

Looking back on that long-ago fall of '79, it's the little things I tend to remember most.

The classes? Who signed on for the classes—although it was certainly hard to ignore a theater class where actress Judi Dench (now DAME Judi Dench, mind you) was the guest lecturer? No, most of us who signed up for that inaugural semester did so just for the chance to travel abroad.

For several years, the charismatic English professor had been taking May session classes to London for whirlwind tours that had made an impression on both sides of the Atlantic. Once when he phoned ahead to the box office at the Royal Shakespeare Company to order tickets, the ticket agent said she didn't need his name—he was the only American who would call trans-Atlantic to order that many theater tickets at one time.

But a semester in London? That was his dream and something of a risk for everyone. A semester is a long time. Nobody at JMU had done such an audacious thing back then. By now, the program (which has expanded to Florence, Salamanca, and beyond) has probably grown its own bureaucracy and—I trust—its own traditions. But that fall, the program seemed to be run out of Ralph's ever-present briefcase and his rich imagination.

He made the formal part seem a breeze. He had no trouble lining up top-flight British professors willing to moonlight with a group of wide-eyed American students. And the travel? Ralph knew more about the back roads of England than any of those "Let's Go" travel guides. Who else knew the legal right-of-way through the pastures between Upper Slaughter and Lower Slaughter in the Cotswolds? Naturally, he insisted we stop for a picnic. And who else knew just the right pub in Southwark to stop at on a pub-crawl? "Yes," he'd tell us during an impromptu lecture, "this pub stands on the very spot where in Shakespeare's day . . . ."

The real trick, though, was simply managing us. Ralph wasn't just a professor or even just a program director. He also had to be something of a surrogate dad, counseling us to watch our money—that first week we blew our cash at expensive dinners at the Oodle's Café on Oxford Street until we finally got the hang of the exchange rate and realized how deep in the hole we'd put ourselves. Or even cracking the whip of discipline—maybe it's best we not go into that here.

If we started out as pioneers in London, we ended up as colonists of a sort, figuring out how to make the place a home away from home.

We claimed the Princess Louise as "our" pub—some of us regulars at last call.

We adopted the Casserole in Tottenham Court Road as "our" other hangout, where we took late-night tea (we did pick up a few English habits) and quizzed the Burmese waitress about why she'd fled her homeland.

We made a point of frowning any time we caught one of our fellow students sneaking into the McDonald's in Oxford Street, which some did in a moment of weakness. And the fourth Thursday in November may not have meant anything to Londoners, but we spent the morning in a game of touch football in Regent's Park.

And we ended the year sleeping on the sidewalk. Somehow, we learned that tickets to a Paul McCartney concert were going on sale the next morning at the Virgin record store on Oxford Street. Paul was an "oldie" even in those days (punk was in its heyday), but after spending a semester inspecting castles and palaces from one end of the U.K. to the other, we'd grown fond of museum pieces. Who could turn down the chance to see one of the Beatles—in an auditorium no bigger than Wilson Hall, to boot?

All day we sent out scouts to keep an eye on the store. About dinnertime, word spread from floor to floor. The queue is starting. Blankets were spirited out of the Arran House to shield us against the cold. By the time we awoke about dawn, the queue snaked around the corner, but there we were, close enough to the front to buy up a row full of tickets when they finally went on sale.

We missed our hearty English breakfast of Major Richards's eggs that morning. But, as I recall, that time we didn't mind.

DWAYNE YANCEY was in the initial *Semester in London* group in the fall of '79. He is now a writer and editor for *The Roanoke Times*, and the author of *When Hell Froze Over*, a book about former Virginia Governor Douglas Wilder.

JMU's ROTC program, begun in 1976, involved not only physical training and principles of military leadership, but classroom work as well. The cadets drew no small audience whenever the rappelling began from the roof of Shorts Hall. (Photo: JMU Special Collections)

Theatre to full houses. He began, "Art isn't any one thing—it's everything": then held forth on music, theater, art, architecture, radio, television, and film. The next night, he drew another full house in Wilson Hall for a lecture on "Villainy"— his movie villains being audience favorites. The series also exposed students to music and dance, with such imports in 1981 as the Cleveland String Quartet and the Ohio Ballet.

On every front, JMU was expanding student horizons and working toward a strong balance between quantity and quality. The *Daily News-Record* issued a special insert on March 14, 1983, for JMU's Diamond Anniversary. The paper reiterated how the Carrier years put students first, asserting, "And that is the attitude, the driving force, which has propelled James Madison University into parity with every other college and university in the state."

Carrier predicted key challenges ahead in funding and restructuring the curriculum to reflect new technology. For example, every student should have a chance to become computer literate and every curriculum should include writing skills. In addition, the school should institute an honors program for outstanding students.

The *Daily News-Record* editorialized that the dramatic changes that had characterized the Carrier years would be a hard act to follow, but the momentum was still there. "And," Carrier added, "it has to keep going."

IN THE LATE '70S, the once leisurely pace of life in many small towns in America began to accelerate around ever-expanding centers of business, government, learning, industry, and population. Ironically, children of a generation who had fled those same small towns in record numbers suddenly longed to recover something missing in their prefab lives. Yet their transition to more rural areas endangered the very quality of rolling fields and open space they sought and threatened rural traditions of place and culture. In Harrisonburg, still a small town in the heart of the Shenandoah Valley, two men would be instrumental in holding one special space against urban assault.

During Dr. Carrier's first decade, moving from college to university, faculty and programs expanded in quality and quantity. The student population more than doubled and the gender gap closed to forty-five percent male. Twenty new buildings had been or were under construction—including a new Convocation Center to showcase basketball teams or rock concerts. But the university had not lost its rural character. Thanks to former President Tyler Miller's foresight, land remained available for continued expansion. In 1952 Miller had persuaded the Commonwealth to spend $70,000 to purchase 235 acres of the remaining Newman Farm—the landholding from which the original campus had been formed in 1908. Carrier had special plans to preserve a part of that land as an open area.

The second key figure in the plan was longtime botany professor Dr. Norlyn Bodkin. He had won his undergraduate and master's degrees at West Virginia University, where two men in particular had influenced his future, Dr. Earl L. Core, head of West Virginia's biology department, and Dr. Roland Guthrie, director of the Core Arboretum. They had convinced Bodkin of the value of an arboretum for a community as well as for higher education.

So from his first days as a professor at Madison in 1964, Bodkin had been campaigning for the college to establish an arboretum, devoting renewed effort after Carrier arrived on campus. Now, Bodkin's tenacity would pay off.

"He plagued me continually," recalls Carrier. "Then one afternoon as I was running along the trail through Newman Woods, I was dismayed by the moving of earth and great clouds of dust rising not distant from where I ran. In that moment it seemed absolutely clear that someone had to make a stand for nature. I called Norlyn to say, 'Lets's do it.' "

The divide between the *saying* and the *doing* proved wider than expected. Seven years elapsed before receiving the first two major contributions to fuel development. Bodkin met with biology department head Dr. Gilbert Trelawny for input as he drafted a formal proposal for an arboretum. Both had been working with classes in the fields of the Newman farm and College Woods, so they knew the area well. He also sought advice from Dr. James Grimm, who was running entomology studies in the pond. Finally in the spring of 1984, the Commission on Planning and Development at JMU approved the establishment of an arboretum.

In the meantime, Carrier also promoted the idea in conversations with friends and legislators. He would need the backing of both groups. For the arboretum, envisioned as a partnership with the community, private funding was essential—and offered supporters not involved in athletics an opportunity to contribute. Two of Carrier's earliest conversations paid off. Once the Commission approved the concept, local poultry producer Charles Wampler and his wife, Dottie, donated a challenge gift of $25,000. Friend and business rival Charles "Chip" Strickler and his wife, Judy, matched the Wampler largesse with another $25,000. Development could begin.

On April 5, 1985, Harrisonburg contractor Cecil Mongold's team fired up bulldozers and backhoes and moved in. Mongold understood the concept of controlling the heavy machinery to leave what trees he could and to curve, not

The beautifully curved entrance drive to the arboretum, created in 1985, guaranteed a slower pace. (Photo: Edith J. Carrier Arboretum)

to channel, the entrance road to the parking lot. By noon his job was finished and the establishment of an arboretum had truly begun.

The next year's construction included trails and the Interpretive Center, a rustic pavilion with a deck. Fraternity boys hauled brush to open major trails and bridges. "They worked well if they brought dates and you promised beer later," Bodkin related later. In the 1980s, alcohol was still permitted on campus.

The ongoing routine was to beg for dollars and go on. Mark Daniel, Class of '85, happened to be taking a class with Bodkin, who didn't discriminate against students when asking for funds. "My granddad has money," Mark said. His granddad just happened to be U. S. Representative Dan Daniel from Danville, Virginia.

"By next week we were invited to lunch in D.C. and, before we left the restaurant, we had a check for $5,000. It was a real shot in the arm," said Bodkin.

Another shot in the arm came in 1986 with a grant of $17,500 from the Virginia Environment Endowment for the purchase of plants and educational materials. Volunteers operated without an overall plan and Bodkin worked out of three file cabinets in Trailer #4 as an office. Yet he had little time for paper-

Formally known as "The Interpretive Center," this rustic pavilion is a focal point where formal receptions, impromptu picnics, instructional brown-bag lunches, or any variety of events take place. (Photo: Edith J. Carrier Arboretum)

work as he was still running a chainsaw, buying and planting plants, and teaching full time.

When he purchased an old equipment building for storage, it elicited, "Boy, that's an ugly building," from Dr. Carrier. "Yes, but it only cost $1,400," came Bodkin's retort. Not that he had much equipment to store. He brought his own wheelbarrow from home, and physical help came from "Junior" Higgs, head of JMU's grounds, and staff members who volunteered. In fact, they planted the first major addition of $1,700 plants by the light of cars and trucks, trapping friends and students to help. But another shot in the arm was at hand. October 2, 1986, brought the first meeting of an Arboretum Advisory Committee that would become a lifeline to eventual success.

At a luncheon in Chandler Hall, Dr. Barbara Pass welcomed major donors Charles Wampler and Judy Strickler, nationally acclaimed horticulturist Andre Viette, and, from the university, professors Emily Baxter and Norlyn Bodkin, vice president of academic affairs Russell Warren, associate vice president for development Don Moore, and university and external programs vice president Glenda Rooney. They were charged with presenting ideas for the development and operation of the arboretum, giving input on program development for education, research, conservation, and aesthetic development. They could design promotional activities to transform the garden into an active public facility. The first big public acclaim came with the arboretum's designation as a Living Legacy by the Commission on the Bicentennial for the United States Constitution on September 17, 1987, as part of the national celebration.

For the entrance gates, sculptor and JMU professor Ken Beer cited the advantages of Cor-Ten™ (an alloy of steel and copper) as its strength and natural oxidization to a dark, reddish patina that blends well with the surrounding woodland. (Photo: Edith J. Carrier Arboretum)

Steadily, work progressed. When the JMU Arboretum officially opened on April 28, 1989, there were actual gates to open. In fact, the gates would become a signature part of the facility. Until then, only a single sixteen-foot steel pipe secured to a post by a chain marked the entrance.

Ken Beer, an art professor at JMU, had long been recognized as an outstanding sculptor. His sculptures had garnered awards in juried shows around the nation. His works also marked corporate headquarters and academic institutions, including JMU and the Harrisonburg headquarters of ROCCO (now Cargill Inc./Georges Foods). His proposal for steel gates at the Arboretum's entrance received enthusiastic and unanimous endorsement by the Arboretum Executive Committee as well as the JMU Administration. He worked on campus for six months outside the old machine shop in a Harrison Hall annex.

"It was a lonely job—getting your hands cold working outside. You didn't draw crowds, since it's a sheltered area. People passing probably figured it was just junk," Beer recalled. "Then I spent the next months chained in the air. Had to build scaffolding."

A parallel challenge to the gates themselves was something to hang them on. With a private donation plus gifts of stone from Luck Stone in Elkton, Virginia, and labor by Michael Long, work on the pillars, rock walls, and entryway began. Beer left details to the architects who constructed stone pillars with steel reinforcement. He said, "Judy [Strickler] did a good job as overall coordinator."

Judy Strickler and her husband "Chip" had funded the project, which used Cor-Ten™ steel, the same steel chosen by the great American architect Eero Saarinen for the headquarters of Deere and Company in a wooded valley near Moline, Illinois. The alloy of steel and copper oxidized to a darkly reddish protective patina that, as Saarinen saw it apropos a tractor company, evoked memories of "an old harrow rusting in the American landscape." Strickler said, "It was exactly this same ambience that Beer and the Arboretum Execu-

After its initial planting, the Arboretum herb garden more nearly resembled the quad in 1909 than the area a writer from *Southern Living* magazine would in 2001 call "a hidden gem" and an "exit for serenity." (Photo: Edith J. Carrier Arboretum)

tive Committee hoped would artistically and aesthetically make a statement about James Madison University's Arboretum."

To observers outside campus life, the arboretum seemed a natural extension of the transformation of campus grounds by exceptional landscaping. In "Junior" Higgs, President Carrier had found the right man to implement his dream of JMU becoming one of the most eye-pleasing campuses in the nation. Beyond the quad, the raw thrusts of new construction were softened by shrubs, trees, and flowers. Every building was edged with plants and every entrance welcomed visitors with color and form. For example, brilliant red *arborvitae*, one of the first North American trees introduced into Europe, lined the road to the Convocation Center near the arboretum.

Since most non-ornamental trees take thirty years to grow to worthwhile size, JMU enjoyed a distinct advantage from the first in starting its arboretum with an established woodland. In its 125-acre reserve, eighty-seven acres held eighty- and ninety-year-old oaks and hickories that Bodkin believed had seeded around the start of the twentieth century.

Another advantage was Bodkin's connection to London. When on educational leave in 1990 to conduct research at the British Natural History Museum in London, he had identified and assembled the more than 500 native Virginia plants that the New World's major botanist John Clayton had collected over two centuries ago.

Clayton (1694–1773) grew up in England but arrived in Virginia in 1705. As an amateur interested in plants, he began traveling the wilderness to collect specimens. Soon the amateur had evolved to the expert botanist, had become the man Thomas Jefferson praised as having "contributed more than any other botanist who lived." His work formed a significant basis for *Flora Virginica*, the first publication devoted to plant life in the New World, co-authored by respected Dutch doctor Johann Friedrich Gronovius and Swedish botanist Carolus Linnaeus. Clayton's significance was not lost on those working at JMU. The arboretum has a John Clayton Trail and features the Linnaeus discovery "Spring Beauty" that bears Clayton's name. In addition, the fundraising arm of the arboretum is officially the John Clayton Botanical Society of the Arboretum.

After Bodkin's induction in December 1991 into the Linnean Society in London, England—the oldest scientific society in the world devoted to natural history—the arboretum group celebrated his immense honor at a banquet in Harrisonburg in May of '92. Internationally known daffodil specialist Brent

ARBORVITAE

Arborvitae, like those planted along the entrance to James Madison University, hold significance in American history. They were among the first North American trees introduced into Europe. French explorer Jacques Cartier carried them back for cultivation in Paris.

His fascination began during 1535–36 when his entire ship's crew had become deathly ill of "Scorbute"—scurvy, the plague of ocean voyages then. Walking ashore along the St. Lawrence, Cartier encountered an Indian named Domagaia, who had been so ill ten days earlier that Cartier hadn't expected him to live. He recalled, "knees swolne as bigge as a child of two years old, all his sinews shrunke together, his teeth spoyled, his gummes rotten and stinking."

Yet here he was well. Naturally, Cartier asked how he had healed himself so that his ailing men could follow the same path. Domagaia replied that he "had taken the juice and sap . . . of a certain Tree . . . to take the barke and leaves of the sayd tree, and boile them together, then to drinke . . . every other day, and to put the dregs of it upon his legs that is sicke."

Cartier didn't understand why it worked, but he followed the directions. We know now that his men were cured of scurvy by the vitamin C in the *arborvitae* sap.

Heath delivered the keynote address. He cited the honoree's contributions in the classroom and in the field, including his work with the arboretum and discovery of a rare variety of flowering plant named the "Shenandoah wake robin" or *Trillium pusillum* var. *monticulum*. He also thrilled his audience with a surprise announcement. He pledged to name a new variety "Daffodil O'Bodkin."

The John Clayton Exhibition displayed in Sonner Hall in March 1993 brought Virginia's history of botanical exploration to Virginians for the first time. Dr. Charles Jarvis, the British Natural History Museum's "keeper of botany," accompanied the collection. In addition to Clayton's exploration, the exhibit showcased botanical literature, line drawings, and watercolors of plants of the 1700s from the Hunt Institute for Botanical Documentation at Carnegie-Mellon. The exhibit drew plaudits and more than 600 visitors.

Every project begins with a plan—and dollar donations. Dr. Carrier and major donor Charles Wampler listen to Dr. Norlyn Bodkin assess the first rendition of several "Arboretum Master Plans." (Photo: JMU Special Collections)

Activity continued to mark the days within the arboretum and beyond. Volunteer hours increased while Glenda Rooney and her assistant Becky Hilton proved a valuable support team from the university. Within her first year helping to develop the program of the arboretum, Rooney had moved from novice to authority on plants. She brought a creative and strong management style to "coordinating volunteers, budgets, and details of organization with a minimum of interruption," according to advisory board chairman Strickler.

On the grounds, native plants proliferated, donated at random from generous individuals and rescue projects. Throughout the entire arboretum, guided tours led hundreds of students and community groups along the ever-growing network of trails—25,000 visitors in the first two years. Volunteers continued investing sweat equity to boost dollar donations. And Bodkin expanded the continuing education tours that he began in 1988 heading groups to the Galapagos Islands and the Amazon rain forest.

Then in 1990, a new problem compounded the ongoing dilemma of the mud-laced pond. The city's plan for a potential public road connector unveiled a new threat. The City of Harrisonburg faced mounting traffic congestion. Of its 115 miles of streets, only twenty-five could handle large numbers of cars and trucks. Many local citizens felt that JMU contributed to the problem, so the school should be happy to contribute to the solution. And one solution was to run a connector road through the arboretum. Carrier and Bodkin argued against that answer—Bodkin publicly, Carrier behind the scenes.

Other voices rose in disagreement. Nearly 1,500 people signed a petition opposing the proposed eastside connector to link Stone Spring and Port Republic roads and East Market and North Main streets and cut through the arboretum. At a meeting of the Harrisonburg Planning Commission, Bodkin reminded the public, "It's not a university facility, folks. It's a community facility for the people in the Central Shenandoah Valley."

Letters to the editor supported saving the arboretum. For example, on July 25, 1990, Julie Swope of the Greenvale Garden Club reported the group's unanimous opposition to the proposed road. She hit on fiscal irresponsibility, writing, "Not only will this be destroying an area of natural beauty, but it will serve as a waste of taxpayers' money which has recently been spent on this project, just to turn around and spend more of our money to destroy it."

Lining the pond became the final answer to a pond that wouldn't hold water. (Photo: Edith J. Carrier Arboretum)

Carrier held discussions with city manager Marvin Milam and assistant city manager Roger Baker seeking compromise. Finally, the City Council withdrew road plans. On April 9, the *Daily News-Record* headlined "Dead End/City Won't Run Connector Road Through Arboretum At JMU." On April 11, the paper editorialized, "For now, nature lovers have prevailed. We hope their victory is a just and meaningful one. But don't be surprised if the debate resurfaces some day. It could happen when the city announces the new price tag for an alternate route that will accommodate progress while keeping the flowering trillium and may apples safe from the bulldozer's blade." The writer was wrong.

So one threat was solved, but the pond's problems increased. Bodkin complained he was constantly treating "a mudhole." Designed in 1988 with the assistance of the U.S. Soil Conservation Service, the 0.4-acre pond had inspired high hopes for its becoming a habitat for dozens of aquatic and semi-aquatic plants in addition to being a scenic attraction to lure tourists. But a major setback surfaced at once. The pond wouldn't hold water. The solution called for full excavation of the pond area, deepening the bottom, widening the edges, extending the size—and adding a plastic liner.

Once lined, the pond held its water—muddy water. The color ranged from golden yellow to deeper brown. Siltation problems mounted due to private development on the upper slopes of the watershed. Bodkin contacted the city about sediment flowing into the pond. Baker identified thirteen property owners behind the mall who were not in compliance with erosion rules. But runoff from erosion didn't end. The pond was situated in a floodplain, and deposition came from all sides. Brown or yellow had become the pond's dominant color. In fact, in May of 1992, Bodkin said he tried adding a nontoxic, algae-control compound to counter the effects of rains and erosion. It held an aqua blue until the next rainstorm. In addition, heavy rains and some lesser ones blocked a grate in the culvert above, causing water to build up until it gushed over the levy carrying mud down the hill and across the parking area. The highly visible pond drew more "tsk-tsk's" than "ahh's."

In spite of the color, however, one aspect brought success. Fish flourished. Exotic Japanese carp came to the pond in 1991 when Dr. Stephen Wright donated four Koi carp and envisioned future sales to help with habitat upkeep. Since Koi average 100,000 to 400,000 eggs a spawn each spring—though only .1 percent reach maturity—hundreds of brilliantly colored offspring swim about today. Fascinated onlookers along the bank cast handfuls of food from a coin-operated dispenser nearby. Their coins cover the food supply. But the fish habitat remains a muddy indentation in the landscape.

The Koi Festival in 1991 began with Dr. Stephen Wright's contribution of four fish to spawn a population of hundreds that entertain visitors today. Saving old bread to feed the fish is a favorite habit of children and adults in the community. (Photo: Edith J. Carrier Arboretum)

Although Carrier and Bodkin had been driving forces behind the establishment of the arboretum, community volunteers' infusion of time, as well as money, proved the lifeblood of its operation. By 1995, volunteer participation had increased 300 percent since 1985, and the advisory council presented its first Trowel Service Award to Ron Brown—who set a benchmark for others. Brown, a retired director of the former Farmers Home Administration, became a volunteer who worked full-time, planting, sowing, pruning, and building trails. He also donated more than 3,000 plants, with an emphasis on native varieties. Over the decade, what had begun with a small team of dedicated local citizens evolved into a diverse network of community participants.

Volunteers proved essential—and continue to be so. Workshops enhance their knowledge and enthusiasm. And current arboretum sponsored trips do the same, although not as far afield as the earlier Natural History Studies Tours to the Galapagos Islands and twelve summer days in Ireland. The annual journeys now offer a variety of day trips closer by.

Any year's agenda confirms the value of the community partnership. For example, a random example from Bodkin's annual report for 1993 listed eighty wide-ranging events for more than 2,900 participants. Eleven couples wed, Shakespeare Express performed plays, English students read poetry at midnight on Halloween, and so on. In addition, seventy sections of formal JMU classes used the facility while classes from county and city schools, garden clubs, alumni, and other community organizations held tours. And casual visitors continued—in the thousands yearly. Throughout the decade, activities continued to multiply.

In 1995, current director Dennis Whetzel joined the staff and added expertise in heirloom perennials, herbs, and antique roses. Something of a workaholic, he admits dependence on the volunteers as he combines "career and my lifetime obsession—gardening almost twenty-four hours a day."

As activities proliferated, the advisory committee suggested a newsletter. From JMU's publications office, *Montpelier* editor Pam Brock created the format and wrote copy. *The Understory* established a hit with Volume 1, Number 1, Spring 1995. Bodkin's first column, called "Overstory," explained the botanical names:

> In 200 B.C. Theophrastus, the father of botany, wrote about the layering of vegetation as "trees, shrubs, undershrubs, and herbs." Later forest stratification [used] the terms *overstory* for the top stratum of tall trees, *understory* for the next layer, then the *shrub layer*, and finally the lowest stratum, a *groundcover* of herbaceous plants including wildflowers.

Of the special gardens throughout the grounds, the Larkin Smith Rock Garden established in 1992 is one of the most unique. Layers of sandstone

shale and limestone form a shale barren featuring seven of the fifteen-plus
strict endemic species that thrive only under a shale barren's extreme conditions of harsh, direct prolonged sunlight heating the surface to more than 100
degrees. No other arboretum in the nation can claim such distinction. The

One of two footbridges to the Andrew Wood Memorial Garden, established in 1994 to honor the 1980 graduate from Richmond. (Photo: Edith J. Carrier Arboretum)

garden perpetuates the memory of deceased JMU student Larkin Smith, daughter of Wilton J. and Linda Smith of Falls Church, who died in a tragic diving accident at the close of her junior year in June 1991.

Another sudden death, that of Andrew Wood in a rafting accident on the New River in West Virginia, led his family to fund a memorial garden in his name with the largest single gift for a garden in the arboretum's history. The commemorative space honoring the 1980 graduate and biology major was dedicated in May 1994. Two footbridges access its eighty-four species of shrubs and more than 1,000 wildflower specimens. His parents, Mr. and Mrs. George Wood of Richmond, and his widow, Marie Scott, funded the memorial.

Fifteen specialty areas form the gardens of the arboretum, in addition to the groves of giant hickories and oaks. They range from the April Walk Daffodil Garden, a forty-yard circular path above the pavilion established in 1988, to the latest Rose Garden set in 1999 near the entrance with thirty varieties of heirloom selections. The August 2001 *Southern Living* magazine termed the arboretum "an exit for serenity" and a "hidden gem . . . a welcome oasis less than five minutes off the interstate." This hidden gem may one day draw 80,000 visitors annually, if the advisory committee and Dr. Carrier's plans reach fulfillment.

In the fall of 1998, both the arboretum and its oak-hickory forest were officially designated to honor two people integral to the development of the university and the arboretum. That September the forest was named for founding director Norlyn Bodkin. He had been the primary force behind the grounds' transformation into a successful, respected teaching facility and popular community attraction. Bodkin said, "This [naming] means more to me than anything else could. The forest epitomizes my love for nature and natural environments. It's wild—a little like me." He had retired the prior July but planned to continue his support of the arboretum.

The JMU Board of Visitors bestowed the second honor by naming the arboretum for Edith Johnson Carrier, wife of JMU President Emeritus Ronald E. Carrier. She had served as JMU's first lady from 1971 to 1998. The board passed a resolution saying that Mrs. Carrier served "with grace, elegance, wit, wisdom, and affability." She had raised three children and assisted her husband during the university's enrollment and building boom. She organized and hosted receptions and gatherings at "Oakview" for alumni, parents, professors, and visiting dignitaries. In the process, she transformed the institution's concept of catering and entertaining to suit its growing reputation and status. She often attended official events in her husband's stead and was increasingly called on as a speaker in her own right. She also shared her husband's deep concern for the arboretum.

While the Board of Visitors had intended to honor Mrs. Carrier for her years of service, their act also assured Dr. Carrier's continued involvement after he left the presidency. As Edith Carrier said, "Ron had the initial vision for this marvelous preserve of nature. And, as his wife, I can safely say he never lets things fail and he'll never stop supporting the arboretum."

Bodkin agreed, "Because of the Carriers, JMU and the community have a nature preserve in their midst for all time."

In May 1999, the formal dedication of the arboretum gathered to celebrate the official name change from James Madison University Arboretum to the Edith Johnson Carrier Arboretum. In thanking friends and well-wishers who honored her by their presence, after introductory remarks, Mrs. Carrier said:

> One of my grandchildren asked me what was so great about
> keeping a woods and plants. He pointed out that garden centers
> are filled with them. I tried to explain that a natural landscape can't
> be rebuilt. Think about it. You can cut down trees and build a
> parking deck or erect a building and then take that down and
> rebuild another and do it again and again. Anything people can
> erect can be destroyed and replaced over and over. But a natural
> woodland can't be re-created. It takes a hundred years for an inch
> of topsoil, a century for moss and ferns to take hold, generations
> for trees to mature.

This is the only arboretum on a state-supported school in the Commonwealth. Planting began in 1985 . . . and enhancement continues. That's one of the wonderful aspects of an arboretum—it's always *becoming,* is never finished. And I pledge to you that I will work to be worthy of this honor by committing myself to making this beautiful natural preserve the best it can possibly be. . . .

The Edith J. Carrier Arboretum has become a personal as well as a community pledge to the future.

FROM DR. CARRIER'S REMARKS AT THE DEDICATION OF THE ARBORETUM ON APRIL 11, 1997:

For all mankind, in all times and places, natural preserves have been rejuvenating counterpoints to the press of buildings, the essence of cities. Ancient Persians created artificial mountains covered by hanging gardens. The Greeks set aside hunting parks—one-fourth of Alexandria for that purpose. In Baghdad nearly 1,000 little walled gardens held fountains, plants in boxes, scented blooms, and mechanical trees and birds. Europe followed suit and England turned king's parks into public gardens.

In our own nation, New York's Central Park breathes life into and sustains the urban surroundings. Nature nourishes us physically and spiritually. Yet although it's always present, it must be perceived to have meaning. Our perception, however, is too often filtered through a screen of its usefulness to us. Too often the cash nexus is the only connection between man and land. A field or farm or woodland is seen only as a mall or subdivision waiting to happen.

But some of us subscribe to a land ethic to provide for land beyond its economic return. Just as we become patrons of theater and art galleries and concerts, we become patrons of the landscape. We see them necessary to the balance of life.

And the most beautiful landscapes are those that convey life—that resonate with seasons of growth and change and living forms. Aldo Leopold's classic book, *A Sand County Almanac,* asserts that "a thing is right when it tends to preserve the integrity, stability and beauty of the biotic community. It is wrong when it does otherwise."

We have tried to do the right thing here. We are building an arboretum that will resonate with growth and life. I say "building" because it's never finished. An arboretum is always unfinished, is always coming into being.

Edith and I grew up in small rural towns in Tennessee. They were, in the words of Russell Baker, "a poor place to prepare for a struggle with the twentieth century but a delightful place to spend a childhood." And, I would add, they were good places to learn values, to form character. But they're disappearing. I remember one of the most exciting places of my boyhood days was the swinging bridge across the Holston River. With a span the length of two football fields, you'd thrill to its swinging. You'd feel as if suspended in space, nothing holding it or you in the air.

I'm lucky—that icon of childhood still remains. But the train no longer stops in Bluff City. The depot's torn down; the quaint, rambling river I once fished is now a lake. I'll always miss the wildness of the river, Island Park in the middle where I'd swim to explore and camp.

Each of you probably can recount similar losses from childhood. All around us land-use changes come too fast, loom too large. And people become disheartened by the changes. They sense their lives in disarray.

So this piece of land, this arboretum, is dedicated to stabilizing and balancing the lives of those living around it. It's not only for people on the forty to fifty guided tours each year or the sixty to seventy class sections that use the grounds. It's not only designed to accommodate the countless visitors doing research or the lovers strolling or those sighting birds and wildflowers.

This space is also dedicated to the needs of ordinary people who seek renewal, who simply need an infusion of nature to better handle their days.

I F THE FIRST HALF OF THE '80s seemed the best of times, the best only got better. Freshmen applications told the story. In 1970–71 when Dr. Carrier arrived, there were 3,565 applications for admission; by 1988, they had increased to more than 13,000. Dr. Fay J. Reubush, associate vice president for academic affairs, pointed out that admissions standards hadn't changed, but the quality of students had improved: "The current students not only have better SAT (Scholastic Aptitude Test) scores, but they, in general, rank higher in their class and have taken a stronger program of study in high school." She also credited Carrier's "marvelous leadership" in attracting students, his risk-taking, and his ability "to see opportunities which many other people simply were not aware of . . . looking beyond where the rest of us were looking."

The change in public perception had not gone unnoticed nationally. JMU license plates (the department of motor vehicles offered a chance to buy them) no longer generated "JM who?" from strangers. *Virginia Business* magazine for December 1989 pointed out how, in his color commentary, then CBS announcer John Madden always referred to Redskins' player Gary Clark as playing his college ball at "Big JMU." The magazine explained:

When Clark first started scoring touchdowns for the Redskins in 1985, Madden referred to the wide receiver's alma mater as "Little JMU." Offended by that choice of words, a JMU graduate cornered Madden in a Washington restaurant and informed him that JMU has more than 10,000 students.

Madden seldom misses a chance to tell that story, and he usually tops it off with an enthusiastic endorsement of

Chapter Twenty

The Accolades
Accumulate
(1984–1989)

Before the advent of phone registration in the spring of '89 and later computers, registration meant long lines and endless cards to shuffle. Upperclassmen got first choice and freshmen got all the eight o'clocks. (Photo: JMU Bulletin 1978–79)

Whenever NFL color commentators mentioned JMU in connection with these former JMU stars—(top left) Charles Haley, (top right) Scott Norwood, and (bottom) Gary Clark—they thrilled Dukes everywhere. (Photos: '83 and '89 *Bluestone*)

the university. "It's a great school," he says on national TV. "It's in Harrisonburg, right in the middle of the Shenandoah Valley. Beautiful country down there. . . ." Clark did his part by carrying the JMU banner into the NFL, but it was an anonymous alumnus, not a superstar, who transformed that good publicity into *great* publicity.

That was publicity worth a million dollars according to Fred Hilton, director of media relations.

More media attention drew national recognition. The May 1986 issue of *Money* magazine named JMU one of "Ten Public Colleges with an Ivy Twist," a public school "lately striving to attain higher marks and greater recognition—and earning them. . . . an exceptional value. . . ." Accolades came from *U.S. News & World Report; Barron's Guide to the Most Prestigious Colleges; Barron's Guide to the Best, Most Popular and Most Exciting Colleges; Peterson's Guide to Competitive Colleges; Changing Times* magazine, and from Edward Fiske, education editor of the *New York Times.*

Faculty, too, were winning individual awards and their departments were gaining wide recognition. Dr. Jackie Driver, associate professor of psychology, became a delegate to a five-day White House Conference on Aging. At the graduate level, the psychology department conferred the greatest number of degrees, 23.4 percent of the total. There were more programs than there had been students when the graduate school opened in 1954 with only twenty-nine enrollees.

The foreign language department's Dr. Elizabeth Neatrour was asked to lead a group of U.S. State Department and Foreign Service officers on a tour of Russia in 1982. Five years later, the Soviet Russians awarded her an honorary medal for her work with cultural exchange. In 1985, President Ronald Reagan and Soviet Premier Mikhail Gorbachev signed a U.S.–Soviet Union international exchange agreement, making JMU one of three colleges (with Bryn Mawr in Pennsylvania and Grinnell in Iowa) participating in exchange with the Herzen Institute in Leningrad (St. Petersburg). Neatrour directed the first exchange of secondary language teachers in 1989.

Also in '81, Dr. Barkley Rosser, professor of economics, had taken a leave of absence to serve as consultant for Prince Khalid of Faisal in Saudi Arabia, and Dr. Devin Bent, professor of political science, had taken leave to spend the year at the Pentagon evaluating management, budgeting, and utilization of studies produced by the army. In 1989, the federal government relied on Dr. Karen Forcht, professor of information technology, to review computer crime documents for the National Institute of Justice. Her final documentation would be used to train U.S. Justice Department personnel to investigate and try cases and promote a computer code of ethics. Dr. Elizabeth Ihle, professor of education, produced four modules on "History of Black Women's Education in the South," developed under a $23,000 grant from the U.S. Department of Education.

Grants proliferated. In 1988–89, the National Endowment for the Humanities awarded $120,000 for faculty development; the Department of Agriculture $312,785 to administer a literacy program for workers within the local poultry industry; the Virginia Department of Economic Development $100,000 to

Professors won acclaim in distant lands as well as nationally. Top: Dr. Elizabeth Neatrour and her mother, fifth and sixth from left, chaperon students in Russia. Bottom left: Dr. Jackie Driver smiles at her invitation to the White House. Bottom right: Dr. Barkley Rosser rides a camel in Saudi Arabia. (Photos: Courtesy of Drs. Driver and Rosser and *Montpelier* magazine archives)

create a small business center. That same year, local philanthropist Fred Funkhouser donated twenty-seven acres of land along Main Street with an estimated value of $350,000.

Intense excitement reigned for JMU's archeologists. Each year saw students traveling to archeological projects in field schools around the state; for example, digging at Jefferson's Monticello in an eight-week program to focus on what archeology could reveal about servant life and craft history, or unearthing Indian and white settler sites along the Jackson River, a tributary of the James

tucked high in the mountains of Bath County. There the decade began with Dr. Clarence Geier and his team working against the clock and rising waters as the U.S. Army Corps of Engineers constructed the Gathright Dam. The JMU cadre worked to retrieve all they could about the people and history of the past 10,000 years in the Jackson River basin before it was gone. Contracted for a two-year project with the Corps of Engineers, JMU professors Geier and William Boyer, Jr., directed between sixty-five and eighty JMU staff members, field school students, and a few others in the largest archeological project ever undertaken in Virginia. Boyer remembers it as "the best of times."

Catherine King-Frazier, part of the National Science Foundation expedition to Antarctica in '85, unfurled the JMU banner outside her tent and impressed an audience on campus and beyond when TV news carried the story. (Photo: JMU Special Collections)

Other accolades accrued. In 1985, Catherine King-Frazier, a geology lab technician at JMU, was tapped to accompany the National Science Foundation expedition to Antarctica to collect meteorites preserved in the ice mass. She proudly posed with a JMU banner in front of her tent. Education professor Mildred G. Dickerson was named Outstanding Woman of Virginia in 1986—the same year that art professor Rebecca Humphrey's handmade-paper works were exhibited and garnered awards nationwide. Year by year citations mounted. Heather Dow, assistant field hockey and lacrosse coach, finished her playing career on the U.S. team that won the World Cup Lacrosse Championship in Perth, Australia, in 1989. Women's basketball coach Shelia Moorman was named coach of the West Team for the 1990 Olympic Festival in Minneapolis–St. Paul.

The '80s was also the decade Dr. Carrier left—temporarily, that is. At a packed press conference the second Friday of April 1986, Carrier announced,

The 1985–86 season began a six-year period that saw JMU win four straight Colonial Athletic Association championships and advance to NCAA play five times. The Dukes had a combined record of 151-34 during those seasons and advanced to the NCAA Tournament's "Sweet 16" four times. JMU completed the 1985–86 season with a 28-4 record and the 1990–91 campaign with 26-5 mark. The Dukes were 27-4 in 1986–87 and 1987–88 and 26-4 in 1988–89. Left: Coach Sheilia Moorman's intensity fueled the Dukes through several winning seasons, and the women's basketball team twice posted major upsets in the NCAA Tournament. Below left: In 1986 the Dukes competed in the post-season event for the first time and beat regional top-seeded Virginia 71-62 in the second round. Below right: In 1991 in second-round play the Dukes defeated Penn State, the nation's top-ranked team, 73-71. In the game at Virginia, JMU took a 33-22 halftime lead and held on for the win. At Penn State, the host Nittany Lions led 11-0, 24-9 and 41-29 (halftime) before a 22-6 scoring burst put the Dukes in front to stay. From 1982–97 Coach Moorman's record was 302-134. She was CAA Coach of the Decade from 1985–95, in 2001 was inducted into the JMU Sports Hall of Fame, and in 2004 became JMU's asssociate athletics director. (Photos: '89 *Bluestone* and JMU Sports Media)

"I have accepted a temporary position as president of the Center for Innovative Technology. This appointment is effective Monday, April 14, and will be for a one-year period. At the end of that time, I will return to my duties as president of James Madison University."

Boards of both JMU and CIT approved the arrangement, but the public raised questions. Several print editorials pointed out that they didn't doubt his sincerity but did wonder whether he would really return. In 1984, his JMU success had led then-Governor Charles Robb to ask him to run for the Senate against Senator John Warner. Carrier refused—as he had earlier refused lucrative offers to assume the presidency of Florida State University and the chancellorship of the University of Arkansas-Fayetteville. Obviously, at fifty-three, he was at his prime for a major professional change. In 1986, Governor Gerald Baliles counted on him to pull in high-tech research money and rebuild a state organization in chaos (some pundits called it "TCIT, for Troubled Center of Innovative Technology"). Success on this mission would certainly raise the ante for future offers.

CIT offices near Dulles International Airport had been set up two years earlier to coordinate research between high-tech industries and state universities. *The Breeze* pointed out that Carrier would meet leading corporate officials from this country and abroad and quoted him as saying, "While I may be the president of CIT, I probably will not miss any opportunity to promote our students and our faculty with these individuals. If . . . I can do a good job, it certainly will reflect very favorably on the university."

The campus paper also assessed Carrier's strengths for the new position: his knowledge of universities, ability to deal with the diversity of state leaders, and administrative skills. "I think I've demonstrated here that I can take a plan and implement it," he said. Since the leave was for only one year, there would be no "loss of continuity."

Continuity was maintained under acting president Dr. Russell Warren, vice president for academic affairs, with Dr. Robert Shapiro, dean of the College of Letters and Sciences, serving as vice president and Dr. Carl Harter, associate dean of the College of Letters and Sciences, acting as dean of the college. "Since Dr. Warren was a bachelor, it made housing easier," Carrier said. The board resolved to let the Carriers keep the president's house during his leave, and rented Warren an apartment.

But the board's generosity also led to problems. Both the Carriers had longed to redecorate "Oakview," and used Carrier's year away for that opportunity. Neither had ever felt comfortable with the ornate and luxurious style left by Mrs. Marvin Poster, from whom the University Foundation bought the house. For example, Mrs. Carrier's bathroom had a sunken tub beside a full window next to the garden. One wall was completely mirrored and small statuettes lined the edge of the tub. Mirrors also defined one wall of the den downstairs where the other walls were papered with silver and red graphic designs. The Carriers had longed for a lighter, airy look to welcome guests, plus renovation of less functional areas. The renovation costs raised an uproar from some faculty and public. Nevertheless, Edith Carrier, who had majored in art in college, dedicated her year to redesigning the interior to improve its function and create a handsome setting for official social occasions. JMU's first lady arranged and presided over so many events that she wanted the house to give guests a favorable opinion of JMU. Soon the residence reflected the Carriers' warmth and style.

After Carrier's return from CIT, they hosted frequent guests from the community and all over the world. "Oakview" might be the setting for a poolside supper to honor the student senate, a buffet supper for the faculty senate, a luncheon for the Irish ambassador, or a formal dinner for any other visiting dignitary. Louise Heeb, coordinator of special programs for the office of the president, recalled one month at "Oakview" included hosting "a reception for Senator John Warner, a dinner honoring artist P. Buckley Moss, a dinner for officers of the Student Government Association, a social for the Women's Club, and an afternoon tea for members of the Bluestone Society—in addition to the myriad events they [the Carriers] had to attend."

Before serving the Irish ambassador, Heeb called the State Department for guidelines. "I also got a book just coming off the press on protocol that they suggested," she said. Heeb always recognized Edith Carrier's indispensable role, saying, "Her value as first lady is to bring the University community the balance that is there when an outstanding couple serve as its leaders. In her way she is just as important to this school as Dr. Carrier."

Heeb also remembered varied challenges:

> One year—it had to be 1989—Mark Warner was assistant to the president and I worked under him. Dr. Carrier wanted to have a meal for the Board of Visitors at a football game between JMU and William and Mary in Williamsburg. And of course, as he always does, he wanted to do everything right, so he needed a tail-gate [type of party]. That complicated things because they left here on Friday and the tailgate wouldn't be until Saturday at noon.
>
> So I got boxes—not quite as big as a shoebox—and prepared them with a roll, one bag of potato chips, one bag of pickles and olives, one brownie, a purple napkin, plastic flatware, and Mark was to add a piece of chicken, a container of coleslaw, and baked beans. Now the baked beans was the story.
>
> I had a good baked beans recipe I had done in my crockpot. So I prepared the beans here in my kitchen, put 'em in the crockpot all ready and cooked them to the point where all he had to do was

plug it in that night before he went to bed and cook them all night long. So we managed baked beans for twenty-four people! Every time he got up during the night he was to stir them—he and his wife did, and I think they still use the recipe.

From "tailgates" to more elaborate menus, served on linen using Waterford crystal with sterling silver, Heeb managed to bring a special panache to any affair originating from the president's office. The last year of Madison College, she received the first Award of Merit from the Madison College Women's Club.

As promised, Carrier returned to JMU at the end of his year's leave. He had worked the necessary miracle of putting CIT in financial and organizational order. He dismissed the hoopla accorded his first day back on campus saying, "This is my job. This is what I do, how I make my living. So it isn't strange when, on April 1, I told the Board of Visitors I would come back to do my job that I show up at 8 o'clock in the morning to do my job. And it isn't a media event; it's exactly what I said I would do. As usual, I couldn't find a parking space," he added with a grin. "I probably have a ticket, but it's a CIT car, so they can tow it."

In one respect, however, he returned a lesser man than when he left. Surgery on his jaw in late December left him about thirty-five pounds leaner. "For those of you with a weight problem, I have a recommendation," he said, his voice still husky. "Just wire your mouth shut for six weeks." His obvious delight at the spring homecoming spilled over into his commentary on how well Dr. Warren had done: "Dr. Warren was doing such a good job I was afraid that any day I'd get a telegram saying 'Things are going well at JMU. Stay where you are.' I was making sure Dr. Warren didn't get the full recognition he deserved by getting the 'acting' removed from his job," Carrier joked.

He presented Warren with a gold Constitution medal developed for the JMU bicentennial. Then the two men held each other's hands in a long, firm gesture of regard while 300 faculty members rose to a standing ovation. In his subsequent address, Carrier reminded the audience that what made JMU distinct was not buildings or salaries or equipment or any concrete item. He said, "What sets Madison apart is passion—passion for James Madison University and passion for greatness. . . . It was easy for me to return."

Certainly Carrier's passion burned as hotly as before. Professor of psychology Dr. David Hanson summed up the atmosphere at the close of the decade: "The 1980s saw the American hostages in Iran released, a tremendous military build-up in tandem with a large tax reduction to create the nation's largest deficit ever, the Iran-Contra scandal, Oliver North, Star Wars talk, Gorbachev's peace initiatives [even talk] of dismantling the Berlin Wall and reunification of Germany, the most serious stock market crash since 1929, an ever-increasing

Celebratory moments became a common sight for the men's soccer team in 1989. They posted a 15-3-3 season and competed in the NCAA tournament. (Photo: '89 *Bluestone*)

drug problem across the nation, and the largest earthquake in the San Francisco area since the turn of the century. At JMU President Ronald Carrier has plans underway for a College of Applied Sciences and Technology."

As Dr. Warren said when Carrier returned from CIT, "I think he has had an opportunity to see a glimpse of the future and bring it back here, and in that sense help JMU's curriculum." That curriculum for the future would soon emerge—to mixed reviews.

Shortly after Dr. Carrier's arrival on campus, technology would take on a new emphasis, culminating in his plans for the new ISAT campus. Shown here (circa 1972) a student works on one of JMU's first computers, the legendary and popular IBM 1130 Computing System, first introduced in 1965 with an addressable memory of between 8K and 16K. (Photo: *Images of James Madison University 1908–1983*)

BUILDINGS MARK VISIBLE CHANGE. From the original two buildings in 1909, eighty-nine new ones had appeared—fourteen during the '80s decade. Initially, Maury and Jackson halls had met all academic and residence needs, including a dorm apartment for the first president and his wife. But by the century's last decade, the campus encompassed twenty-six residence halls, seventeen Greek houses, forty-eight academic buildings, and a president's home nearby. And the campus boasted the only school arboretum in the state.

Student change was no less visible as the school entered the '90s. The early student body, primarily young girls from small towns and farms seeking a year or two of teaching before marriage, represented the conservative, working-class values of the time. The 1990s campus drew a totally different and diverse population. Now primarily from affluent suburban and urban areas, students of the '90s, male and female, sought careers. Coeds closing the century expected roles beyond housewife and mother.

Yet the rural landscape that girls early in the century longed to leave behind now drew city dwellers. Bob Brummer ('89) endorsed the school's setting amid mountains and fields: "Because it's out in the country, it makes it seem like more of a campus. It's not like in a city where you have to stop and ask 'Is that building part of our campus?'" Not that city lights didn't still attract. As Ken Ashton ('86) said, "Tech's down the road; UVA's down the road; D.C. is two hours away—it's easy to roadtrip anywhere."

Chapter
Twenty-one

"Keep the customer happy"
(1989–1992)

JMU was still a school for women, but not exclusively. In 1990 it was 55.6 percent female. Unlike the keep-off-the-grass campus at the beginning, the modern lawn invites (left) sitting, sun-bathing, and recreation. Right: Women present no fading-violet image, and hold their own in class, in lines, or with graduation honors. (Photos: JMU Special Collections)

Coach "Lefty" Driesell (seated in center), one of college basketball's all-time coaching legends, reviews game strategy with his team. Driesell was hired as JMU's men's basketball coach after leaving the University of Maryland. He coached the Dukes for nine seasons, from 1988–97, and had a 159-111 record. He led the team to the NCAA Tournament in 1994 when the Dukes won the Colonial Athletic Association (CAA) championship and to the National Invitation Tournament in 1990, '91, '92, and '93. JMU played in the CAA title game six times under Driesell, and he was CAA coach of the year in 1989–90 and 1991–92. (Photo: JMU Sports Media Relations)

A headline on January 3, 1990, in the Norfolk *Virginian-Pilot* splashed the school's impact across the front page: "JMU Is Winning Popularity Contest." The article reported Laura A. Hunt's ('90) dilemma in choosing a college as typical. Accepted by both William and Mary and JMU, she was torn between the former's reputation for academic rigor and the latter's "friendly professors, homey atmosphere, and picturesque Shenandoah Valley campus."

She chose JMU, she recalled during her senior year, because "I felt like I *should* go to William and Mary, but deep down I *wanted* to go the JMU . . . I was more comfortable at JMU. I don't regret my decision at all."

The once small-town teachers college had become Virginia students' favorite. Thirty-five percent of those taking the Scholastic Aptitude Test sent their scores to JMU. That was more than to any other college in the Commonwealth, although JMU was smaller than several. Surging applications meant that, although JMU's best freshmen may have scored no better than before, there were more high scores. *U.S. News & World Report* magazine ranked JMU second in overall quality of its freshman class out of 148 southern regional colleges and universities surveyed. JMU also stood sixth in the percentage of entering freshmen remaining to graduate.

Carrier's original adage, "Treat the student like a customer and keep the customer happy," held them on campus through four years. Student comfort remained a priority, from social life to dorm styles to dining options. *Virginian-Pilot* reporter Thomas Boyer pointed out, "JMU's food service is the envy of college administrators. . . . Students uniformly praise the lobster they get once a year, the steak available once a week, and the junk-food snacks offered at odd hours during exam periods." Leisure time was enhanced by 220 student organizations, a sports arena suitable for rock concerts, plus big-time basketball under the controversial but nationally known Lefty Driesell.

Dubbed "Generation X" by former Canadian career counselor David Cannon, students of the '90s possessed a new set of values, new ways to process information, new attitudes toward life. Cannon's label, borrowed from rock singer Billy Idol or writer Douglas Coupland, stuck through the decade. His assessment forced professors to question traditional ways of teaching.

"Generation Xers expect the right answers, the facts, crystal-clear procedures. They want to know 'how to' and they want to know it right now," wrote Cannon in the Winter 1991 issue of the *Journal of Career Planning and Placement*. Growing up with computers and MTV, they found anything boring to be an absolute anathema. "Research" meant choosing sources from lists provided by the professor, not compiling their own lists. They wanted set steps to follow.

While Xers might have difficulty choosing a major, their ultimate career goals were high end—broadcast journalism, international affairs, corporate consulting. Raised in fairly affluent households where both parents worked, their salary expectations often exceeded reality and fear of failure was great. Postponing entering the "real world" as long as possible, many stretched their college days into a fifth year.

Emotionally, students from Generation X developed "a well-managed shell," said Cannon. They tried to convey a confident, in-control image no matter how close to a breakdown. Yet they really needed frequent feedback, and they craved personal approval and reinforcement.

At JMU, fifty-five professors attended a workshop in October 1991 to explore the challenges of teaching "Generation X" students. They probed interdisciplinary studies and the "switched-on classroom."

Assistant directors of JMU's Office of Career Services Mary Morsch and Bruce Matthias recognized the significant shift in student needs over the past two decades. They worked to "meet the students halfway, to key into the things that make sense to them," said Morsch. And new ways of communicating were one key.

Psychology head Dr. James Couch picked up on the trend. Enthusiastically demonstrating his department's new equipment, he prompted a challenge from Dr. Carrier to develop an electronic classroom. The idea was to meld the latest

Technology came wholesale to JMU. The sixty-five-seat planetarium with a thirty-foot dome was established in 1975, then upgraded in 1985, pictured here, with $80,000 worth of automation and auxiliary projection equipment. Elsewhere on campus, professors abandoned slide projectors for PowerPoint, and renovated classrooms accommodated needs from wiring to screens. (Photos: JMU 1993 Viewbook)

By 1991, "Shoot Yourself" became a popular feature of every *Bluestone*. Students arrayed themselves in wacky ways and shot a photo that meant something to the participants, but often left readers mystified. (Photo: '91 *Bluestone*)

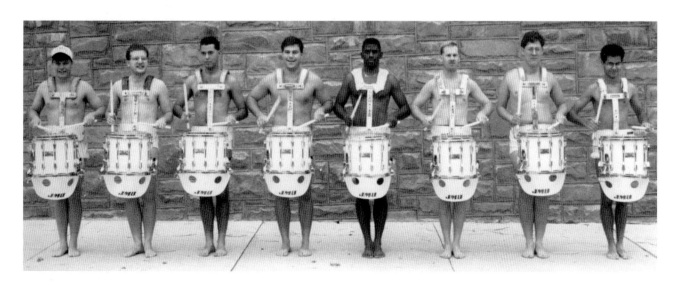

Fears that technology would erode student-professor relationships proved unfounded. Professors remained accessible in labs, offices, and studios as the encounter between art professor Masako Miyata Zapton and a student shows here. (Photos: JMU 1993 Viewbook)

Operating on the principle that a total learning village could produce a technology-savvy workforce, in 1989 the Virginia General Assembly made an unprecedented advance of $4.1 million for JMU to purchase 110 acres east of I-81 for a new College of Integrated Science and Technology. JMU was one of the first universities approved for the creation of the type of college that lawmakers considered essential to keep Virginia in the global economic forefront. Shown here is construction of Carrier Drive over I-81 and the ISAT/CS building. To take advantage of the free publicity afforded JMU by I-81, Carrier Drive is renamed James Madison University Boulevard on the VDOT sign on this bridge/overpass (see the top photo on page 270). (Photo: '96 *Bluestone*)

computer, laser, and compact disc technology. Couch formed a committee to design an interactive classroom with push-button student-teacher communication and wide access to information. Department members Dr. Michael Stoloff, Dr. Charles Harris, and Dr. James Benedict participated, as did Tom Bonadeo, director of technical services, and Dale Hulvey, associate director of academic computing. Their proposal was "a classroom which will include state-of-the-art technology, will be a model for the twenty-first century, and will be the first such classroom in the Commonwealth of Virginia."

In 1988 Governor Gerald Baliles had created a Greater University Commission to answer the question "How can Virginia . . . change within its colleges and universities so they will be ready to meet the demands of life in the twenty-first century?" JMU responded. President Carrier told the Board of Visitors that adding students by simply enlarging programs lacked imagination. He asserted new styles of teaching were needed to respond to the demands of the new century. He knew classroom excellence was key to JMU's success. He said, "The miracle occurs each day as faculty members turn on a student to a new idea, the excitement of learning, or a greater self-image."

From the beginning of his tenure at JMU, Carrier had determined to stay on the cutting edge by not reacting to, but anticipating student needs. He envisioned a College of Integrated Science and Technology as an essential

component of any campus heading into the next century. By 1991 he had persuaded the State Council of Higher Education for Virginia (SCHEV) to approve the new college. Wasting no time, on February 22, 1992, Carrier introduced Dr. Lyle C. Wilcox to the faculty as the first provost of CISAT. Wilcox vowed "to make obvious the value of CISAT to every other department."

His vow was a large order—perhaps an impossible one. Many professors in the liberal arts questioned whether the new college diluted the value of academic standards, whether CISAT would ever be more than a glorified trade school. They also questioned the expense, openly concerned over whether their own programs were being shortchanged. Electronic classrooms or not, the bluestone buildings lining the quad housed cramped offices and classrooms. Limited space limited options for creative teaching. Architectural projections for the new facility set across I-81 seemed light years from the original campus. The faculty senate sponsored an open meeting and panel discussion on the proposed college. The discussion did not quell doubts.

Yet the public perception remained that JMU had to be doing something right. Bumper stickers on cars proudly proclaimed allegiance with phrases such as "My kid and my money go to JMU" or "JMU That's Who!" or "JMU/THE CHOSEN FEW." Alumni giving at 34.1 percent lifted the school to second nationally in 1991. And in the *U.S. News & World Report* special issue on "America's Best Colleges," JMU ranked eleventh regionally overall and third in academic reputation. In addition, campus publications and personnel garnered frequent national acclaim. The quarterly alumni magazine *Montpelier*, edited by Pam Brock, and "A Campus Guide," designed by Wayne Liskey and typeset by Mag Sandridge, took national awards. Dr. Elizabeth Neatrour, professor of Russian and French, received one of the eleven Outstanding Faculty Awards in Virginia (of which Dr. Ralph Cohen had been JMU's first recipient in 1987). And Dr. Carrier was named 1991's Outstanding Virginian.

In spite of the economy's ups and downs, awards multiplied during the decade. Between the '91–'92 semesters, ninety-three grants were awarded. Among those in the spotlight were Dr. Alexander Gabbin, Dr. Brenda Ryals, and Dr. Dan Downey. Gabbin, an associate professor of accounting, became the first recipient of the Adolph Coors Foundation Minority Professorship in JMU's College of Business—part of a $250,000 grant from the Coors Foundation to support minority faculty and students. Ryals, an associate professor of speech pathology, won $100,000 from the National Institutes of Health to bring her total to more than $400,000 for her research on hearing recovery. Downey, an associate professor of chemistry, established the school as a regional site for Research Experiences for Undergraduates with a joint grant for $95,000 from REU and the National Science Foundation.

The University's first postdoctoral student, Dr. Ho Gun Rhie, worked with biology professor Dr. Doug Dennis on a genetic project to clone protein used

ROYAL DUKES, ROYAL RECOGNITION

For women's games at Harrisonburg Teachers College in 1924, the five-member Galek Players chanted, "Got pep, give pep, get pep!" In 1994, the James Madison University Marching Royal Dukes, 320 strong, carried on the tradition with a regal flourish that won national recognition. The John Phillip Sousa Foundation tallied votes of all NCAA member band directors to name JMU's marching band the best in the USA. Receiving the Sudler Trophy for 1994 placed the school on a roll of distinguished previous winners, including the universities of Michigan, Illinois, and Texas, Ohio State, Northwestern, and UCLA.

Under the leadership of Dr. Pat Rooney, the Marching Royal Dukes was the first non–Division I school to be so honored and also one of the youngest programs in competition. Started in 1972, the marching band was part of a series of innovations for Madison College at the start of Ronald E. Carrier's presidency. As Carrier primed the school in new directions, campus buzz centered on the first Faculty Senate, new open dorms, and Coach Chalice McMillan's first football team. The football team wouldn't post a victory until the following year, 1973, but the band's halftime show proved a winner from the start.

Director Malcolm Harris had recruited 100 members during the summer. By September, practice paid off as the Madison Marching Band took first prize in its first competition at the Shenandoah County Bicentennial Parade in Woodstock, Virginia.

Two years later, new director Ken Moulton had 115 members and added eight flag girls performing precision drills plus a color guard. Whether the football team won or lost, the band held spectators in their seats at halftime to watch the marching band perform. They also drew fans along parade routes and to an increasing number of events elsewhere.

Although Moulton moved on, Mike Davis came on board in 1977 and the band continued to attract students and spectators. "Major Mike" directed on campus during the school term, and worked at Disney World through the summer. "He enhanced the program with sparkling choreography and fuller sound," according to current director Rooney. Membership doubled and Davis invited fellow Disney World director Rooney to judge a band contest at JMU.

Rooney was so impressed with the band, the campus, and the area that he applied for Davis's position when Major Mike joined Disney full-time. Appointed to the faculty in 1982, Pat Rooney accelerated the Dukes' rapid stride to the front of collegiate marching bands.

"I saw a sleeping giant, so much potential. There was always the feeling something exciting was going on. The school was creating its own history, not steeped in tradition. Of course, I felt then it might be the first step to a bigger school, but what I didn't know was that JMU would be that bigger school," laughs Rooney.

Over the next two decades his marching performers not only reached an optimum 325 pieces but also expanded audiences. They've entertained during halftime shows for the National Football League teams, been featured with Walt Disney Productions, marched in two Presidential Inaugural parades, played at the Silverdome in Pontiac, Michigan, and the Hoosierdome in Indianapolis. In 1997, they welcomed the New Year in Monaco and in 2000 in Greece.

Asked to assess the magnetic draw for so many talented students, Rooney says, "If you ask the kids what they like best about being in the band, they may say the social part—travel, hanging together. We're small enough to keep a feeling of family. But I think the real appeal is being part of something that's excellent. Just as we've developed a trademark style, a characteristic sound and look that's recognizable now, there's also a pride that can't be denied. It's a thrill to do what we're doing."

The thrill is reciprocal, shared by audiences as well as performers.

The Marching Band achieved international fame when it played cities in Europe, including Genoa (bottom) and New Year's Eve in Monaco (top) in 1998. (Photo: JMU Photo Lab)

Professors winning national recognition crossed the spectrum of concentrations. In 1991–92 they included (top left) Dr. Alexander Gabbin in the College of Business, (bottom left) Dr. Brenda Ryals in Speech Pathology, and (top right) Dr. Dan Downey in Chemistry. (Photos: JMU Photo Lab)

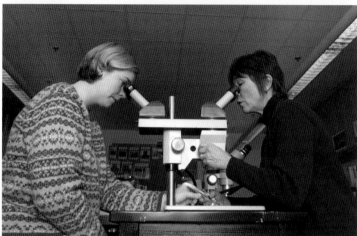

in making plastic. Dennis had cloned a gene in 1988 that led to a bacterial, biodegradable plastic. Using Dennis's gene, researchers at the University of Michigan introduced it into a plant that produced plastic. In January 1993, *Time Magazine* named the Dennis-Michigan result as one of the ten best science advances of 1992. By spring of 1994, Dennis's work earned a permanent exhibit at the Smithsonian and JMU earned a patent that December.

Colleagues across the campus hailed the value of Dennis's work. Environmentalists hailed the ramifications of a plastic that was biodegradable. Business majors recognized the spin-off for new industries.

Recycling had come to the campus in the '90s, and every dorm held bins for aluminum and plastic, every copy machine aligned boxes for used paper. Erin Goewey ('92) became JMU's first recycling coordinator. Under a prior contract, Harrisonburg had agreed to take all JMU's materials and, in return, provide the university steam produced from burned materials to heat its buildings. Recycling became a win-win situation.

Advances in science permeated every aspect of campus life—but one. Telling accurate time by campus clocks was still a challenge. In Wilson Hall a

Above: The thirteenth anniversary of Logan's Run in 1989 found forty-seven JMU students and one alumni on the thirty-four-hour, 150-mile relay from the nation's Capitol to the steps of Rockingham Memorial Hospital in Harrisonburg. The event posted $8,000 for the hospital and pleased the hospital liaison Merv Webb, who is pictured on the extreme right. Webb, who earned his master's from JMU in '83, now serves as vice president of development at RMH and Logan's Run endures today. (Photo: JMU Special Collections)

clock's hands might point to 2:10, while in Keezell clocks read 4:15, and down campus in Godwin, a single clock with four faces exposed two different times to passersby. In the early days, building clocks had been connected to a central time control in Harrison Hall, with the entire campus set together. But over the years, the wires frayed and broke and the clocks slowed down.

Estimates for replacing the old cable conduit proved too costly, so a substitute system was adopted. In 1992, director of maintenance Phillip Deane projected that every building on campus would soon have its own system. Slowly, old cables were bypassed and new clocks, individually set, appeared building by building. The result rendered telling time still an adventure—proof positive that modern science can't always be counted on. To some, those clocks moving irritatingly out of sync symbolized an impending schism of the faculty.

Juli Henner, JMU's 1992–93 female athlete of the year, placed second in the 1,500 meters in the 1996 U.S. Olympic Track and Field Trials and ran at the Atlanta Olympic Games as the first JMU athlete to compete at the Olympic level for the U.S. At JMU, Henner was the first female athlete to earn Division I All-American honors in track. She finished tenth in the 1,500 meters at the 1992 NCAA Championships, was a two-time All-East performer in both the 1,500 meters and the indoor mile (1991, 1992), and won Colonial Athletic Association championships in the 800 (1991) and 1,500 (1991, 1992).

P ARENTS WHOSE CARS SPORTED "My kid and my money go to JMU" were not kidding. Education costs had soared, although at James Madison University tuition remained one of the lowest in Virginia. During the '90s, in-state dorm students shelled out $8,994 a year, while those entering from beyond state borders paid $13,662. Commonwealth grants and assistance, plus Federal Pell Grants and student loans, eased the burden somewhat—as did a long list of JMU Foundation scholarships from every college within the university.

The '96–'97 semesters saw 3,544 students working around campus to help pay their expenses. The average student employee worked ten to fifteen hours per week—hours that forced many of them to add a fifth year to their college days. Jobs in the food-service locations drew between 500 to 700 students each year. Retail services, including the bookstore, became the second-place employer, with the recreation center and police cadets close behind. The only requirements were that each student employee be degree seeking and enrolled full time.

Students not only worked for themselves, but also expanded their personal horizons with volunteer jobs. Dr. Cecil Bradfield's "Seminar in Appalachia" moved from the classroom to Red Bird Center in Clay County, Kentucky—one of the poorest parts of the nation. Students who crossed the area's swinging bridges also crossed cultural bridges from middle-class comfort into poverty. Sixty percent of the county's population existed below the official poverty level.

Shannon May ('95) participated in her sophomore year and said, "I had no conception. I had no idea."

Students held jobs on and off campus— from Carrier Library to D-Hall and Dukes, to downtown Jess's, to Wal-Mart. Left: Sarah Hoyt counted herself lucky to work the information desk in the Campus Center for its central location and flexible schedule. Right: Rob Toomer honed future job skills behind the camera at WHSV-TV, the local ABC-affiliate station. (Photos: '94 *Bluestone*)

She felt her own public education system had fallen short in imparting knowledge that such subcultures existed within this country.

Top and bottom left: Student volunteers reached out to enrich the community—from tutoring, working with the elderly, cleaning roadsides, aiding the SPCA, to painting murals. Alpha Phi Omega, a coed service fraternity, and the Center for Service Learning, a voluntary service organization for the local community, lined up opportunities. (Photos: '96 & '97 *Bluestone*)

Bottom right: Hundreds of students opted for alternative trips during spring break that provided service to those in need. Brian Tetro ('95) and a friend helped rebuild in the Hurricane Andrew–devastated area of Florida. As Paula Pasicvnyk ('94) said, "Service is not a duty or a chore; it is a way of life." (Photo: '94 *Bluestone*)

Other students had alternate eye-opening experiences. Some devoted their spring break to helping build houses with Habitat for Humanity. As a headline in *The Breeze* put it on March 2, 1998, "Students 'spring' at a chance to help others during break." Students also volunteered in local nursing homes and mentored younger students in public schools.

In *The Breeze* article on alternative spring breaks, 100 students had signed up to help others—paying $195 a week for the privilege. Rich Harris, coordinator of Community-Service Learning, said, "These trips are life-changing . . . create a passion for life-long service ethics." Destinations included New Orleans, Puerto Rico, Chicago, and Madison County, Florida. Senior Stacy Grosh felt her experience helping with flood relief in the spring of 1995 had been unforgettable. "You're getting outside of your comfort zone. It opens your mind to differences . . . to so many new ideas through service," she said.

Senior Sheena Mendenhall, trip leader for a 1998 group going to Chicago's South Side, spoke of her prior year's work with HIV children in Miami: "It was incredible to me. I've never worked with children who had so much down in their lives and were still living so much and so happy."

A new JMU mission statement in the late 1990s declared, "We are committed to preparing students to be educated and enlightened citizens who will lead productive and meaningful lives." Certainly alternative opportunities strengthened that goal.

"Doing good," however, did not mean acting solemn. Campus groups combined fundraising for good causes with fun along the way. In 1991, one appeal brought every organization on campus to its aid. Angela Justis came to Alpha Sigma Alpha seeking help for her mother, whose life depended on receiving a bone-marrow transplant. Rene Giese ('92) formed a small committee to head a campus-wide drive to raise the necessary $90,000. The group stuffed mailboxes, posted flyers, and urged friends to be involved.

Soon every organization responded to the appeal, "Help raise money for Angela's mother." The Ski Club donated eighty-five percent of its traditional Ski Swap proceeds. The Cycling Team rode on stationary bikes for twelve hours to bring in dollars. Plus the cyclists' raffle to fund their uniforms and bikes ended with a three-to-one split—Angela's mother on the high end of it. Even "couch potatoes" joined the effort by doing *nothing*. They solicited money by simply sitting on the patio all day. Gen-X opened its collective heart.

But if the generation united in giving, individually its members moved to different drummers. The colleges comprised vastly diverse populations. From living space, to music, to studies, groups formed subgroups around interests that differed widely, with dress often the clue to alignments. Button-down still marked business majors, and tie-dye reappeared on artists. Yet all spoke a "slanguage" of Gen-X expressions.

In women's field hockey, the 1994 Dukes had a dream season, winning an NCAA title championship and making the Dukes the top team in the nation that year. The Dukes outscored North Carolina in a dramatic penalty-stroke "shoot-out" to win the NCAA title on a warm November day in Boston. Top left: In the game's first half, Dukes celebrate Carole Thate's goal that evened the score with 1:33 remaining in the half. The game remained tied 1-1 through two rounds of sudden-death fifteen-minute overtime play and was decided by a series of five penalty strokes, alternating, with a player from each team taking a shot. Top right: Duke goalie Heather Colbert opened the shootout with a kick save on UNC's first attempt; then Thate connected on JMU's initial try to put the Dukes up 1-0. Each team scored on the next two strokes, with Renee Ranere and Kelley Bloomer connecting for JMU, resulting in a 3-2 JMU lead. UNC just missed on its next attempt, and it was left to Gwen Stoltzfus to give the Dukes an insurmountable 4-2 lead in the tie-breaker and to give the school its first NCAA title. Bottom left: Senior Eileen Arnaldo played the entire NCAA tournament with a cast on her right hand. Right: Dukes celebrate the win. Bottom right: Cristy Morgan (right) coached JMU to five NCAA tournaments in field hockey and the 1994 NCAA National Championship.

As Jennifer Johnston ('91) wrote in *The Bluestone*:

> The first and most obvious JMU-Universal terminology deals with the co-mingling and mating habits of the sexes. Certainly everyone has been guilty of "scooping and scanning" the aisles of D-Hall, whether in general or with a specific target in mind. Seeing that certain someone who has that certain something unconsciously earns them the title of "scope."
>
> Once a plan to initiate further contact has formulated, the scanner becomes . . . a "scammer." The scammer's schemes may eventually lead to a date, but more than likely, it will only lead to a "hook-up" (or multiple hook-ups), which may be broadly interpreted depending upon personal experience.

Johnston went on to translate the party scene where "helmets"—guys who weren't smooth and didn't talk to girls—hung out. Parties with numbers of helmets were known as a "Helmet Fest." Terms for drinking included the universal language roiled up from other generations and milieus: "getting wasted," "getting rocked," "hammered," "plowed," "totaled," "toasted," "obliterated," or plain drunk. Groups also evoked slang IDs. People who were environmental or pro-Earth activists were called "granola," or possibly "crunchy." Harrisonburg was easily shortened to "the 'Burg" and parents to "the 'rents." And the point of all their days at JMU was to make students "good to go" in the outside world.

The decade of the '90s also brought big-name music acts to campus. When Live played the Convo Center in April of '96, students from other schools traveled to JMU rather than the other way around. Students camped out to get tickets to see Matthew Sweet perform at the Convo in September '95. Few parents recognized names like Eddie from Ohio, Triggerfish, or Das EFX, but such names held students on campus and attracted others.

Along with music, the mid-'90s resounded to the bang of hammers and the grind of earth-moving machines. CISAT began with massive trailers arriving and setting up for classrooms across I-81. Mathew Keller ('97), who became an ISAT* Distinguished Graduate in 1997's first class, recalled that when he initially visited JMU, program coordinator Dr. Richard Roberds had nothing to show him "but told me their vision for the college and it was one that I could believe in."

*Before the College of Integrated Science and Technology, CISAT began with programs in Integrated Science and Technology, ISAT.

Keller continued:

> The first year we were known as the 'weird techy people' in the trailer park on the other side of the Interstate. The program attracted a lot of students; however, it held on to a special kind of student—students that could see the vision, students that were not afraid to try something different.
>
> We all had our doubts at the beginning with no course descriptions or even a building. But I feel this first class proved we were special. Four years of being guinea pigs let us form a unique and close bond from our shared experiences. We also became close to the faculty. This program taught many things, but the greatest learning experiences were not in the text books but in being part of something new and working to make it the best it could be.

Construction for the first CISAT building started during the summer of 1995, and its dedication was held on October 3, 1997—four months too late for Keller's class. The pomp and ceremony even included a bagpiper. JMU alumnus Peter Wood marched from the top floor to the bottom piping a Scottish air to install good spirits throughout the 92,000-square-foot facility. Dr. Jackson Ramsey, who succeeded Wilcox as dean of CISAT, welcomed a crowd of several hundred to the first building on the East Campus. Housing nine science labs, fifteen classrooms, an auditorium, meeting rooms, and offices for faculty and staff, it was only a beginning. Soon a Student Services Building followed, plus residence halls for 850 students. The spring of 1998 brought construction on a second academic building, scheduled to open in the year 2000. The "weird techies" were there to stay.

The West Campus also pulsed with construction and renovation. On September 29, 1994, even as ground was broken for the new student activities building described as a bridge to connect the West and East campuses, the West Campus drew national attention. Under the leadership of Dr. Joanne Gabbin, the Furious Flower Conference, September 29 to October 1, drew thirty-four acclaimed and emerging African-American poets to JMU and an audience of 1,300. Later called poetry's "coup of the century," the event spun lifelines into the future. Dr. Gabbin, English professor and director of the honors program, subsequently published a book in 2003 titled *Furious Flower: African-American Poetry from the Black Arts Movement to the Present*, and also established the Furious Flower Poetry Center to honor Pulitzer Prize-winning poet Gwendolyn Brooks and attract students and scholars who wish to research African American poetry. In 1998, Gabbin released a four-tape video anthology of that historic gathering which sold well and is now in libraries and English departments of more than 400 colleges and universities across the nation.

The Furious Flower Poetry Conference of 1994 became a watershed for African-American poetry, drawing thirty-four nationally acclaimed poets and more than 1,300 participants. Its title derived from Gwendolyn Brooks's lines, "The time/cracks into furious flower. Lifts its face/all unashamed. And sways in wicked grace." Top left: Dr. Gabbin, conference organizer, and Gwendolyn Brooks. Top right: Amiri Baraka and Sonia Sanchez greet one another. Bottom left: Bernice Johnson Reagon recites a poem. Bottom right: Clyde Taylor talks with the audience. A second Furious Flower conference was held in 2004. (Photos by C. B Claiborne, courtesy of Dr. Joanne Gabbin)

One professor, requesting anonymity, commented that he never felt the need to move to another school, for JMU was always a different place, always evolving into something bigger and better. That professor's sentiments, however, may have been a minority view as growth burgeoned in two directions, carving new roles at CISAT and shifting alignments of existing programs elsewhere. Both directions drew critics.

In spite of his clear success in lifting JMU from a small, regional college to a nationally ranked university, President Carrier came under fire from his faculty. The first serious concern was prompted by a curriculum proposal from CISAT. The curriculum committee of the faculty senate turned it down—a decision based (depending on perspective) either on merit or on jealousy between the programs. Traditional science departments felt they did a good job and saw little need for the new college. So when the Board of Visitors responded by giving Carrier extraordinary privilege for directing the curriculum, faculty members objected. Many agreed with English professor Robin McNallie, who felt Carrier had been accorded "overreaching authority over the curriculum, an authority traditionally belonging to faculty."

Carrier and those supporting his position, both within and without the campus, saw the matter differently. In their view the university was programmatically anticipating and responding to concerns regarding higher education that were being raised within the state—through a committee appointed by Governor Gerald Baliles examining "Virginia's University of the 21st Century"—and nationally. In a report published by the American Association of State Colleges and Universities, a blue ribbon panel appointed by President Bill Clinton called for new programs in applied science, mathematics, technology, and communication to address a "crisis in science education." Carrier, who had to answer to the General Assembly, saw CISAT and the proposed new curriculum as indispensable foundations for JMU's continued ascendancy in the twenty-first century.

On behalf of the administration on January 13, 1995, Dr. Bethany Oberst, vice president for academic affairs, proclaimed at a faculty meeting that changes could not be accomplished without "stresses and strain" and continued, "It is time now for some further steps. Some of these steps are not pleasant but they are needed for the continued success of JMU. . . ."

Under a restructuring plan supported by the State Council of Higher Education and called "one of the best in the state," Oberst announced that JMU would eliminate four major positions: a vice president, two assistant vice presidents, and a college dean. In addition, the College of Letters and Sciences and the College of Communication and the Arts would merge into a single, yet-to-be named college. Furthermore, a major in physics would be eliminated.

By way of defending the decision to omit the physics major, Oberst pointed to a national study of instructional costs and productivity conducted by the University of Delaware which indicated, "the direct instructional cost per student in physics at JMU is $5,838, which is $2,109 above the average cost for comparable institutions. This excess beyond the national average is by far the greatest of any of the JMU departments." She added that most physics graduates were prepared for graduate school, not employment.

Dr. Jack Armistead held the dean's position that was to be eliminated. He was a popular English professor, and the faculty cried "foul." Colleagues also rallied to the defense of the physics department and its ten full-time faculty members. Although the department had averaged only five graduates a year for several years—while the biology department, by comparison, with a faculty of twenty, averaged ninety graduates annually during the same period—comparisons proved odious and the numbers irrelevant to many faculty. Traditionally, colleges support a comprehensive curriculum depending "on popular majors to offset the lower student-attracting programs, such as, in addition to physics, the studio arts, philosophy, and some foreign languages," said McNallie, recalling the events years later.

From Carrier's perspective, the faculty seemed unaware of the external world in which legislators had determined that schools must become demonstrably cost effective. Moreover, as he knew, the faculty did not have to face those legislators in Richmond to justify expenditures, nor coax grants from the private sector. Most faculty-parent discussions dealt with students, not finance.

What was happening at JMU, however, was besetting campuses nationwide. In a fundamental way, the curriculum debate challenged 2,000 years of western academic tradition. One side held that learning for the sake of learning needed no defense economically. The other supported marketable results. Article after article in the *Chronicle of Higher Education* and other publications reported that professors felt they were being sidelined as governing boards, presidents, and legislatures repeated calls for restructured institutions within limits of more cost-effective programs.

In 1991, the American Association of University Professors began blacklisting schools that violated the principles of shared governance. By 1998, the AAUP had cited Francis Marion University plus Lindenwood and Elmira Colleges for their presidents' making unilateral decisions of matters of curriculum and tenure procedures. They harked back to a 1966 "Statement on Government of Colleges and Universities" that laid out roles that trustees, administrators, professors, and students should play in "shared responsibility and cooperative action" for running institutions. Following historic patterns, the AAUP stated that professors should have primary authority over curriculum, research, and faculty status—overridden "only in exceptional circumstances."

JMU's administration felt that the explosion of knowledge and technology of the times rendered circumstances "exceptional." As Carrier saw it, he was looking to the next decades, maintaining his focus on the future. His perspective had moved from analog to digital and he expected no less of his faculty. He sought to anticipate the needs of generations *born* during his tenure.

Dr. Richard Whitman, dean of the College of Arts and Letters, recalled:

> The loyal opposition felt they had the best interests of the university at heart. A lot of people in the humanities don't see job placement as part of their purview. People should learn for the

love of learning and they should be there to assist them to satisfy that love of learning. But we're moving in the opposite direction. It's wonderful for someone to enjoy their experience here, but when they leave they should also be employable. I am sure that there are many faculties here that believe we have "dummied down" the curriculum, and we're moving in the direction of a trade school.

With the faculty and the administration at an impasse over control and content of the university's curriculum, tensions mounted. On many campuses a degree of tension inherent between the front office and classroom is productive. That between Carrier and the faculty had become corrosive, and even more so after Oberst's announcement in mid-January of 1995. The rift soon culminated in a faculty referendum taken on January 23 and 24. The results indicated that 197 faculty members circled "Yes" and 305 voted "No" to the statement: "As a JMU faculty member, I have confidence in the ability of President Ronald E. Carrier to responsibly lead James Madison University." Of the total 571 ballots distributed, fourteen were ruled invalid by the referendum committee, fourteen were abstentions, and forty-one faculty members declined to vote. The majority vote of no-confidence reflected a concern about the changes *and* the imperious, top-down manner in which the changes were offered.

Many faculty expected Carrier would resign, as had other college presidents after no-confidence votes—including former JMU dean Russell Warren at Altoona State following a similar referendum.

But those who thought they'd ousted the president had failed to understand Carrier. He remained determined to pursue his agenda for JMU, even as his leadership had been assailed, his pride injured. As one supporter (who requested anonymity) said, "It's a very difficult position—and a very lonely position—to make those kinds of changes at an institution when they're obviously not going to be supported by faculty members. It's a tough role to be in."

In response to the referendum, Carrier replied that he regretted the outcome, and he attributed the vote to the acute discomfort the faculty felt at the enormous transformations being required of higher education from outside economic and societal pressures. He said:

> It is the job of a college president to deal with these changes. At this point in my career, I could have easily avoided the controversy that JMU is now facing but I would not have been doing my job. I don't see the faculty action as a vote against what I have done at the university, but as a vote that represents a longing for a time past where the external challenges to higher education were non-existent, the demand for collaboration among departments purely voluntary, and campus government was conducted over coffee and confined to ivy walls.

Carrier should be applauded

After serving as JMU's president for 27 years, Ronald Carrier announced Wednesday he'll retire when his successor is hired or Dec. 31. More than 500 students, faculty, administrators, staff and alumni witnessed Carrier's 20-minute address.

Carrier never mentioned how he wants his presidency to be remembered during his speech. It's safe to say that was a smart move because when you've been in office as long as Carrier has, it's impossible to control how you will be remembered.

Faculty are quick to criticize him. In recent years, the faculty clashed with Carrier over restructuring in 1993 and the physics department in 1995. On Jan. 24, 1995, the faculty voted no confidence in "Carrier's ability to lead JMU responsibly," according to the Jan. 26, 1995 issue of *The Breeze.*

Some students are quick to point out his faults as well. "His reputation is grounded in his history or legacy, but since I've been here, his last years have been his least productive," senior Jason Robertson said in Thursday's *Breeze.*

It's natural for varying segments of this campus to remember JMU's fourth president for what they perceive he's done or not done.

However, it seems that nobody can, or wants to, remember any of the things Carrier did for this university before 1993.

The Breeze has been particularly hard on Carrier in the last five years for some of the progressive decisions he's made.

Yet it's not fair to look solely at Carrier's last five years when he's done so much for this university over the span of his tenure.

When Carrier arrived at Madison College in 1971, he had a progressive vision to transform a small school into a comprehensive university of distinction, but it was an uphill climb.

"From Day 1, Dr. Carrier had a clear vision for the future of James Madison," former college of education dean Robert Riggs said in 1986. "Initially, few supported his aspirations, but due to his courage, energy and managerial skills, his dreams have been realized."

"From Day 1, Dr. Carrier had a clear vision for the future of James Madison. . .,"

During Carrier's tenure, the school became a university, enrollment more than tripled, 19 degree programs were added, the annual operating budget skyrocketed from $9.1 million annually to its current $168 million, 37 buildings were built. Also, JMU has become one of *U.S. News & World Report's* Best Comprehensive Universities and the total number of faculty members jumped from 250 to 789.

Carrier didn't change; we did. He's done more for JMU than any single man or woman alive, and he's done it the same way for 27 years.

He should be commended for his hard work and dedication. We should stop whining and give this man his due. He's earned every bit of it.

Thank you, Uncle Ron.

The house editorial reflects the opinion of the editorial board which consists of the editor, managing editor and the opinion editor

An editorial and cartoon in *The Breeze,* courtesy of Donna Dunn.

Carrier's views were echoed three years later. The *Chronicle of Higher Education* opined in "Shared Governance Under Siege," on January 30, 1998, "If you want to draw a crowd to a faculty senate meeting, talk about pay, parking, or ousting the president. . . . The concept of professors' playing a role in running their institutions is a cherished idea, but it's under siege." The faculty referendum had marked the eve of Carrier's silver anniversary on campus. It should have been a year for accolades; it turned to a year of acrimony.

Following the vote, the Board of Visitors renewed Carrier's contract with a statement of support. Many JMU parents and alumni heard about or read the news of the no-confidence vote and the rift between the president and faculty with puzzlement. They ignored the issue and applauded Carrier with genuine enthusiasm whenever he spoke at orientation or graduation. Students still responded to his warmth in informal encounters—although those encounters diminished in number. Less and less of Carrier's time was free to roam the campus, poke into classrooms, or greet clusters of students on the lawn. More and more time was spent lobbying in Richmond or soliciting individual or corporate grants. To hold tuition costs level, he turned to the private sector for unprecedented amounts of money to supplement state funding. In 1997, he took a six-month leave to raise funds and left Dr. Linwood Rose at the helm of JMU. When he came back, he had generated less immediate income than he'd hoped, but had laid the groundwork for future bequests.

He returned, nonetheless, to finish his job, as he saw it, determined to enter the twenty-first century with a school ready to meet whatever the next hundred years demanded. Only those who knew him well, however, recognized the personal cost not only to himself, but also to Edith, of his decision to stay the course after the faculty's no-confidence vote.

Top: Dr. and Mrs. Carrier host a poolside supper for CISAT's first graduates in 1997. Bottom: Another of the frequent student receptions held at "Oakview," this one honoring the Senior Challenge, Class of '97. (Photos: Author)

W HEN RONALD CARRIER announced his retirement in the spring of 1998, there were those among the onlookers who wondered what would happen to "the JMU Way"—the sense of spirit permeating the campus—when he was gone. For almost three decades Carrier's name and that of the school were indelibly linked. Student member of the Board of Visitors Daniel Ciatti had once put it, "I know exactly where the JMU spirit originates. It comes from, in a sense it starts with, the president of James Madison University—Dr. Ronald Carrier." Ciatti continued during an interview for the 1994 edition of *101 of the Best Values in America's College and Universities*: "He has such an enthusiasm for the university and such an intense interest in the well being of all those who make up JMU that his sheer presence on campus drives that great JMU spirit." Ciatti expressed, perhaps, what many students and alumni must have thought over the years.

As the *Richmond Times-Dispatch* wrote in an article announcing the committee recommendation for Carrier's successor, "Ronald Carrier is the Cal Ripken of higher education." But this very success was what enabled him to leave. The university continued to garner top national rankings. No longer the small, predominately female teachers college Carrier assumed leadership of in 1971, JMU was now a major comprehensive university.

Graduates were making headlines nationwide. Dr. Marcia Angell ('60) edited the prestigious *New England Journal of Medicine*. Robert Christopher "Phoef" Sutton ('81) continued a career in Hollywood after making his name writing and producing the award-winning TV show *Cheers*. Movie producer and director Steve James ('77) toured with his extraordinary documentary *Hoop Dreams*. Space pioneer Elizabeth Wilson Gauldin ('50) led at NASA. NFL pros Charles Haley ('87), Gary Clark, and Scott Norwood ('82) collectively played in nine Super Bowls and won seven championship rings. In 1997, Sherman Dillard ('78) came back to move JMU's men's basketball into the NCAA once more. And in 1998 the National Teacher of the Year, Philip Bigler ('74), returned to address the first faculty meeting of the new session. On and on, the lists of notable JMU alumni lengthened.

Under Carrier's tenure, enrollment had increased from 4,041 to 13,714 with minority enrollment rising from 1.4 to eleven percent and male students from twenty-five to nearly forty-five percent. All this took place with an increased

In November 1999, Visiting Scholar Dr. Marcia Angell ('60), editor of the *New England Journal of Medicine*, dined with JMU President Rose. In a personal letter to emeritus faculty Dr. Crystal Theodore, Angell fondly recalled the value of the education she received at JMU: "Dr. William Mengebier was a great favorite of mine—we argued constantly but I learned a great deal from him. . . . Madison was unusual in the caliber of its faculty when I was there, despite its isolation. After I graduated I found I could hold my own with people who went to Harvard, Yale, Oxford, etc., because the faculty at Madison took teaching seriously. They didn't assume education would simply rub off on you by virtue of being thrown together with all the right people. I particularly remember Annette Wilcox (math), Martha Fodaski (literature), a tyrant named Marie Louise Bouget (English), and Raymond Dingledine ('There were five causes of the Civil War: List them'), and of course, you and David Diller (art). (Photo: JMU Photo Lab. Quote: Courtesy of Dr. Crystal Theodore)

quality of students. Average SAT scores for entering freshmen rose from 987 to 1,174. In addition, the Carrier decades added forty major facilities with a replacement value of $210 million. The full-time faculty and staff increased from 500 to 1,750 and the annual operating budget soared from $9.1 million to more than $200 million.

Not that Carrier had achieved all his goals. As he saw it, that moment could never arrive in his pursuit for "the Ultimate University." But his accomplishments had satisfied many.

Tributes followed his retirement announcement. A column in the *Richmond Times-Dispatch* quoted its former reporter Gail Nardi, who defended Carrier's record against the final years of discord between him and the faculty:

> In recent years, I've watched from a distance with disappointment that a lot of faculty members have made it their habit to take potshots at him. That's too bad because every one of us—and trust me, faculty members are no exception—has a bad day or parts of their personalities that are less attractive than others, and when someone has an oversized personality, that becomes exaggerated.

> But the fact is a lot of universities James Madison's size vanished over the past twenty-seven years—and James Madison thrived. And anyone who thinks there is more than one force behind that is either sadly petty or hugely blind.

From former governor the Honorable Linwood Holton came high praise and the reminder, "Your Bluff City heritage synchronized with mine from Big Stone Gap, and even then I predicted great things for you. What became the 'University' in the future far exceeded even my great expectations, especially considering the creation of the College of Integrated Science and Technology as the final, or near final, icing on a beautiful cake."

Dr. Christopher Janosik, former vice president of student affairs at JMU and now assistant to the vice president at Villanova University, e-mailed three paragraphs including, "I hear people at Villanova talk about the contemporary demands of the presidency. . . . A few will 'charitably' acknowledge that 'one

In 1998, Phil Bigler ('74) was named National Teacher of the Year and honored at a White House ceremony with President Bill Clinton. Over the years, Bigler's enthusiasm for teaching, coupled with student success, won numerous recognitions. He subsequently returned to JMU to open and direct the James Madison Center. (Photo: Tyler Mallory, *Montpelier* magazine)

CHANGES DURING THE PRESIDENCY OF
DR. RONALD E. CARRIER

1971–98

Headcount Enrollment	4,041	13,714
Male/Female Student Ratio	25/75	44/56
Percentage of Minority Students	1.4 %	11%
Applications for Admission	3,800	15,313
Average Freshman SAT Score	987	1,174
Number of Degree Programs	70	89
Number of Faculty Members	250	789
Total Number of Employees	500	1,743
Faculty with Terminal Degrees	50%	85%
Average Faculty Salary	$12,100	$52,519
Annual Operating Budget	$9.1 Million	$168 Million

BUILDINGS CONSTRUCTED AND RENOVATED DURING DR. CARRIER'S PRESIDENCY

1971-Warren Campus Center. Honors Percy Warren, former professor and Madison's first dean. A focal point for student activities.

1971-Weaver Hall. Honors Russell Weaver, rector of the Board of Visitors when Carrier was hired. Residence hall.

1972-Godwin Hall. Honors Virginia Governor Mills Godwin and Mrs. Godwin, a JMU alumna. First major athletic center.

1972-Ikenberry Hall. Honors J. Emmett Ikenberry, Head, Mathematics Department, then vice president for Academic Affairs. Residence hall.

1973-White Hall. Honors Helen Mugler White, vice rector, Board of Visitors, and alumna. Residence hall.

1974-Chandler Hall. Honors Wallace Chandler, former Board of Visitor rector, president of the JMU Foundation.

1975-Miller Hall. Honors former Madison College president G. Tyler Miller. Residence hall.

1975-Bridgeforth Stadium. Honors Ed Bridgeforth, former member, Board of Visitors, donor of the first full athletic scholarship at JMU.

1978-Greek Row. Fraternity residence halls lining Newman Lake.

1978-Mauck Stadium. Honors Leonard Mauck, former member, Board of Visitors. Long Field honors Ward Long, first basketball coach.

1979-Grafton-Stoval Theatre. Honors Martha Grafton, former president of Mary Baldwin College and former member, Board of Visitors, and Daryl Stoval, former member, Board of Visitors.

1980-Roop Hall. Honors Inez Roop, former member, Board of Visitors, alumna, and benefactor.

1982-Bell Hall. Honors Francis Bell, former rector, Board of Visitors. Residence hall.

1982-Carrier Library Addition. Renamed library honors Ronald and Edith Carrier, JMU president and first lady, 1971–1998.

1982-JMU Convocation Center. Athletic and entertainment center.

1984-McGraw-Long Hall. Honors Wally McGraw, former rector, Board of Visitors, and Nell Long, member, Board of Visitors, and Madison College alumna.

1985-Phillips Hall. Honors Adolph Phillips, vice president for business, 1968–1981.

1987-Hillside Hall. Coed residence hall.

1987-Edith Johnson Carrier Arboretum. Honors former JMU first lady.

1989-Music Building

1990-Sonner Hall. Honors Ray Sonner, senior vice president of JMU, former president of the JMU Foundation.

1991-Showker Hall. Honors rector, Board of Visitors, and benefactor Zane Showker.

1993-Taylor Hall. Honors Dr. James Taylor, former rector, Board of Visitors. Student center for events and conferences.

1994-CISAT Modular Building

1994-Wampler Hall. Honors Charles Wampler, member, Board of Visitors, and benefactor. Residence hall.

1996-Student Activities Building

1997-CISAT First Permanent Building

1997-Facilities Management Building

1998-CISAT Student Services Building

1998-CISAT Residence Hall

2000-CISAT Second Academic Building (Completed under Dr. Rose's presidency)

Under Dr. Carrier's tenure, renovations also were carried out on Maury, Jackson, Converse, Cleveland, and Burruss halls, Gibbons Dining Hall, and the Campus Health Center.

man can't do it all.' My memory of time at JMU and my brief encounters with you always bring a smile to my face. I never fail to respond, 'I worked for one that could, and I bet he still can.' "

Plaudits also arrived by campus mail to swell the hundreds from off campus. In one, Dr. Joanne Gabbin, director of the JMU Honors Program, responded to Carrier's final commencement address as president, writing how inspired and moved she felt. "I sat there and thought about the meaning of a good life, a life well lived because it has reached out to build, to teach, to lead, to inspire, and to serve. You have done all of those things. . . . I want you to know that even though you may not hear it as much as you should, you are a mountain of a model for us to emulate."

The Breeze, which had been particularly critical of Carrier during the previous five years, urged applause. An editorial enumerated many of his accomplishments and ended with thanks for his hard work and dedication.

The Board of Visitors on Friday, March 27, 1998, accepted Carrier's request to step down as president and designated him the first James Madison University chancellor. Board members assured him that his experience and knowledge of the university were too valuable to lose, if he were willing to continue serving.

As chancellor, Carrier would define the new position as he went and imagined he'd serve primarily as a consultant on raising private support for the school. For more than a decade he had emphasized that JMU's future success depended on increasing that private income. Traditional sources from taxes and tuition remained stationary, but costs continued their upward spiral. His success in his new role would be tied directly to his success tapping outside corporations and foundations. He announced his initial goals as "securing grants as well as developing international partnership for students and faculty."

His semester leave in 1997 to concentrate on fundraising had confirmed how essential such efforts were to enable the university to maintain its momentum and position. At the first faculty meeting after his return to campus in January 1998, he praised and thanked Dr. Linwood Rose for carrying the load as acting president for six months.

But the main thrust of his remarks revealed his conviction that JMU needed to develop partnerships with the government, industry, business, and philanthropic organizations. He said:

> There is a tremendous amount of intellectual power and energy
> on our campus. We need to match that with the energy and power

Fortunately for JMU, Dr. Ronald Carrier and Dr. Linwood Rose brought different strengths and personalities to the presidency, illustrating an anonymous aphorism: One of a kind isn't much of a poker hand, but it's a good description of a real leader. (Photo: '99 *Bluestone*)

of partners who can bring to us the software, the technology and the information that we need . . . .

Educational technology is a way of life. Nearly 130 years ago President [James A.] Garfield observed that true education occurs when there is a master teacher on one end of a bench and a willing student on the other end. While we may long for those days, much more is now necessary for a solid educational experience. The vital role of the teacher will never diminish, but twenty-first century educational experience will be designed differently. Yet as we go about using technology and partnering, we can't forget that the final outcome still depends on the close relationship between a caring teacher and an eager learner.

As chancellor, however, he would no longer be involved in the university's day-to-day operations. To make that position clear, he moved from "Oakview" well before the new president was named, and in September he moved his office off campus. While he had agreed to serve until the selection of his replacement or until December 31, he wanted his successor to feel total control, never to sense someone watching over his shoulder.

In addition, the chancellor's role would carry part of the responsibility for relations with the federal government, plus international educational affairs. Carrier's resignation as president came one year short of the twentieth anniversary of JMU's overseas involvement. Former students were already planning a grand reunion the following summer in London, where the program began in 1979.

From that tentative foray overseas, JMU had moved to second place nationally among master's-degree-level universities for the number of its students who include credit-earned study outside the United States. Committed to the principle of enhancing students' global perspective, the school offered four international options: semester-abroad programs, exchange and consortium programs, short-term study, and internships. The *Chronicle of Higher Education* reported that JMU, with 391 study-abroad students, or 3.3 percent of its enrollment, ranked just behind the University of St. Thomas, which sent 410, or four percent, of its students overseas.

Equally impressive, ties between JMU and the federal government had widened. Numerous federal grants, in addition to state and private funds, infused departmental projects campus wide each year. For fiscal 1997, those awards totaled $5,278,900—no small recognition. But distribution was fairly even among three sources, with federal grants providing thirty-eight percent; state, thirty-two percent; and private sources, thirty percent.

Carrier told one audience in January 1998, "I was reminded yesterday after a visit to the chemistry department how essential it is to have funds and to combine different ones—state, private, corporate funds. A new piece of

From 1979 on, JMU students could take a semester abroad. The international studies program was initiated with semesters in London (top left), but now has expanded to offer other foreign locales, including (top right) Paris, (bottom left) Rome, (bottom right) Salamanca, as well as cities beyond Europe. Time after time, students praised their semester abroad as one major—if not the—highlight of their years at JMU. (Photos: '94 *Bluestone*)

equipment that the chemistry department just installed cost $400,000, but it is the state-of-the-art in that field. Our undergraduate students in chemistry have an opportunity to work with that piece of equipment where at other schools—almost all other schools—a student wouldn't get to touch it until he or she was a graduate student. It takes partnerships and funding from various sources to make this possible."

Carrier's reference was to the new nuclear magnetic resonance spectrometer, or NMR, that allowed students to examine the molecular structure of compounds and had led to a four-college partnership. The NMR was so molecule-trait specific that it could analyze—to students' delight—a sample of vodka to determine whether it was made from grain or potatoes. Familiarity with nuclear magnetic resonance had become crucial to a chemistry student's preparation for either graduate school or industry. The $424,000

instrument united JMU with Harrisonburg's Eastern Mennonite University, nearby Bridgewater College, and Staunton's Mary Baldwin College into the Shenandoah Valley Regional NMR Consortium to benefit each school's chemistry students.

Joint partnerships promised future vitality. Certainly the Humanitarian Demining Information Center housed in CISAT under Col. Dennis Barlow represented one major federal-industry link. The Center received $588,200 in early 1998 to continue working as a major "information hub" in the global effort to rid war-torn nations of dangerous, deadly land mines. In addition, it received $9,000 to create a mine-awareness module compatible with the Demining Support System.

The Center's mission under a subcontract from the Essex Corporation of Columbia, Maryland, was to assist the Department of Defense in the removal of millions of lethal land mines worldwide, left over from wars since World War I. On a visit to the university in January 1997, assistant secretary of defense H. Allen Holmes reminded his audience in Wilson Hall that the mines posed "a humanitarian problem of epidemic proportions."

Holmes pointed out that the land mine crisis had developed principally because of the way the mines were used over the past fifteen years. "Indiscriminately laid by militaries, paramilitaries, and insurgents, in some cases, they've been employed specifically as weapons of terror against the civilian population." Regardless of the source, they kill or maim an estimated 1,200 to 2,100 men, women, and children each month.

"Last year 80,000 mines were removed," Holmes said, raising hope. Then, before the audience drew a breath of relief, he added, "But maybe more were planted. At our current clearing rate of 100,000 anti-personnel land mines per year, it will take over 1,000 years to clear the land mines in the ground today."

At JMU's center, approximately fifty faculty members and students continue coordinating efforts from diverse disciplines in this worldwide cause. In 1997, health sciences head Steven Stewart, Essex Corp. staff, and JMU students produced videos showing how to treat landmine injuries. They also produced a series of drawings on how to apply tourniquets. Those illustrations, silk-screened on linen scarves, were to be worn by workers in the fields.

Others, led by Mary Kimsey in the Center for Geographic Information Science, surveyed and modified existing software that helps locate and monitor mine fields to be used more effectively on site. Lennis Echterling, a noted expert in disaster psychology, produced a critical stress debriefing report for deploying American troops.

JMU psychologist Anne Stewart's team prepared alphabet cards and a comic strip designed to teach children to stay away from deadly mines. Computer scientist Mark Lattanzi launched three electronic information vehicles. Political scientist Kay Knickrehm headed an outreach program to monitor and respond to needs of the large and diverse group of participants in the demining community—especially the United Nations and private volunteer organizations, such as CARE, Refugees International, and the International Red Cross.

At the end of the twentieth century, an amazing transformation had occurred. A provincial small-town teachers college for young women had evolved into a coed regional university with cross-cultural ties and international impact. Napoleon Bonaparte defined a leader as "one who deals in hope." James Madison University had become a leader. Through the arts, humanities, sciences, and sports, JMU generated hope for growing numbers of students. In the supporting offices and surrounding communities, it carried hope beyond campus boundaries. In the worldwide striving of mankind to survive and to dream, it extended hope across oceans.

Walter Lippman once wrote, "The final test of a leader is that he leaves behind in other men the conviction and will to

The new president, Dr. Linwood Rose, with his wife, Judith, and sons (left to right) John and Scott in the driveway of their new home, "Oakview." (Photo: JMU Photo Lab)

carry on." Through the span of nine decades, JMU's presidents—from Burruss to Duke to Miller to Carrier—had passed the test. They had left behind for those following not only the conviction and will, but also the innate joy to carry on.

On September 9, 1998, the Board of Visitors appointed Dr. Linwood Rose the institution's fifth president, to lead the way into the new century.

An aerial view of the campus as Dr. Rose began his presidency, a grand expansion of the original architectural vision of 1908 that projected twenty-five years into the future. (Photo: Edith J. Carrier Arboretum)

W ITH HIS INAUGURATION as JMU's fifth president on September
17, 1999, Dr. Linwood H. Rose brought a new style to campus—one as right for the new age of information as his predecessor Dr.
Ronald E. Carrier's had been right for an earlier time. Carter Melton, head
administrator at Rockingham Memorial Hospital, once described Carrier as a
cross between revivalist Elmer Gantry and former U.S. President Lyndon Johnson. An article in *Montpelier* magazine sustained that view, assessing: "Carrier—
sometimes through sheer force of will and personality—created a dynamic,
bursting-at-the-seams James Madison University not unlike himself. . . ."

So even as it bid respectful farewell to Dr. Carrier, the university warmly
embraced its new president. Less flamboyant, but equally able to charm an
audience, the urbane and reflective Rose listens intently and watches broadly to
definitive purpose. A perpetual student with a wide-ranging intellect, his
vision is clear and his methods reflect a remarkable combination of objectivity
and imagination.

Rose's inaugural address outlined four key goals for the university's future:

1. To preserve the prominence of the student in all that we do.

2. To secure a higher level of resources to support the faculty,
   staff, and progress.

3. To embrace the concept of institutional effectiveness . . . [and]
   accountability.

4. To unite or align in a common direction so that we might
   maximize our potential and achieve beyond our expectations
   and those of others.

His first five years in office brought achievements toward each
desired objective. Like his immediate predecessor, Rose set student
needs as the litmus test of operation and programs. Unlike all his
predecessors, however, he sought no student growth, hoping to sta-
bilize enrollment at a steady level between 15,000 and 16,000.

Epilogue

Linwood H. Rose:
Approaching JMU's
Centennial in 2008

His second goal forced recognition that the pressure of fundraising would limit his time on campus. As never before, presidential energy needed to be channeled to seeking private endowments for a public institution that public funds could no longer fully support. His first year in office proved successful. JMU received more than $5 million in donations to the newly named Madison Fund—all before the school's first $1 million contribution from Steve and Dee Dee Leeolou, for whom the new alumni center would be named.

For the third goal, Rose underscored that the institution had maintained academic quality but now needed to raise that bar. Assuming his duties as president in advance of the official inauguration ceremony, he called upon a seventy-member Centennial Commission to help his administration and Board of Visitors define an ideal James Madison University for the future. Commission members drew from across generations, talents, and fields of expertise by including professors, students, alumni, parents, donors, community volunteers, and both business and government leaders. Working with an intensity and enthusiasm to match Rose's own, the commission delivered its report on May 11, 1999. Rose's inaugural address reflected that collective vision for JMU's future.

The fourth goal of unity and alignment spoke both to enhancing collaboration and broadening diversity—not only by gender and culture, but also by educational disciplines. Rose said, "The '90s were devoted to Science and Technology. Now is the time to return to the other side of campus and put equal effort and energy on the arts."

On election day in November 2002, Virginians overwhelmingly approved a $900.5 million bond issue for higher education facilities. That vote meant authorization of $99.9 million in projects at JMU—a new library for the East Campus, major renovations of Harrison and Burruss halls, extensive infrastructure work, and increased handicapped accessibility, plus a two-building complex for the arts. The latter, a center for the arts and a music recital hall, will receive $51 million. The projected cost, demanding an additional $10 million from donations, prompted JMU's largest gift in history: Charles E. Estes of Richmond donated $2.5 million to honor his wife, Dorothy Thompson Estes ('45), who died in 1996. The theater-dance building, adjacent to a new music performance center, will be named for her. Dr. Rose asserts, "The arts are fundamental to total education because they are directly connected to the human experience." And he quotes Norman Cousins, "Without the arts, education is not education, but vocational training." Clearly, the new arts complex, across the quad on South Main Street, will benefit not only JMU, but also the entire Shenandoah Valley.

Complementing the arts projects, a projected athletic center adds another dimension to equalizing programs. The $9.8 million athletic performance center will drain no tax dollars, with $7 million derived from private gifts and

$2.8 million gleaned from fees and JMU reserves. The 48,000-square-foot facility will provide academic support for all student athletes, a sports medicine complex, a strength-training area, a new football locker room, and offices. The building will be named for faithful JMU supporters Robert E. and Frances W. Plecker of Harrisonburg who donated $2 million to the school.

Each quarterly issue of JMU's award-winning alumni magazine *Montpelier* carries a letter from the president. In it, Dr. Rose candidly shares his feelings as well as campus news and needs. In the spring of 2000, he focused on five professors, relating cumulative individual honors and professional achievements by J. Patrick Rooney (school of music), Gina M. MacDonald (department of chemistry), William C. Wood (department of economics), Jane S. Halonen (school of psychology), and Allan Berg (department of computer science). Then he ended his message as follows:

> My principal ambition is to create an environment in which great teachers can work their special magic with students. . . . Rather than ten buildings, $10 million, or ten new programs, I would prefer to be responsible for creating the conditions for ten faculty members to flourish at JMU and to alter the lives of the students they teach.

As James Madison University approaches its centennial celebration in 2008, its fifth president is shaping an institutional future worthy of its past.

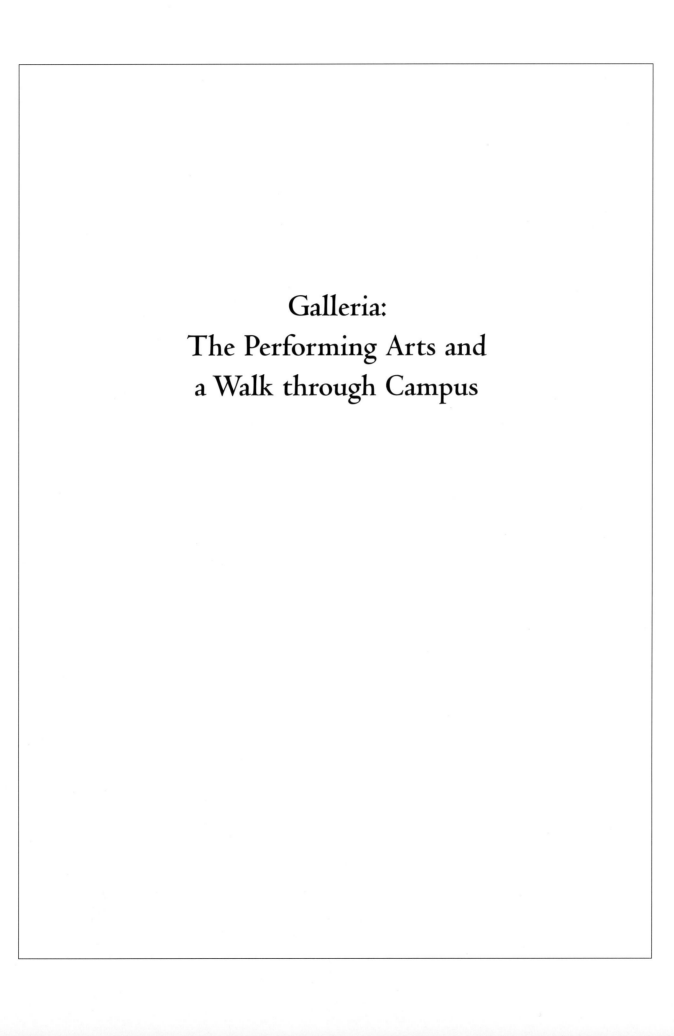

Galleria:
The Performing Arts and
a Walk through Campus

The performance of *Passifflora Gracilis*, choreographed by renowned guest-artist Li Chiao-Ping, as part of a concert by the Virginia Repertory Dance Company of JMU. (Photo: Richard Finkelstein)

The production of *Medea* by the School of Theatre and Dance. (Photo: Richard Finkelstein)

The JMU Symphony and Chorus perform in historic Wilson Hall. (Photo: JMU Photography Services)

The JMU Jazz Ensemble performs in Wilson Hall. (Photo: JMU Photography Services)

The production of *The Glass Menagerie* by the School of Theatre and Dance. (Photo: Richard Finkelstein)

The production of *Lilly's Purple Plastic Purse* by the School of Theatre and Dance, as part of its ever-popular Summer Children's Playshop. (Photo: Richard Finkelstein)

Many official campus visits begin at the statue of James Madison situated between Varner and Roop halls, at the south end of the walkway that passes between Wilson Hall and the Quad. (Photo: George F. Thompson)

Touched by seasonal reds, autumn foliage adorns the entrance to the Carrier Library. (Photo: George F. Thompson)

Facing southwest toward Roop Hall from the front of Maury Hall. (Photo: George F. Thompson)

The back of Wampler Hall from Bluestone Drive. (Photo: George F. Thompson)

The view on a Saturday morning in October, looking northeast across the Quad
toward Keezell Hall. (Photo: George F. Thompson)

Students congregate on the walkway (and former two-lane road) in front of Wilson Hall.
Burruss Hall is pictured (center) in the background. (Photo: George F. Thompson)

Converse Hall dominates the southwest entrance to the campus, as it faces South Main Street (U.S. 11) and Bluestone Drive (shown in the foreground). (Photo: George F. Thompson)

The long shadows of autumn extend toward Burruss Hall (left) and the original, pillared front entrance and building of the library (right). In the early 1980s the university expanded the library into today's Carrier Library, and rerouted the main entrance. (Photo: Diane Elliott)

The view across the Commons, behind Gibbons Dining Hall (left), with Hillcrest
in the background. (Photo: George F. Thompson)

As one leaves Carrier Library and heads west toward the original campus entrance on
South Main Street, the distinctive red-tile roofs dominate the view. (Photo: Diane Elliott)

The walkway behind Gibbons Dining Hall affords a beautiful view of campus grounds and of Massanutten Mountain in the background. (Photo: George F. Thompson)

The ground floor of the Phillips Center houses one of the popular food venues on campus. (Photo: George F. Thompson)

Through the trees rises the cupola of Wilson Hall, as seen from a walkway that leads up from the Commons and Warren Campus Center. (Photo: George F. Thompson)

The view from Jackson Hall across the Quad toward Sheldon (left) and Alumnae (center) halls.
(Photo: George F. Thompson)

The walkway above the Commons on a clear day offers a welcoming view toward Warren Hall (left) and the tower of the new ISAT/CS Building on the east campus across Interstate 81. (Photo: George F. Thompson)

Aside the Carrier Library, looking west over the red-tile rooftops of Alumnae, Sheldon, and Johnson halls as well as the Music Building. (Photo: Diane Elliott)

Whatever the season, JMU's Edith J. Carrier Arboretum offers a welcome sanctuary to students, alumnae, faculty, travelers, and residents of Harrisonburg and Rockingham County. Here the leaves of an oak are illuminated against the backdrop of the arboretum's pond. (Photo: George F. Thompson)

These 1993 JMU alums return regularly to the campus with their children, and they always take in the sights, sounds, and smells of an autumn afternoon in the arboretum. (Photo: George F. Thompson)

Overlooking the greensward from University Boulevard that sweeps down to the pond in the arboretum. (Photo: George F. Thompson)

A view of the oak and hickory forest that honors biology professor Norlyn J. Bodkin, who, along with former JMU President Ronald E. Carrier, was instrumental in envisioning and creating the arboretum. (Photo: George F. Thompson)

The daughter of a JMU dance professor sets out across the popular swinging foot bridge in the arboretum. (Photo: George F. Thompson)

An inviting bench along a trail near the arboretum's pond. (Photo: George F. Thompson)

A JMU student and her younger
brother from Connecticut look
at the resident turtles and fish
from the bridge that spans the
pond at the arboretum.
(Photo: George F. Thompson)

The walkway alongside the impressive University Recreation Center, with the new ISAT/CS Building
in the background. (Photo: George F. Thompson)

Looking across Newman Lake from Bluestone Drive (left to right): The cupola of Wilson Hall, the parking deck beside Bridgeforth Stadium, and Shorts and Chandler halls. (Photo: George F. Thompson)

The main entrance to Showker Hall, along Bluestone Drive. (Photo: Corinne Diop)

The stylish architecture of Sonner Hall (right) as seen along Newman Lake.
(Photo: George F. Thompson)

The new JMU Bookstore near Godwin Hall. (Photo: Corinne Diop)

A familiar sight to generations of JMU students: The railroad tracks that run along the base of Bluestone Hill through the heart of campus. (Photo: Diane Elliott)

The award-winning Dukes Marching Band is always a highlight of JMU football games in Bridgeforth Stadium.
(Photo: JMU Photography Services)

Whereas the original bluestone campus fronts U.S. 11, Harrisonburg's Main Street, the new technology campus rises to the east along busy Interstate 81. (Photo: George F. Thompson)

Looking west toward the ISAT/CS Building (left) and Health and Human Services (right) on the new east campus. (Photo: George F. Thompson)

The tower of the ISAT/CS Building is a prominent architectural feature of the new east campus.
(Photo: Diane Elliott)

The landscaping of the east campus reveals its newness but provides an unimpeded panoramic view of
(left to right) the College Center and Potomac and Chesapeake halls. (Photo: JMU Photography Services)

The College Center in the late afternoon of an autumn day. (Photo: JMU Photography Services)

(Left to right) Leeolou Alumni Center, the College Center, and Potomac Hall on the east campus.
(Photo: Diane Elliott)

The main entrance to Chesapeake Hall, a state-of-the-art-dorm on the east campus. (Photo: Diane Elliott)

The graceful curvature and fenestration of the College Center and a glimpse of Massanutten Mountain in the distance and of Harrisonburg's commercial development where it bumps up against JMU's northeast boundary. (Photo: George F. Thompson)

A late winter afternoon highlights the beautiful architecture of the University Recreation Center, a major asset to the JMU community. (Photo: Randall B. Jones)

Duke Hall, pictured on a winter's day, is the home to the distinguished Sawhill Gallery and Latimer-Shaeffer Theatre. The sculpture on the left is composed of newspaper and was installed as part of a public art display on campus. (Photo: Randall B. Jones)

The South Main Street (U.S. 11) entrance to campus and Converse Hall through a screen of icy trees and a thick blanket of winter snow. (Photo: JMU Photography Services)

May 2004 graduation exercises on the Quad in front of historic Wilson Hall. (Photo: Randall B. Jones)

List of Patrons

The Community Foundation of Harrisonburg and Rockingham County gratefully acknowledges anonymous donors and the following patrons:

The Arts Council of the Valley

Nancy Revercomb Brubaker ('56)

J. Ted ('90) and Stephanne Strickler ('93) Byrd

Dr. Ronald E. and Edith Johnson Carrier

Paul Cline ('82)

The Daily News-Record

Mensel ('70) and Linda Taylor ('71) Dean

O. Dean and Joanne Ehlers

The Denton Family Charitable Foundation

Scott and Anne Marie Strickler ('91) Elles

Joe and Sallie Ewing ('67) Funkhouser

A. Wesley and Glenna Graves

Bonnie Neff Hoover ('48)

Larry and Pat Hoover

Lisa Brubaker Hopkins ('86)

Andrew M. Huggins

Hugh ('73 & '80) and Nancy Bowman ('71) Lantz

Kathy Moran ('87)

John and Linda Neff

Nielsen Builders, Inc.

Robert and Frances Plecker

Larry ('79 & '81) and Ramona D. ('85, '88, '90, '05) Rogers

W. Raymond "Buddy" ('50) and Dolly Rutherford ('54) Showalter

Zane Showker

Judith Shreckhise Strickler ('60)

Lorraine Warren Strickler ('52)

Winston ('71) and Bonnie Weaver

WRITING APPEARS A SOLITARY ENDEAVOR but capturing the history of a place and time seldom happens alone. I am grateful for all the voices along the way who contributed to my search for facts and feelings and for those who gave candid reviews as the manuscript emerged. First, of course, I'm grateful to Dr. Ronald E. Carrier for commissioning "a popular history," which I interpreted to mean "remind alumni why they care about JMU." Next, I'm glad to have had an ongoing committee to offer comments chapter by chapter. My sincere thanks to the original advisory committee members identified by their positions at the book's inception:

Fred Hilton, Director of Media Relations; Chris Bolgiano, Special Collections Librarian; Dr. Dorothy Boyd-Rush, former Dean of the Graduate School and Professor of History; Dr. Paul Cline, former Professor of Political Science; Emily Dingledine, former faculty wife and Harrisonburg City Council member; Dr. George Leffel, JMU alumnus; Donald Lemish, Vice President for University Advancement; Patty Sarb, Director of the JMU Bookstore; Sarah Schaeffer, Director of Alumni Relations; Dr. Ray Sonner, Senior Vice President Emeritus; Dr. Linwood Rose, Senior Vice President. In addition, I'd be remiss not to include subsequent advisors Dr. Barbara Castello and Glenda Rooney.

My greatest source for details of the school's first fifty years was the definitive history Raymond C. Dingledine published by that name in 1959. I make no pretense to his level of research and scholarship. His is a marvelous book and an absolute must for serious forays into the past.

In addition to Dr. Dingledine's volume, I found delight in the school yearbooks—first *The Schoolma'am*, then *The Bluestone*, from the beginning years through the current times. Also, copies of *The Breeze, JMUniverse, Curio, Montpelier, Virginia Teacher, Daily News-Record,* and even *The Fixer* have provided insight to the times and people. Naturally, interviews with alumni and faculty, in person or by mail, deepened my understanding and allowed color commentary throughout. Added thanks is due Melanie Rowan for photographic research and the many resources at JMU who opened files to us, especially Chris Bolgiano in Special Collections, Margaret Buse for the history of ISAT, and Gary Michael in Sports Media Relations. Also I thank Robin McNallie and Christine Edwards for close reading of the manuscript and advice that I sometimes took—especially curing me of "conjunction-itis," my too liberal use of *buts* or *ands*.

I close with special thanks to Judy Strickler, who encouraged me to publish, and to Stephanie Strickler Byrd and the board of The Community Foundation of Harrisonburg and Rockingham County for underwriting publication, in order that the book could be published through the Center for American Places. Both nonprofit organizations took a leap of faith to invest in this project. At the Center, many thanks to its president and publisher George F. Thompson. My debt is also overwhelming to my son Randall B. Jones, who served as the book's project director, for his editorial skills in shepherding me through the selection of the more than 300 photographs herein and his assistance in providing the captions. My thanks as well to my other son, Martin F. Jones, for proofreading and indexing the book. Their insights and attention to detail, coupled with boundless patience, not only made their mother proud, but also made the book possible.

Fox, James W. (faculty), 144, 147, 151
Francis Marion University, 231
Frank, Helen (staff), 85
Franklin, Nancy, *146*
Frederick College, 136
Fredericksburg, Virginia, 4, 96
Frederikson, Edna Tutt (faculty), 114
Frederikson Hall, 155
Frederikson, Otto F. (faculty), 155
Fredricksburg State Teachers College, 80
Friddles Restaurant, 48, *48*, 76
Fritz, Phil, *181*
Front Royal, Virginia, 107
Frye Building, 155
Frye, Lucius C., 155
Fulton, Mary Jane, 97
Funkhouser, Fred, 206
Funkhouser, Mary (faculty), *162*
Furious Flower Conference, 228, *229*

Gabbin, Alexander (faculty), 219, *221*
Gabbin, Joanne (faculty), 228–9, *229*, 239
Galapagos Islands, 194
Galax, Virginia, 77
Gannon, Justin, *181*
Garber Hall, *146*, 155
Garber, Dorothy (faculty), 88, 105, 110, 155
Gardner, Marie (staff), *145*
Garner, Tom, 96
Gathright Dig, 206–7, *207*
Gauldin, Elizabeth Wilson, 235
Genoa, Italy, 220
Gentis, Lorraine, 58
geography department, 12, 110, 122
geology department, 110, 122
Georgetown University, 179
Georgetown, Texas, 46
GI Bill, effect on Madison College, 95, 107
Gibbons Hall, 138, 155, 238
Gibbons, Howard K. (staff), 99, 114, 135, 155
Gibson-Geiger, Nancy, 84
Giese, Rene, 225
Gifford Hall, 120, 155
Gifford, Walter John (faculty), 67, 99, 114, 122, 139, 155
Giordano, Kenny, *176*
girl-break dance, 73–4
Gladin, Mabel B. (staff), 95
Godwin Hall, *180*, *182*, 238
Godwin, Mills (Virginia governor), 159, 170, *170*, 238
Goewey, Erin, *221*
Good, P.B.F. (Virginia delegate), 4
Gordon, Margaret (faculty), 126
Gordonsville, Virginia, 55
Grady, Jean Raup, 92
Grafton, Martha (Board of Visitors), 238
Grafton-Stoval Theatre, 238
Graham, Martha, 85
Grand Caverns, 120
Granddaughters Club (subsequently Sesame Club), 76, 89, 96
Grandle, Ed, 117
Grandy, Jean Bell, 73
Graves, Glenna, *190*
Graviano, Frank, *176*
Greece, 220
Green, Walter, III (medical staff), 146, 147
Greenvale Garden Club, 195
Gregg, Rachael (faculty), 29
Gregory, Dennis, 151
Griffith, Linda, *148*
Griffin, Pat, *146*
Griffin, Robert (staff), 151–2
Grimm, James (faculty), 188

Grinnell College, 205
Groseclose, M., *111*
Grosh, Stacy, 225
Grottos, Virginia, 31
Guthrie, Roland, 187

Haban, Mary (staff), *172*
Habitat for Humanity, 225
Haley, Charles, 180, *204*, 235
Halifax County, Virginia, 23
Hall, Roger, 169
Halley's Comet, 18
Halonen, Jane S. (faculty), 247
Hammond, Lee, 151–2
Hampton-Sydney College, 119
Hankins, Mary Coles, 23
Hanson Hall, 155
Hanson, David (faculty), 212
Hanson, Raus McDill (faculty), 92, 155
Happy the Man, 165
Harambee, *150*, 151
Harkins, Sue Anne, *148*
Harley-Davidson, 28
Harmon, Priscilla, *56*
Harnsberger, Ann Virginia (staff), 114
Harper's, 94
Harrington, Michael, 183
Harris, Charles (faculty), 218
Harris, Elizabeth (faculty), 33
Harris, Malcolm (faculty), 220
Harris, Rich (staff), 225
Harrison, Albertis S., Jr., (Virginia governor), 136
Harrison, Gessner, 27, 54, 80
Harrison Hall, 14, 27, 28, 31, 37, 45, 51, 54, 55, 56, 63, 66, 68, 89, 92, 115, *115*, 119, 192, 222, 246
Harrison, Thomas, 80
Harrison, William Henry (U.S. President), 80
Harrisonburg Chamber of Commerce, 43
Harrisonburg Club, 16
Harrisonburg Courthouse, 19
Harrisonburg Fire Department, 3, 5, 7, 24
Harrisonburg High School, 55, 57, 58, 96
Harrisonburg Junior High School, 125
Harrisonburg Municipal Building, 57
Harrisonburg Planning Commission, 195
Harrisonburg State Teachers College. *See* State Teachers College
Harrisonburg, Virginia, City of, *121*, 195, 221
   alumnae living in, 46
   blackout in, 24–5
   Council of, 5, 196
   fires in, 7
   School Board at, 43
   School System of, 123
   site for State Normal School, 3, 4, 7
Harter, Carl (faculty), 210
Hartman, Jane, 97
Harvey, Sue, *146*
Hatch, David (faculty), 122
Haydon, Richard (faculty), 129, 131, 135
Heath, Brent, 193–4
Heatwole, Cornelius J. (faculty), 43
Heeb, Louise (staff), 211, 212
Hellen/Ellen Club, 35
Henner, Juli, 222
Herzen Institute of Leningrad, 205
Hess, Irvin (medical staff), 146
Higgs, "Junior" (staff), *190*, 193
Higgs, K.M., 59
Hiking Crowd, 18
Hillcrest (President's house), 6, 25, *25*, 29, 37, 42, 47, *47*, 54, 55, 98, 103, 105, 110, 139, 142, 175
Hillside Gang, *171*, 180
Hillside Hall, 238

Hilton, Becky, 194
Hilton, Fred (staff), 172–3, 205
history department, 12, 122
Hite, Shere, 183
Hocking, W.E., 93
Hoffman Hall, 155
Hoffman, Margaret Vance (faculty), 88, 114, 155
Hollar, Ethel, *56*
Holmes, H. Allen, 242–3
Holsinger, Virginia, *56*
Holton, Linwood (Virginia governor), 236
Home Economics Day, 143
home economics department, 26, 37, 89, 110, 122
Hook, Grover, 61
Hoover, H. Mae, 34, 37–9
Hoover, Pearl S. (staff), 115
Hoover, S. B., 134
Hotel Roanoke, 129
Hounchell, Paul (faculty), 114
household arts department, 12, 14, 34
Hoyt, Cliff, *176*
Hoyt, Sarah, 223
Hudson, Ruth (faculty), 58
Huffman, Charles H. (faculty), 122, 155
Huffman Hall, 155
Hulvey, Dale (staff), 218
Humanitarian Demining Information Center, 242
Humphrey, Rebecca (faculty), 208
Humphreys, C.C., 169
Hunt Institute for Botanical Documentation, 194
Hunt, Laura A., 216
Hurricane Andrew, 224
Hursey, R.F., Jr. (faculty), 143

Iceland, 127, 128
Ihle, Elizabeth (faculty), 205
Ikenberry Hall, 238
Ikenberry, J. Emmert (faculty), 122, 238
Indiana University, 44
International Sports Medicine Encyclopedia, 143

Jackson Hall, 5, 10, 14, 16, 18, 26, 35, 38, 54, *146*, 238
Jackson River, 206–7
Jackson, "Stonewall", 26, 54
James Madison University
   75th anniversary of, 186
   aerial view of, *244*
   alumni donations to, 219
   alumni of, 235
   applications for admission to, 203
   arboretum at. *See* Edith Johnson Carrier Arboretum
   assets of, 236
   baseball at, 180, 181
   basketball at, men's, 179, 216
   basketball at, women's, 208–9, *209*
   Board of Visitors of, 211, 212, 218, 230, 234, 235, 238, 239
   budget allocations for, 172
   College of Integrated Science and Technology at, 213, 214, 218–9, 227–30, 234, 236, 242
   colors, selection of, 16
   concerts at, 227
   cycling team of, 225
   enrollment at, 172, 173, 235–6, 245
   extracurricular activities at, 179
   facilities of, 187, 215
   faculty, number of, 172, 236
   field hockey at, 182, 226, *226*
   football team of, 168–9
   fundraising for, 173
   golf at, 181
   housing at, 173
   lacrosse at, women's, 180, 208

The Center for American Places is a tax-exempt 501(c)(3) nonprofit organization, founded in 1990, whose educational mission is to enhance the public's understanding of, appreciation for, and affection for the natural and built environment. Underpinning this mission is the belief that books provide an indispensible foundation for comprehending—and caring for—the places where we live, work, and explore. Books live. Books endure. Books make a difference. Books are gifts to civilization.

With offices in New Mexico and Virginia, Center editors bring to publication 20–25 books per year under the Center's own imprint or in association with publishing partners. The Center is also engaged in numerous other programs that emphasize the interpretation of landscape and place through art, literature, scholarship, field research, and exhibitions. The Center's Cotton Mather Library in Arthur, Nebraska, its Martha A. Strawn Photographic Library in Davidson, North Carolina, and a ten-acre reserve along the Santa Fe River in Florida are available as retreats upon request. The Center is also affiliated with the Rocky Mountain Land Library in Colorado.

The Center strives every day to make a difference through books, research, and education. For more information, please send inquiries to P.O. Box 23225, Santa Fe, NM 87502, U.S.A., or visit the Center's Website (www.americanplaces.org).

ABOUT THE BOOK:

The text for *Rooted on Blustone Hill: A History of James Madison University* was set in Centaur with Gill Sans display. The paper is acid-free Korean Tripine Matte text, 150 gsm weight. The book was printed in Korea through Global Ink, Inc.

FOR THE CENTER FOR AMERICAN PLACES:

George F. Thompson, president and publisher
Randall B. Jones, independent project director
Lauren A. Marcum, Kendall B. McGhee, and Ernest L. Toney, Jr., editorial assistants
Judith Rudnicki, of Skyboat Road Company, Inc., manuscript editor
Martin F. Jones, indexer
David Skolkin, book designer and art director
David Keck, of Global Ink, Inc., production coordinator